LINUX FOR NON-GEEKS™

LINUX FOR NON-GEEKS™

A Hands-On, Project-Based, Take-It-Slow Guidebook

by Rickford Grant

NO STARCH PRESS

San Francisco

Publisher: William Pollock
Managing Editor: Karol Jurado
Developmental Editor: Hillel Heinstein
Cover and Interior Design: Octopod Studios
Technical Reviewer: Joseph Arruda
Copyeditor: Andy Carroll
Compositor: Wedobooks
Proofreader: Stephanie Provines
Indexer: Kevin Broccoli

For information on book distributors or translations, please contact No Starch Press, Inc. directly:

No Starch Press, Inc.
555 De Haro Street, Suite 250, San Francisco, CA 94107
phone: 415.863.9900; fax: 415.863.9950; info@nostarch.com; http://www.nostarch.com

Library of Congress Cataloging-in-Publication Data

Grant, Rickford.
  Linux for non-geeks : a hands-on, project-based, take-it-slow guidebook / Rickford Grant.
      p. cm.
  ISBN 1-59327-034-8
  1. Linux. 2. Operating systems (Computers). I. Title.
    QA76.76.063 G723 2004
    005.4'32--dc22

                                                                        2003024732

DEDICATION

This book is dedicated to the memory of my uncle, Boris Ivan Pavlovich, who always seemed to me the incarnation of what being young-at-heart meant, and to Herr Harry Kennedy, my German teacher at Los Angeles City College — suave, cool, open-hearted, and the kind of teacher I have always tried to be. He not only taught us German, but also brought us into the world of Candide, Schweik, and Wolfgang Hildesheimer.

ACKNOWLEDGMENTS

I always thought that the acknowledgments sections in books were a bit pretentious — something like the never-ending list of thank-you's of an Academy Awards acceptance speech. However, once you get down to writing a book, you realize that there actually are a lot of people who help you along the way, and the desire to thank them is real and right enough. For that reason, I too want to offer my thanks now to all those who helped out in one way or another, whether directly or indirectly.

First and foremost, I want to thank my wife Sumire for encouraging me to put my knowledge to use and write, rather than just goof around on the computer, and for putting up with being a little ignored while I was writing this book. Then, of course, I must thank my mother, Dixie Angelina Burckel-Testa, for being one of the reasons this book got started and for helping out with some of the initial proof-reading. And then, of course, I must also thank my aunt, Danica Lucia Zollars, for uttering the two words that are the reason you are reading this now: "Publish it."

Of course, the folks at No Starch Press were the ones who actually did "publish it," and so I really want to thank Hillel Heinstein, Karol Jurado, and William Pollock for making it possible, guiding me along, pointing me in some new directions, and making the whole process seem not only like a team effort, but also a whole lot of fun.

My interest in computers and the sum total of my knowledge about them is really the culmination of the experience I gained from, or in the company of, a number of people I would be dreadfully selfish to leave out. These include a number of friends and colleagues from my various phases as a computer user and enthusiast: Sheldon Rudolph, from the good old Atari XL600 days; Donald Hammang, from the Commodore 64, Windows, and OS/2 days; Russel Park (who first took me online), Keith Hagan, and Tracy Nakajima from my early Mac days; Masaki Kameko, who was my Unix command guru when I first got started in the world of Linux; and Andrzej Kozlowski, from my Mac OS X days, who is actually inadvertently responsible for getting me into the world of Linux, whether or not he realizes it.

It would also be terribly remiss of me not to thank my work colleagues, Setsu Uesaka and Toshiko Takagi, for lending me bits of hardware here and there during the writing of this book. Yes, they lent me everything from paper punches to laptop computers, and all they got out of it was a recipe for killer martinis. Sweet vermouth just doesn't cut it, Toshiko san.

I would also like to thank Paul Helbert, who kindly shared his chapter-by-chapter experiences with the first printing of this book and brought a few typos and other points to my attention.

Then there are also those equally important souls who did their part by lending an ear when I couldn't shut up, pushing me on when I lost my way, and doling out the tea and sympathy when I needed it most: my friends and colleagues Karen Fedderholdt, James Porcaro, Lisa Snyder, Hiroshi Sakamoto, and my former linguistics professor at Portland State University, Kimberley Brown, who gave me the confidence to write, and encouraged me to do so.

Special thanks are also due to those people who had a more indirect effect on the production of this book but were ultimately a great influence in the total scheme of things — Anders Grant, Stephanie Garrabrant-Sierra, Steven Young, Dick Petrie, and Kimberly Jo Burk.

Finally, I turn to the kitties. Yes, Muju, my cat, who had to forsake her late-night grass-eating walks on a leash while I busied myself writing, and the Great Saw (aka Melissa), who is the living definition of "simple kitten ways."

BRIEF CONTENTS

CONTENTS IN DETAIL

3

A NEW PLACE TO CALL HOME

4

MORE THAN WEBBED FEET

5
DRESSING UP THE BIRD

6
GUTENBIRD

7
PUTTING YOUR DATA ON ICE

8
RPM ISN'T A 1980s ATLANTA-BASED BAND

9
SIMPLE KITTEN WAYS

10
YES, YET ANOTHER WAY!

11

DINING ON TARBALLS

12

DATA ON ICE REVISITED

13

TUX ROCKS

14
BRUSH-WIELDING PENGUINS

15
PENGUINS BACK AT WORK

16

FONT FEATHERED FRENZY

17

TUX SPEAKS YOUR LANGUAGE

18

TUX UNTETHERED

19

LEAVING THE NEST

20

WHAT TO DO IF TUX STARTS ACTING UP

A
LAUNCHER SPECIFICATIONS

B
RESOURCES

INDEX
299

A NOTE ABOUT FEDORA VERSIONS
313

PREFACE

My own computing life began long ago in the Commodore/Atari days. The purchase of my first machine, no doubt inspired by Alan Alda's television commercials at the time, was an Atari XL600 with a cassette drive for storage, and 16KB of RAM — more than I thought I would ever need at the time (ha!).

Most of my time on that machine, I must admit, was spent playing cartridge-based games and typing in pages and pages of machine code from the now-defunct magazine *Antic* to create even more games. Eventually, my interest in computers increased, especially after seeing my first, and actually *the* first, Macintosh at the UCLA bookstore. The very in-your-face nature of the Mac's operating system caused me to become an operating-system maniac. To date I have worked with almost every operating system there is or ever was, including Mac operating systems up to and including OS X, every Windows version from 3.1 to XP, and even IBM's much forgotten OS/2.

Though tempted to join the Linux fray, I continued to steer away from it for a long time, because I could not help but see it, as so many others do, as a system for never-seen-the-light-of-day-faced, late-night Dr. Pepper–drinking, Domino's-pizza-eating compu-geeks. Moving to Japan and being surrounded with machines loaded with Japanese versions of Windows, however, presented me with numerous problems, such as language constraints. As everything, including help files, was written in Japanese, I ended up using only a fraction of the full potential of most software. Then there were those annoying Windows-type problems, such as the constant freezes and restarts, and the gradual system slowdowns, which were eventually only remedied by reinstalling the system. Getting the software I needed to do the things I wanted to do also took its toll on my wallet, and I began to rethink my initial resistance to Linux. With Linux's multilingual support, system stability, and extensive and free software packages, there were plenty of incentives for me to get over my obsession with the stereotypical Linux user.

After a few failed attempts at getting Linux to work on the oddball Frankenstein-like collection of junk that was my computer, I finally succeeded the safe way with a CD-based Knoppix distribution, which worked well enough to hook me in a little further. I then moved on to Mandrake, as that was claimed to be the most newbie-friendly version, and then tried out SuSE as well, which I found rather quirky. Eventually, I tried out Red Hat Linux and stuck to that, as it just gave me no grief; and I, like most others, do not need any more grief than necessary.

I started off with my three desktop machines at work and home set up as dual-boot systems running both Linux and Windows, but I gradually found myself using only Linux. Although I had expected to encounter numerous limitations in Linux that would force me to return to Windows often, I instead found that I had actually increased my productivity. Other than lack of native support for Windows streaming media, I was actually able to do more due to the extensive software base that was now installed on my machine. Without having to fork out money that I could ill afford to spend, I was able to manipulate my digital images, rip songs from CDs, create vector drawings, create PDF files, and do a variety of other things that I wasn't able to do under Windows. It was only a matter of a little time before my dual-boot setups became full Linux-only setups. I ceased to be a Windows user.

Of course, during the course of my adjusting to the Linux environment, I had to learn a lot. I was, after all, alone in a sea of Windows users with a Mac island or two on the horizon. What I needed to know I had to find out on my own. The basics, of course, were quite easy, as intuition alone seemed to be enough; but, just as with other operating systems, I had to resort to doing some research to learn to do other things. Given the baffling geek-oriented nature of most Linux books at the time, I had to turn to mailing lists, bulletin boards, and the ol' proven and true system of trial and error. As my memory has never been that good, I kept notes of what I had to do in order to get something done so that I could do it again in the future.

The idea of writing a book, however, came a bit later. In fact, the inspiration for the book was, of all people, my mother. My mother had been using an old Windows 95 machine of mine for years, but it was reaching the end of its days. My mother, being retired and of fixed income, found buying a new machine a bit beyond her means, so I told her I would send her one of my extra machines. The only problem was that she didn't have any software or even a system to put on the machine. All she had on her old machine was what I had installed long, long ago, and the installation disks were mere memories.

Buying new copies of Windows, Microsoft Office, and all the other odds and ends that she had grown accustomed to would cost a fortune, so I thought that perhaps I might just set up the machine with a Red Hat Linux system. Of course, I worried at first whether my 72-year-old mother was ready for entry into the Linux world. Thinking of my own experiences, however, I couldn't really see any reason why she wouldn't be. After all, she could handle her mouse as well as the next person, and the process of installing Linux had improved so much from the days when I got started that it had essentially become a no-brainer. Yes, with a set of decent instructions that a beginner could understand, she would do all right.

I told her what I was going to do, and she seemed receptive enough; however, when she said that she would go out and buy a book to get her ready, and asked me for suggestions, I was stumped. Having gone through many a book myself as I got started up with Linux, I couldn't think of a single one that would be of any use to someone like her. Most books then, and even now, tended to follow a similar format: They started with a rudimentary gloss over the basics of installation and usage, and then they suddenly leaped into geek mode, discussing everything in terms of commands and focusing excessively on topics that the average user would be intimidated by (and have little, if any, use for), such as setting up servers. It seemed to me that such books would just confuse her or, worse yet, scare her away. After all, that was what they did to me. I therefore decided to just write up a set of instructions myself — instructions that even my mother could understand and have some fun with. When my auntie got a hold of the instructions, the power of Zeus took hold in her, bringing about her simple edict: "Publish it!" And that is what "inspired" me to take that set of instructions and my notes to myself to the next level and write this book. One must not fly in the face of the power of Zeus . . . or my auntie.

Who Is This Book For?

As you can surmise from the background you've just read, I wrote this book so that a total non-geek, such as my mother, could use a pretty standard Linux distribution without much in the way of pain and grief. Of course, you may be wondering who qualifies as a non-geek, so I will try to clarify the several types I had in mind.

The first type, the Mom group, consists of users who really don't know much about computers other than how to use them for writing letters, sending email, and browsing the Web. Such users just want to be able to use their Fedora system in much the same way they had used their Mac or Windows systems, and to have a bit of fun along the way.

The other type, the me-and-my-friends type, consists of those users who are a bit more adept at using computers but are also new to Linux, and thus want to know how to get things done in the manner they are accustomed to, while at the same time wishing to learn just enough more so that they have a foundation on which to go further and push the envelope just a bit — the want-to-get-their-feet-a-little-geeky types.

There is yet another type of user I had in mind, and I suppose I could call them the on-the-fence type. The on-the-fence users are not really users at all. They are people who have read or heard about Linux and are wondering whether or not they are ready to deal with it, perhaps being held back by the Linux-is-for-geeks stereotype. These on-the-fencers need a reason to make the switch and a bit of reassurance that they will be all right once they do. To such folks, I can say right now, cliché though it may be, c'mon in — the water's fine.

All of this is to say that this book is pretty much for the average desktop computer user — someone who wants to use their computer for home- and even work-oriented productivity, music, art, and most importantly, fun. As such, there is no discussion of setting up a server or anything of that ilk. When and if you become interested in such things, you will have a lot of resources to turn to, and you will be well prepared to do so once you've read this book.

Instead, I try to explain how to do things within the framework of the comforting graphical interface. To the degree that it is necessary or might be of interest to those push-the-envelope-a-little types, I also provide a brief, though detailed, explanation of how to use the command line, with much handholding along the way. This may even be of interest to someone with some previous experience with Fedora Core or Red Hat Linux, or to a migrant from another Linux distribution.

No matter which of these types of users you are, this book will get you comfortable using Linux. If you are looking for a power-user Linux book, though, try the next book on the shelf.

Concept and Approach

As a language teacher, I have always preferred programming books, mathematics books, and old-fashioned foreign-language-learning texts because of their straightforward, skill-based orientation, in which each chapter builds upon the skills acquired in the previous chapter. I have tried to organize this book in that manner so that you will never be called upon to do something that you have not already learned. I also like such books because they not only teach the reader how to do something, but also provide him or her with the chance to put those morsels of knowledge into practice in the form of exercises. I have therefore included several exercises, or projects, in this book, where appropriate, to give the reader opportunities to apply their knowledge. This book will serve as a reference text and will also provide a dynamic learning experience, so that you can learn by doing, as they say.

The projects throughout the book have a secondary purpose as well — to round out your Fedora Core system so that it can do anything you want it to. As you will see when you install Fedora Core, your new system (despite having more software than you will ever know what to do with) lacks certain applications and support files that you'll need to get the same or greater functionality as you had in your previous operating system. When you've completed all of the projects in the book, that will no longer be the case.

How to Use This Book

It is possible, of course, to use this book as a mere reference text that you only consult when you have a problem to solve, but that would negate the basic concept behind the design of the book. Instead, I recommend that you first go through the entire book chapter by chapter, doing the projects along the way. This will give you a much broader understanding of how things are done (and of how you can get things done), and it will reduce the chance for anxiety, confusion, and, worse yet, mistakes.

Of course, it is best to read this book and complete its projects when you are relaxed and have time to spare. Nothing makes things go wrong more than doing things in a rush. And keep in mind that Linux and the projects in this book are fun, not just challenging work exercises. The whole point of the Linux world, in my opinion, is that it offers all kinds of fun. So, go ahead and enjoy it.

About the Conventions Used in This Book

There are only a few minor points worth noting about the conventions I have used in the book. Words that you need to pay particular attention to, such as file or folder names that you will actually be called upon to use, I have put in **bold** type. Any words or command strings that you will have to type on the keyboard are shown in `monospace` font, while any output from the Linux command terminal, the application you use when you want to type in commands, is indicated by **`bold monospace`**. I have also opted to use the more graphically suggestive term *folder* instead of *directory* — no doubt the legacy of my many years as a Mac user.

Version Compatibility and Updates

This book was prepared for use with Fedora Core, the successor to Red Hat Linux 9 Personal Edition. Despite the new name, Fedora Core is really just the evolutionary next step in the Red Hat Linux line. A Red Hat Linux 8 or 9 user will feel right at home in Fedora Core — just think of it as a constantly evolving Red Hat Linux 10 with a name change. (I will explain the reasons for the name change and the new features of Fedora Core in Chapter 1.)

For those of you who are still using Red Hat Linux 9 (and who don't feel the need to upgrade to Fedora Core), I should point out that all of the projects in the book were also tested and are compatible with Red Hat Linux 9 Personal Edition; the links and procedures, when different from those for Fedora Core, are noted in the text.

The world of computers is an exceedingly dynamic thing, however, and there may be changes in the software or the links to the files for projects in the book after the book is released. Any such changes, as well as other updated information and cool software finds, will be posted at the Web site for this book: http://www.edgy-penguins.org/non-geeks.

About the CDs Accompanying This Book

Linux for Non-Geeks comes with a full Linux distribution on two CDs that includes more than enough software to keep you busy for, as Opie's Aunt Bea used to say, a month of Sundays. Once you have used the CDs to follow the installation steps in Chapter 2, your computer will be loaded with a fully functional and up-to-snuff Linux system based on the 2-disk Fedora Core Publisher's Edition. This will allow you to follow along with all the projects in the book and get everything else you want to get done . . . done.

I should also make it clear that the version of Fedora Core that accompanies this book, Fedora Core 1, is no longer the most recent version available, because FC2 is already out and FC3 is soon on its way. This is primarily irrelevant, however, because this is not a Fedora book. It is a book on learning to use Linux, and in my mind the relatively bug-free FC1 is a much better tool for that task than its buggier younger siblings.

That doesn't mean that you cannot or should not try one of the newer versions of Fedora Core on your own. I would strongly recommend that you wait until you have worked through the projects in this book with FC1 and have a little experience under your belt before moving out on your own. When you are ready (or if you're just curious), I have provided more information about the most recent versions of Fedora Core in the section "A Note about Fedora Versions" at the end of the book.

1

BECOMING A PENGUINISTA

Welcome to the World of Linux

Now we begin our project to get you up and running in the world of Linux. If you have already made the commitment and have Fedora Core installed on your machine, then you are essentially ready to go. Others of you might have made the commitment psychologically, but have yet to install anything on your computer. And some of you are probably reading these words in the aisle of a bookstore, wondering about Linux and about whether you should spend your money on this book or on a latté every morning for the next couple of weeks. For those in this last group, I can only say, "Get this book." Save the wear and tear on your stomach and nerves.

In any case, the first thing we need to do is get you up to snuff on what this Fedora Core thing is all about, why you might want to install and use it, and what you will need in order to do so. I expect you will have lots of questions along the way, and if you are like most people, a few doubts. I hope that by the time you finish this book and have your Linux system up and running, your doubts will be gone and your questions, for the most part, will be answered. For the time being, just relax, don't worry, and go with the flow.

What Is Linux?

Your computer, despite being a collection of highly sophisticated parts, is really just . . . well, a collection of highly sophisticated parts. On its own, it can do nothing other than switch on and off and spin a disk or two. In order for it to do anything else, it needs an operating system (OS) to guide it. The OS takes an essentially well-endowed but completely uneducated hunk of a machine and educates it, at least enough so that it will understand what you want it to do.

You already know of, and have probably used at least one of the many operating systems that exist today. Windows, DOS, and the Mac OS are all such operating systems, and Linux is yet another. Linux is, however, different from these other operating systems, both in terms of its capabilities and its heritage. Linux was not created by a corporation or by some corporate wanna-bes out to make money. It was instead created by a Swedish computer enthusiast living in Finland, Linus Torvalds, who wanted to create a better Unix-like system that would work on home computers, particularly his. Rather than keeping his creation to himself, Torvalds opened it up to the world, so to speak, and the system was then expanded and improved on by compu-geeks around the globe who worked to make the system better and more powerful.

Linux has acquired many fans and followers since its creation in 1994. Such devotees praise Linux for its many features, as well as for its being robust, reliable, free, and open. Despite these positive characteristics, however, Linux is, on its own, just a text-based system. There is no pretty desktop, and there are no windows or charming little icons to make you feel safe and comfy once you are behind the keyboard. Powerful though it may be, Linux is still strictly a black-screen, command-line-driven operating system. I guess you could think of it as DOS on steroids, though a Linux purist will surely cringe at the thought. Sorry.

Although you can use Linux by itself, accomplishing all your tasks by typing in commands on a black screen, you don't have to. It is fair to say that with the advent of the Macintosh and its easy-to-use graphical user interface (GUI, pronounced goo-ee) in 1984, users of other operating systems began suffering something akin to GUI envy. They began clamoring for a GUI to call their own, and Windows, which gave DOS a GUI, eased many command-wary users into the Microsoft world.

Similarly, many members of the Linux world felt the need and desire to go graphical, and various software mechanisms were developed by the community at large to bring about the change. The graphical desktop environments that are included in your Fedora Core distribution, GNOME and KDE, are examples of the fruit of that development.

About the Penguin

You may have been wondering about the penguin in the chapter title, so I might as well explain that now. The penguin is the Linux mascot, and his name is Tux (see Figure 1-1). This explains not only the ornithological references and graphics throughout the book, but also why there are so many penguin icons in Linux distributions and so many programs that include "penguin" or "Tux," like TuxRacer, XPenguins, and Pingus. This also explains why Linux users are sometimes referred to as Penguinistas.

Figure 1-1: Tux, the Linux mascot

Why Should I Use Linux?

People use Linux for many different reasons. For many it is a matter of power, stability, multilingual capabilities, or even personal philosophy. However, for many others, crass as it may sound, it is a matter of money. Just think for a moment about what it costs to get started up with another operating system. Go to wherever it is you go to buy software, and take a walk down the aisles. Make a list in your head of all the things you want to buy and how much each costs: an office suite, a game or two, and maybe a graphics program with which to make yourself look better in your digital photos. Now do the math.

After you pick yourself up off the floor, you will understand that we are talking big bucks here. On the other hand, for the price of this book you will have all of those things you wanted and more in the Linux world. Despite the worries that many people have, making the move to Linux means not only savings for you, but also more computing versatility — you will not be hamstrung at some point along the way because you don't have this or that program when you need it most — you'll have it all from the get-go!

You might counter with the fact that there are a lot of freeware applications out there for other operating systems, but c'mon, let's face it, these are often rather limited in terms of their capabilities. The programs with a little more oomph are mostly shareware, and most shareware programs these days are limited in some way, or they only let you use them for a month or less, unless you are willing to pay for them. Sure, their costs are relatively low, but $25 here and

$35 there eventually adds up to a considerable chunk of change. In addition, at least in my experience, the majority of such programs are hardly worth the money asked. The only shareware program I ever found worth buying was Lemke Software's GraphicConverter for the Mac.

Is It All Just About Money?

While money is important to the average user, it is certainly not the only reason for taking the Linux plunge; there are a variety of other reasons as well. As I mentioned before, Linux is noted for its stability. Try running your present system for a month without restarting occasionally and see what happens. Linux has been known to run for over a year without a hitch or decrease in performance. With its multilingual capabilities, Linux is also a perfect choice for language students or users in a multilingual environment.

In addition, Linux is infinitely customizable: You can get your system to look and act the way you want it to without being wizarded to death. And then there are the applications that come with most Linux distributions. In addition to there being a wide variety of them, most are well up to industry snuff, with some, such as Evolution and the GIMP, being sources of envy for those outside the Linux world.

But Is Linux Really Ready for the Desktop?

This question pops up quite often, and that's fair enough. But consider this: When you install a program on your present system and get an error message saying that the program can't run because some .dll file is missing, or when you connect a piece of hardware and can't get it to run, no one asks if that operating system is ready for the desktop.

In my own experience, I have found no reason to doubt that Linux is ready. Sure, Linux has its occasional quirks, but so does every other operating system. Linux is ready and able. If my mother, hardly a computer whiz, can do the work she needs to do and can keep herself amused till the middle of the night using her Linux system (without blowing the whole thing up), then I think it's pretty safe to say that you'll do all right too.

What Is a Distribution?

An operating system consists of a lot of files that perform a lot of different functions. And because there is no Linux Corporation to package and distribute the files that make up Linux, the task of getting Linux onto your computer in working order, along with the applications that you are likely to want, has fallen to a varied group of entities — companies, universities, user groups, and even private individuals. The Linux system and application collections they create are called *distributions*, or *distros*. You could bypass such distros and try to collect everything you'd need to set up a system all on your own, but you would undoubtedly lose your mind in the process. Most people, even the geekiest, opt for the distros.

The majority of these distros, whatever their ultimate target audience, basically consist of the same main elements: the Linux kernel itself, some sort of installer program to get all the system parts and applications properly installed on your machine, the X Window System to provide graphical interface support, one or more graphical desktop environments, and then a series of applications, such as word processors, audio players, games, and all the other files needed to make these things work.

There are, of course, a large number of distros. Some are geared to a specific audience, such as businesses, educators, gamers, students, programmers, system administrators, and specific language users. What makes each distro different is the specific software that is bundled with the Linux kernel, as well as other convenience features, such as the installer. Some distros are especially appropriate for home users due to their ease of installation. Mandrake, SuSE, and Fedora/Red Hat Linux are probably the three most popular in this regard, with Fedora/Red Hat Linux being cited as having the most users in the American market. While many of these entities charge for their distros, most also provide them free for download.

What Is Fedora Core?

Red Hat, the company, essentially had two different Linux product lines: a consumer product for personal desktops and workstations (Red Hat Linux 8 and 9, for example), and a separate product for corporate users (Red Hat Enterprise Edition). The corporate product is and always has been Red Hat's cash cow, as companies pay for the system on a subscription basis along with various support services. The consumer version, despite its great popularity, was essentially a money loser because most users would just download it for free, rather than buy it.

In the first half of 2003, Red Hat announced that it would no longer package and sell the consumer product as a boxed item, and instead set it off as a semi-autonomous unit under the Red Hat umbrella called the Red Hat Linux Project. The new project would continue producing the consumer version, but as a totally free product developed by the project with Linux community involvement. Most saw this as a positive move, as it would allow greater input into and more rapid development of the distribution. Work then progressed on what most people were then calling Red Hat Linux 10.

Shortly after the establishment of the Red Hat Linux Project, however, work began on a merger between that project and another completely separate community project, the Fedora Linux Project. The Fedora Linux Project, rather than building a distribution of its own, worked to prepare application packages (RPMs) for use with Red Hat Linux. As the goals of the two projects were overlapping, the two projects merged. The result is the Fedora Project, which is still under the Red Hat umbrella. Rather than continue using the name Red Hat Linux, however, the Fedora Project opted to use the more all-encompassing name *Fedora Core* as the name of its distribution.

Is Fedora Core Different from Red Hat Linux?

Fedora Core, at this point, is essentially what Red Hat Linux 10 was going to be, just with a new name. It is hardly a startling departure from what has come before. Red Hat Linux 8 and 9 users should feel completely at home with Fedora Core, as it retains the look, feel, and functionality of Red Hat Linux 9. To paraphrase the folks at the project, changes will be evolutionary, not revolutionary. This is certainly the case so far.

Of course, with every new version release, there are a few changes, but other than the updated Bluecurve theme and the inclusion of a couple of new applications, most of the changes will not be readily apparent.

Why Fedora Then?

With so many distros out there, you may wonder why you should opt for Fedora Core. Well, I've tried quite a few distros, and Fedora Core is the one that pleased me most. As for the reasons, they basically come down to these:

Ease of installation   The Mandrake distro is often cited as the easiest distro to install, and perhaps in terms of setting up a dual-boot Windows/Linux system, that might be true to some degree. However, I have to give the nod to Fedora. Though I do not advocate doing this, one could just press ENTER at every stage of the Fedora Core installation process and end up with a perfectly usable system. What could be easier than that? Even if you screw up, you don't.

RPM based   As you will soon learn, RPM (Red Hat Package Manager) provides a very easy way of installing additional software and related files.

RPM availability   Perhaps because of its market share, there are many more RPMs out there for Red Hat Linux and Fedora than for any other distro.

Dependable and robust   I know these terms come across as mere hype, but after you smack things around in your Fedora system a bit, particularly when using GNOME, you come to understand what they mean. Knock things down and around, and they bounce right back — this is very important for beginners who often have a knack for screwing things up. Nothing turns a new user off more than a twitchy system that has to be velvet gloved all the time.

Good selection of applications   Fedora Core comes with more applications than you will know what to do with, and most are configured so that they will work as soon as you run them.

One last point worth mentioning is that the Fedora/Red Hat community of users is actually even larger than the number of people who use Fedora Core or Red Hat Linux. Many other distros are actually Red Hat–based, meaning that they are essentially Red Hat Linux distributions with all the Red Hat references and logos being replaced and with certain software packages added or removed to customize the distro for its targeted audience. JAMD, Yellow Dog, and Alt Linux are all Red Hat Linux–based distros. In theory, even *you* could create your own Red Hat–based distro. Red Hat, the company, is pretty cool in that sense, and as the

Fedora Project is continuing that same policy, you could even create your own Fedora-based distro and call it something like Boaz Linux, for example, once you know what you are doing.

Hardware Compatibility

Well, enough of this background babble; it's time to get things rolling. If you haven't installed Linux on your machine yet and are wondering whether you can, it is relatively safe to say that Fedora Core will run on most machines out there today. Of course, this statement comes with a major caveat: You just never know till you get up and running. There are so many minor parts to your machine that it is difficult to say whether each part will cooperate with your installation. Ignoring peripheral devices for the time being, there are video cards, sound chips, LAN cards, monitors, and so on, and they all need to be considered.

If you are really worried about compatibility, you can search the Web to see if your hardware is supported by Linux. Of course, before you can do this, you need to know what model of hardware you have. You should know at least what motherboard, processor (CPU), and monitor you have if you want to be able to find out anything of value. Identifying your CPU and monitor should be easy enough, but the motherboard may require a bit more searching. If you have no documentation that clearly states what kind of motherboard you have, then just open up the case of your computer and look at your board. You needn't worry about damaging something because you don't need to touch anything (so don't). You may need a flashlight to find it, but the model name and number should be stamped on there somewhere, either in the middle of the board or around the edges. Mine, for example, says quite clearly in the middle of the board, "AOpen MX46-533V." You should be looking for similar information.

Once you have that information, you can do a variety of things to check out your motherboard's compatibility with Fedora Core. You can simply do a Yahoo or Google search by typing in your motherboard's make and model plus the word "Linux." This works for other hardware devices too. You can also post a question to one of the various Linux forums or mailing lists on the Web. A listing of some of these is provided in Appendix B at the end of this book. Just write that you are a newbie and want to know if anyone has had any experience using Fedora Core or Red Hat Linux with the board (or other hardware) in question. You will probably get quite a few responses. Linux users are usually rather evangelical in terms of trying to draw in new users.

If you are going to buy a new machine to run Linux on, then it is reasonable enough to check things out first, but if you are going to install it on the machine you have, I recommend just diving in. Being the reckless character that I am, searching the Net to figure out whether things will work seems a bit of a nuisance to me. You can spend hours poking around and still end up not being sure. You might also be misled into thinking that Fedora Core won't work on your machine, when in fact it actually will. You can find out for sure by just trying to install it. If it works, it works; and if it doesn't, it doesn't.

Hardware Requirements

All worries about compatibility aside, there are some minimum hardware requirements that you will need, and thus want, to meet:

- Pentium II processor, 400 megahertz (MHz) or above for a graphic-mode system
- About 3GB of hard disk space, though having at least 10GB would be more comfy
- Sufficient memory (RAM)

I have a bit to say about RAM. The official specs tell you that you need a minimum of 192 megabytes (MB) to run Fedora Core (though 256MB is recommended to run it comfortably). Yeah, right. That might do the trick if all you want to do is stare at your desktop, but I have yet to find anyone who is inclined to do only that. This underestimation doesn't mean that the folks at the Fedora Project are trying to sucker you. It is just one of those OS things. The fact is that no matter what OS you are dealing with, whether it be Windows or Macintosh or Linux, whatever they tell you is enough memory is sure to be too little. My basic rule of thumb, no matter what OS I am dealing with, is that you need the recommended (not the minimum) memory plus at least 128MB. Regardless of what the official specs say, put in more. You won't regret it.

Saying that the more memory you have, the better, may sound a bit simple, and perhaps even cavalier, but trust me on this one. When you have too little memory, no matter what system you are running, weird things happen: applications seem to take years to open, or don't open at all; menus take forever to render their little icons; and freezes and general system meltdowns just happen much more often.

To be realistic and exceedingly honest, I would say that 256MB is the absolute minimum you want to have. I personally would recommend that you have at least 384MB of RAM in order for things to move smoothly and comfortably. It is such a waste to have a pretty speedy CPU and not be able to appreciate it because its hands are tied by a lack of memory. It is sort of like trying to do jumping jacks in a broom closet. Sure you could do it, but you would be all contorted, and you'd be smashing your hands into the walls every 1.4 seconds.

Memory is relatively cheap these days, so go for it. Since you're saving money on applications by installing the Fedora Core system, you should have enough extra cash to make your life easier. After all, a 128MB DIMM (memory chip) will set you back less than $30, and a 256MB DIMM less than $45 (according to Hardware Planet, www.compwarehouse.com, and 18004 Memory, www.18004memory.com, as I write this). At those prices, just imagine how much memory you could buy for the price of the most popular Windows Office suite.

Where Do I Go from Here?

Now that you know more about the world of Linux, it's time to get down to it. If you have already installed Fedora Core on your machine, just flip ahead to Chapter 3. If your machine is still Linuxless, though, it's time to commit. Strap yourself down in front of that computer, clip on your spurs, and go straight to the next chapter. It's time to become a Penguinista!

2

MAKING COMMITMENTS

Installing Linux on Your Machine

If you have already installed Fedora Core (or even Red Hat Linux 9) on your machine, you can skip right over this chapter and go on to the next one. If, however, you haven't installed Fedora Core yet and are ready and raring to do so, then you had better stay right where you are and read on. In this chapter, I will guide you through the installation steps and review everything you need to do before that in order to get Linux up and running on your machine.

Protecting You from Yourself

Before beginning the installation of Fedora Core, you must decide upon a root password, a user account name, and a user password. You will be asked for this information during installation, so it will be good to get it out of the way here.

You may wonder what this *root* business is all about, so I will explain. Generally, Linux asks that you have at least two accounts: a *root* account and a *user* account. The root account is there automatically; all you have to do is come up with a password. The root account is used for system administration chores, such as installing programs or changing system settings.

As for the user account, this you will set up yourself during the post-installation process at the end of this chapter. You decide on your own username and password. The user account is the one that you use for your everyday computing chores.

In general, if you are doing anything other than altering the system setup in some way, you should be using your user account. This is Linux's way of protecting you from yourself, so that in the course of your everyday computer use you will not damage the system by doing anything dumb. If you screw anything up, it will only affect your personal data; the system will remain intact.

With your root account powers, you can create additional user accounts at any time. Let's say that your family wants to use your computer, but you don't want them messing around with your files or, worse yet, blitzing the whole system in some way. You could use one account for yourself, and then add additional accounts for your daughter (Erika), your son (Jethro), and your spouse (Pat).

Under this system, when any one of them starts up your computer, they will only be able to log in to their own account, from which they will have no access to the system itself or to any of the files in anyone else's account. Jethro cannot read Erika's private letters; Erika cannot find out what Jethro has bookmarked in his Web browser, and your beloved Pat cannot pop open one of your spreadsheet files to find out how you are squandering the family fortune — all very safe and convenient. Of course, because you set up the computer and, thus, also have access to the root account, you can log in as the root user and enter any of their accounts to see what is going on. This may not be fair to them, but that is just the way things are.

Now that you understand the root/user distinction, decide upon a root password and a user password. You will be using the user password every time you log in, so make sure it is something that you won't forget and, more importantly, won't mind typing in every day. The root password you won't really need to use as much, although you will be using it quite a bit while doing the projects in this book. Still, it should be something that you will remember, because it is very important.

You will also need to come up with a username for yourself. It could be as simple as your initials (my username is *rg*) or the name of your favorite tropical fish, such as *neontetra*. Whatever you choose, it will appear on your desktop once you've logged in, so make sure it is a username you don't mind seeing every day. Having to see "stinky's Home" on your desktop day in and day out could prove a little annoying if not embarrassing. By the way, your username cannot have any spaces and must be all lowercase.

Once you've decided upon your username and your root and user passwords, make sure that you write them down on a piece of paper or in a book, and keep it at hand until the installation process is over and you have gotten the swing of things. After that, you can store it in some safe place — but don't forget, as I am prone to do, where that safe place is. The information is very important, and it is easy, as time rolls by, to forget such things, which you definitely do not want to do. Holding on to your root password is most important of all, because without it you won't be able to install packages, add users, or even change your printer settings.

Single- or Dual-Boot Setup?

If you don't have Windows on your machine, you can skip right over this section. If you do have Windows installed on your machine, the first thing you are going to have to do is decide whether or not you want to keep it.

It is possible to have both Windows and Linux installed on the same machine and for them to happily coexist. In my own case, I started out with just such a dual-boot setup. In time, however, I found that I used the Linux side of things exclusively. Having so much disk space being taken up by a Windows system I didn't use seemed a waste of prime real estate, so eventually I just dumped the whole thing and went for a straight Linux-only setup. My feeling is that unless you have some application that you really need that is not available on the Linux side (probably some game), then go for the Linux-only setup and just forget about Windows. Linux has most of what you will need anyway, and because OpenOffice can read and write MS Office files, you'll be well enough connected, if that is of concern to you.

You may be thinking that if you do as I suggest and dump your Windows system when you install Linux, you might have to reinstall Windows if you don't like Linux or if you can't get it installed properly. That would be a considerable waste of time and energy, to be sure. However, believe it or not, there are advantages to my suggestion even if your no-go scenario turns out to be the case.

You may have noticed that your Windows system, as you've used it over time, has gotten sort of gunked up — it is no longer the quick little kitten it used to be. Menus don't pop open as quickly as they used to, things take longer to start up than they did before, and you find yourself saying "what the Sam Habberdack is that!" all the time, as mysterious things happen with increasing frequency.

This is just the nature of the beast, and a very good way of getting things back to normal is to reinstall the whole thing. So even if you do decide to come back to Windows later, you'll be doing yourself a favor, because it should run better than before. It's a little more work up front, but in the long run you'll be a happier camper.

If, on the other hand, you opt for running both Windows and Linux, you will be greeted by a Linux boot-selection screen when you start up your machine, from which you can choose to continue booting up Linux or choose Windows in its stead. After that, boot-up proceeds as normal for the system you selected. This setup works fine, so you needn't worry.

Of course, in order to create a dual-boot setup, you will need to have either two hard disks (preferable) or at least two partitions on one hard disk. The disk or partition on which you intend to install Fedora Core (the non-Windows, or *target,* partition) will also have to be at least 5 gigabytes (GB) in size. If you don't have a single partition of that size available but do have two or three that you can use, that will do too. And if you don't have any of these, you can either install another internal hard disk or create another partition with some partitioning software, such as Partition Magic, before trying to install Fedora Core.

The state of your target partition or disk will determine what creating a dual-boot system means for you during the installation process. If, for example, the target partition or disk is just unformatted free space, the installation process will be much like a straight Linux-only installation. If, however, the target hard disk or partition is already formatted in a DOS file system, such as Fat16 or Fat32, then you will have a bit more work cut out for you during the installation process. The dual-boot installation process is explained in the "Dual-Boot Installation" section later in the chapter — read through that section to get an idea of whether or not you'll feel comfortable doing what needs to be done.

Pre-Installation: Can You Boot from CD?

Before you go on to the installation, make sure that your computer is set up to boot from your CD drive. Most machines these days are set up to do this, so you probably don't have to do anything special. If you're not sure and don't feel like tinkering around, you can just find out by going right to the installation steps in the next section. If the installation starts up, you can just keep going. On the other hand, if you suddenly boot up in Windows, you will have to make some adjustments.

Probably the only thing you have to do is restart your machine and then press whatever key the screen tells you to in order to enter your BIOS setup. This is usually DELETE or F1, but not all machines are the same. If the onscreen information passes by so fast that you miss it, you can check your user's manual to see what the correct key is. Once you get into the BIOS setup, change the boot sequence so that your CD drive is first.

In the extremely unlikely event that your machine cannot boot from a CD at all, you will have to create a 3.5-inch boot diskette. To do this, you must first boot up your machine in Windows. Once you are at your Windows desktop, insert the Fedora Core Install Disk 1 and look for and open the **dosutils** folder on that CD.

In the **dosutils** folder, you will find another folder called **rawwritewin**. Open that folder, and you will find a utility program called **rawwritewin** (that's no typo: two w's in the folder name, but three in the application name). It has a little penguin as its icon. Double-click the penguin, and RawWrite will open up as shown in Figure 2-1.

Figure 2-1: RawWrite under Windows

To create the boot floppy, put a 1.44MB floppy disk in your floppy drive. In the **Image File** input box in the RawWrite window, type D:\images/bootdisk.img (if your CD drive is not the D drive, change this accordingly) or use the **...** button to locate the file graphically. Once you've done this, click the **Write** button, and RawWrite will create a boot floppy for you. Once it's done, be sure to label the diskette accordingly.

Doing the Deed

Let's get down to the actual Linux installation. Put Install Disk 1 in your CD drive (and if you needed to make a boot floppy, stick that into your floppy drive too) and keep the other installation CD and a blank floppy disk next to your computer. Set this book on your lap so you can follow along, and get ready for action. It's time to do the deed!

To keep things as simple as possible, I will ask you to let me be the captain here. Don't worry about what to do unless I specifically ask you to check or decide something on your own. If any of the selections I ask you to make sound odd, there is a reason, so don't worry. Trust me here. I am going to have you install your system in a way that will allow you to do all of the projects in this book, that will keep you out of trouble, that will give you greater flexibility in the future once you're on your own, and that hopefully will make things run a tad faster than they might otherwise. We will be installing the KDE desktop environment in addition to GNOME, so you will have the chance to use KDE in the future as well. Once you know a bit more about what you are doing, you will be able to make changes to system settings and add or delete software packages as you choose.

When you look at the following steps, the installation may look like a long and cumbersome process. It is not. It will be over more quickly than you can imagine. Installation steps 1–23 combined take me less than five minutes to complete. As a beginner frequently referring to this text, you might take a bit longer, of course, but don't worry. All in all, the whole process is faster (and I think easier) than that for Windows XP or Mac OS X. And keep in mind that with XP and OS X, you are installing the operating system with just a few bundled applications. In a Fedora Core Linux installation, you are installing not only the operating system itself, but also most of the applications you will ever want or need to use. You will thus be getting a lot done in one fell swoop.

One more thing before we start. Some people approach installing a system with a good deal of trepidation. The process makes them nervous, as if the house is going to go up in smoke if they click the wrong thing somewhere along the line. Needless to say, there is no need for such concern. As long as you have backed up your data, you will be OK. If you screw up the installation the first time out, so what? Just start over again. No harm done, as you have nothing to harm. Just make sure that you give yourself more time than you need for the process. Don't start installing one hour before you have to be at work, or before you have to meet your friend downtown. Rushing makes people do weird things. Make things easy on yourself by giving yourself plenty of time . . . and by backing up any data you would mourn the loss of.

That said, let's get to it!

1. **Start 'er up**   If you haven't already done so, place Install Disk 1 in your drive (and a boot floppy in your floppy drive, if you need one), and start your machine.

2. **Choose install type**   After a bit of scrolling white text, you will arrive at your first semi-graphical screen. Here you select the type of installation you want to perform. Just press ENTER on your keyboard for a graphical installation. Some white text will then flow down the screen for a while.

3. **Media check**   If you are installing Fedora using the disks included with this book, you will not be presented with this step, so skip on down to step 4. If you are using disks burned from downloaded disk images (ISOs), you can either perfom the media check by pressing ENTER, or skip it by using your TAB or cursor keys to highlight the **No** button and then pressing ENTER. Either way, it's up to you, though, personally, I wouldn't bother.

You will now be treated to a blue screen with the words "Welcome to Fedora Core" at the top. This screen will just sit there for a few seconds, and then the bottom quarter of the screen will turn black and be filled with a short stream of scrolling white text. After a few more seconds, you will have a total blackout, but don't panic, as this is all normal and will only last a few moments. Then you will see an X in the middle of the screen, followed by a graphical Fedora Core splash screen with a blue background. This will disappear on its own in a couple of seconds, after which you will see the first graphical installation screen, "Welcome to Fedora Core."

NOTE *If you are using an LCD flat-panel display or an old or unusual monitor, it is possible that the installer won't know how to deal with it. In that case, the black screen mentioned previously may never disappear, or you might be greeted by a screen full of distorted-looking junk that you can't make heads or tails of. If so, restart your machine, and then at the semi-graphical prompt mentioned in step 2 type* linux lowres *after the **Boot:** prompt ("Boot:" will already be on the screen; you don't have to type it) and press* ENTER. *Things should work after that. If, however, they do not, restart your machine and, when you get to the semi-graphical prompt again, type in* linux nofb *after the **Boot:** prompt and press* ENTER.

1. **Welcome to Fedora Core**   Just click **Next** to proceed.

2. **Default language for the installation**   Choose the language you want to use during the installation process, and then click **Next**. You will be able to choose additional languages to install later, so don't worry about that.

3. **Keyboard configuration**   Select your keyboard layout, or accept the default if it is correct, and click **Next**.

4. **Mouse configuration**   Select your mouse type, or accept the default if it is correct, and click **Next**.

NOTE *If you have a laptop with a two-button trackpad, then 2 Button Mouse (PS/2) is most likely the correct choice.*

5. **Monitor Configuration**   You will most likely only see this screen if the installer cannot determine what kind of monitor you have. In this case, it will select **Unprobed Monitor**. If so, select one of the settings in the **Generic** groups.

6. **Upgrade examine**   If you are installing Fedora onto a hard disk that does not already have a Linux system installed, you will most likely not see this screen. If you do, choose **Install Fedora Core** and then click **Next**.

7. **Installation type**   Choose **Workstation** and then click **Next**.

8. **Disk partitioning setup**   **Automatically Partition** should be the default. If so, and you're not setting up a dual-boot system, click **Next**.
   For a dual-boot system, things are a little different. If you're installing Fedora Core on a partition or hard disk that is not formatted (i.e., free space), then you can proceed to step 11. If, however, your target partition or hard disk is already formatted, select **Partition Manually with Disk Druid**, click **Next**, and follow the steps in the "Dual-Boot Installation" section later in this chapter. Once you've done that, you can come back to step 11 of this installation process.

9. **Automatic partitioning**   Select **Remove all Linux partitions on this machine** and click **Next**. If you want to clear your entire hard disk and make it Linux only, select **Remove all partitions on this machine** instead.
   At this point, a small window will pop up asking you if you really want to do this. Click **Yes**. This will be followed by another small pop-up window telling you that your boot partition might not meet the booting constraints of your machine. Just click **OK**.

10. **Partitioning your disk**   Accept the defaults by clicking **Next**.

11. **Boot loader configuration** If you are not setting up a dual-boot system, accept the defaults by clicking **Next**.

On dual-boot systems, every time you boot up after installation, you will be presented with a menu from which you can choose to boot either into Windows or into Fedora. If you do nothing, the boot loader will automatically boot you into Fedora after a few seconds. If you would prefer the boot loader to automatically boot you into Windows if you do nothing, click the checkbox next to **DOS** as shown in Figure 2-2.

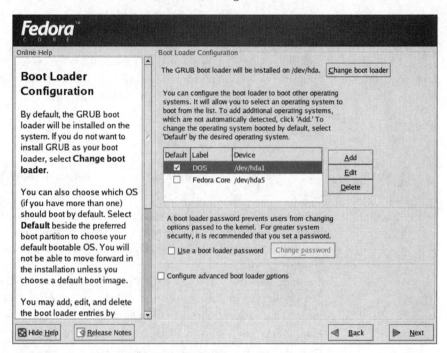

Figure 2-2: Setting the default OS on a dual-boot system

12. **Network configuration** Accept the defaults by clicking **Next**. Note that if the installer doesn't find a compatible network (Ethernet) card, this screen will not appear.

13. **Firewall configuration** Click **Next** to accept the default firewall. This will protect your system from intruders.

14. **Language support selection** If you want to set up a multilingual machine, you can add additional languages here. You can choose as many additional languages as you like. You will be able to boot up in any of the languages you select, after which the system interface, most applications, and, very importantly, the help files will appear in the chosen language (read Chapter 17 for more information if this is of interest or concern to you). If you don't want a multilingual machine, accept the default language, which is the installation language. In either case, finish your selection by clicking **Next**.

NOTE   *As you will find out in Chapter 17, it is easy to add foreign language support for most foreign languages after you have installed your system. However, if you are considering installing support for Chinese, Japanese, or Korean, it is much better and less cumbersome to do so now.*

15. **Time zone configuration**   Click the yellow dot closest to your place of abode (or at least in the same time zone as where you live) and then click **Next**.

16. **Set root password**   Enter the root password you've decided upon in both boxes and then click **Next**.

17. **Package installation defaults**   Your computer will take a few seconds as it searches for packages. Once it's done, select **Customize the set of packages to be installed** and then click **Next**.

18. **Customizing your package selections**   At this point, you are going to add a group of programs and other packages that are not part of a default Fedora installation, but are necessary, or at least useful, for following along with the projects in this book. When the Package Group Selection screen (shown in Figure 2-3) appears, do the following:

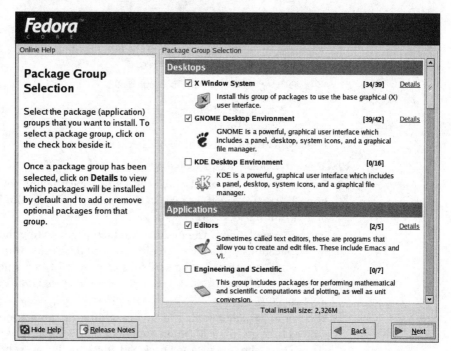

Figure 2-3: Selecting programs and packages to install

a.   Check the box next to **KDE Desktop Environment**.

b.   Scroll down to Sound & Video and click the **Details** link to the right. A window with details of the audio/video packages will be displayed (see Figure 2-4 on the next page). Check the boxes next to **grip** and **xcdroast**, and then click **OK**.

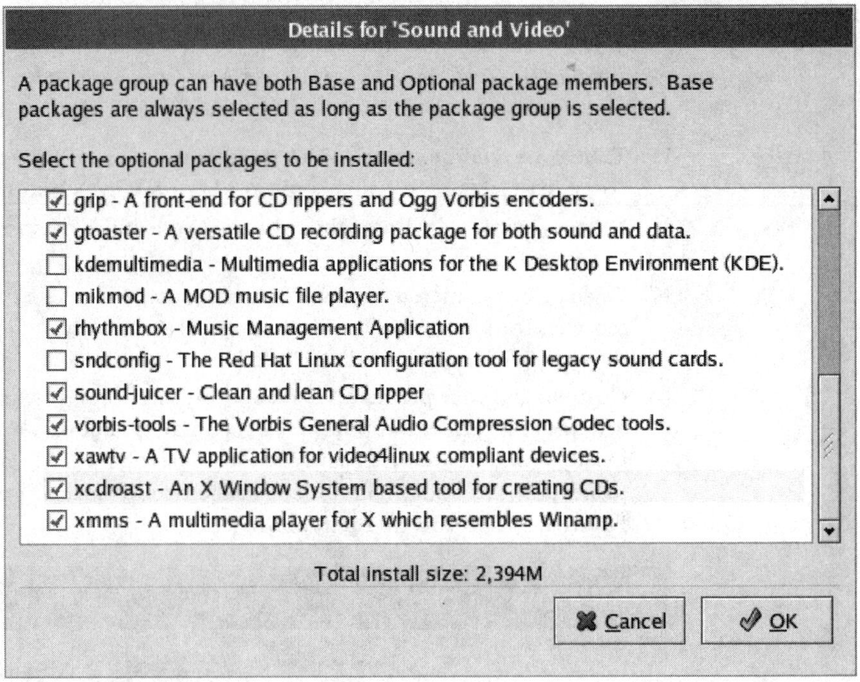

Details for 'Sound and Video'

A package group can have both Base and Optional package members. Base packages are always selected as long as the package group is selected.

Select the optional packages to be installed:

- ☑ grip - A front-end for CD rippers and Ogg Vorbis encoders.
- ☑ gtoaster - A versatile CD recording package for both sound and data.
- ☐ kdemultimedia - Multimedia applications for the K Desktop Environment (KDE).
- ☐ mikmod - A MOD music file player.
- ☑ rhythmbox - Music Management Application
- ☐ sndconfig - The Red Hat Linux configuration tool for legacy sound cards.
- ☑ sound-juicer - Clean and lean CD ripper
- ☑ vorbis-tools - The Vorbis General Audio Compression Codec tools.
- ☑ xawtv - A TV application for video4linux compliant devices.
- ☑ xcdroast - An X Window System based tool for creating CDs.
- ☑ xmms - A multimedia player for X which resembles Winamp.

Total install size: 2,394M

✖ Cancel   **✔ OK**

Figure 2-4: Selecting sound and video package details

    c.   Finally, scroll down to the System section and check the box next to **System Tools**.

When you are all done with these steps, click **Next**.

19. **About to install**   Just click **Next**.

20. **Required media**   A small window will now appear telling you which installation CDs you will need. Just click **Continue**, and the partitioning and formatting of your hard disk will begin.

21. **Package installation**   The installer will then begin writing the system and all the applications you selected to disk. You will be greeted with a series of screens (all variations on Figure 2-5), some with witty messages, and you will see an even more constant series of darting blue progress bars showing you what is being installed at any given moment.

You can sit back and watch this stream of progress, go get yourself a sandwich, or go to the TV and watch reruns of *Green Acres*. Whatever you choose to do, be sure to come back and check on things every ten minutes or so, as you will be called upon to change CDs. The whole process should, depending upon the speed of your hardware, take less than 20 minutes.

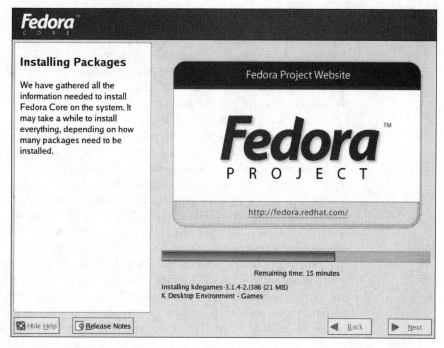

Figure 2-5: Installing Fedora Core

22. **Boot disk creation** When the system and apps are all installed, you will be
asked whether you want to make a boot diskette. You might as well do this
just to be safe, so click **Next**. A little window (see Figure 2-6) will then pop up
telling you to stick a floppy in the drive, so do that. It doesn't matter if the
disk is blank or not (as long as you are willing to sacrifice any data that's on
it) or whether it is formatted or not. After you've put the disk in, click the
Make boot disk button, and the installer will start erasing, formatting, and
then writing your boot disk.

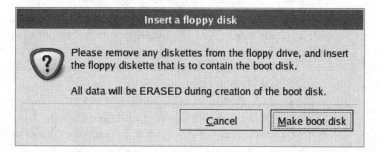

Figure 2-6: Creating a boot diskette

23. **Congratulations, the installation is complete** This ends the main
installation process. All you have to do now is remove the CD and the
floppy disk from their respective drives, and then click **Reboot**. Be sure
to label that floppy.

Dual-Boot Installation

If you've decided to keep Windows on your machine and install Linux on another partition or on another internal hard disk, then you need to follow these installation steps, as was mentioned in step 10 in the previous section. If you are doing a Linux-only install with no Windows on your machine, you can ignore this section and move on, unless, of course, you're just interested.

As I mentioned before, in order to create a dual-boot setup, you will need to have an additional hard drive in your machine (preferred) or at least 5GB of space (10GB would be better) on a partition that you are willing to commit to Linux (other than the one where you have Windows installed). If you do not have a second hard drive or an additional partition, you will either have to install another hard drive or add another partition to your present drive with a partitioning program, such as Partition Magic, before trying to install Fedora. You do not need to format or clear the target partition or disk before proceeding; just make sure you have one. And again, remember that any data on the partition or disk which you are allocating to Linux will be erased for good.

The following steps will prepare your disks for dual-boot installation. This may seem complicated, but it isn't bad at all. Just follow the directions as laid out, and you should have no problems. You can always go back to change things once you're done, so don't get too stressed out. The process is rather forgiving.

1. **Select a disk or partition**   On the screen shown in Figure 2-7, you select your target disk or partition. The disk layout in the figure, of course, will depend on your drive setup. Select the target partition or disk that you will use for your Linux installation by clicking the partition name in the list or by clicking the graphical map of your disk setup. Your Windows partition will most likely be hda1 (for an IDE drive) or sda1 (for a SCSI drive), so your target will probably be hda2 or, in the case of a separate hard disk, sda2, hdb1, or sdb1. Once you have made your selection, click the **Delete** button in the middle of the right half of the screen, which will clear all data and formatting from the partition or disk you have selected.

2. **Confirm partition delete**   A small warning window, as shown in Figure 2-8, will then pop open. Click the **Delete** button to remove the partition. If you think you've made a mistake after doing this, you needn't worry because your disk isn't actually changed at this point. You can still use the **Back** button and start all over again.

3. **Select free space**   Your target partition should now appear as free space. Select that free space by clicking it, and then click the **New** button. An Add Partition window, as shown in Figure 2-9 on page 28, will then open.

4. **Create a swap partition**   In the Add Partition window, click the **File System Type** drop-down menu and select **Swap**. In the **Size (MB)** box, type a value that is double the size of the random access memory (RAM) on your machine. Thus, if you have 256MB of RAM, type 512, and so on. Once you've done this, click **OK**.

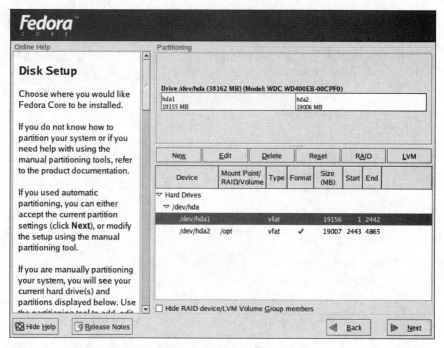

Figure 2-7: Choose the installation disk or partition

5. **Create a boot partition** Select the remaining amount of free space by click-ing it, and then click the **New** button. The Add Partition window will again open, but this time, for the **Mount Point**, select **/boot** from the drop-down menu. In the **File System Type** drop-down menu, select **ext3**. Finally, in the **Size** field, type 100. When you are finished, click **OK**.

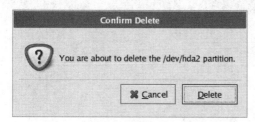

Figure 2-8: Confirm the deletion of the partition

6. **Confirm boot disk creation** A small warning window will open to tell you that you might need to create a boot disk. You will be doing this at the end of the installation process just in case, so click **Continue** for now.

7. **Create a root partition** Select the remaining amount of free space by clicking it, and then click the **New** button. Again, an Add Partition window (see Figure 2-10 on the following page) will open. For the **Mount Point** set-ting, select **/** from the drop-down menu. For the **File System Type**, select **ext3** from the drop-down menu. Finally, select the **Fill to maximum allow-able size** option in the **Additional Size Options** section. When you are all done, click **OK**.

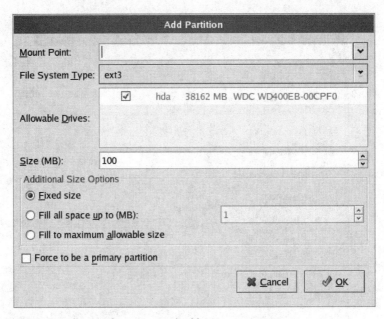

Figure 2-9: Select the free space and add a new partition

8. **Partition your disk**   The partition setup you have just created should look
something like the one shown in Figure 2-11. (Of course, yours will probably
look a bit different, depending on your hardware setup.) If all seems to be as
it should, click **Next**. If something looks odd to you, or if you, for some per-
verse reason, just want to do it all over again, click the **Back** button and start
over from the beginning.

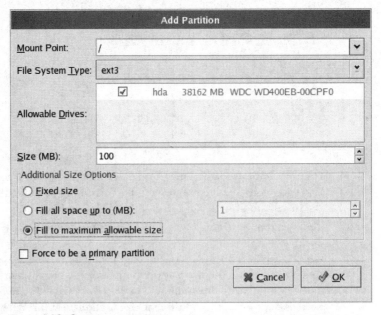

Figure 2-10: Create a root partition

9. **Return to the main installation steps** You are now done with the dual-boot setup. Go back to the single-boot installation process and continue with step 11.

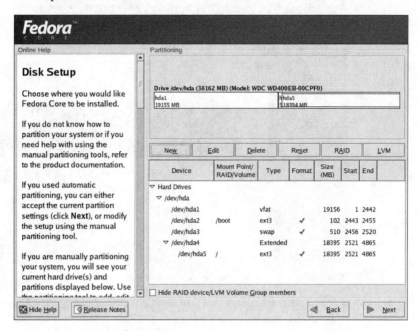

Figure 2-11: A completed partition setup

Post-Installation Steps

Once you have completed all of the installation steps and your computer restarts itself, you will be greeted by the boot loader screen. If you've set up a Linux-only machine, just press ENTER (or just wait a few seconds). If you are a dual booter, select Fedora Core with your cursor keys, and press ENTER. After a short while, a new Welcome screen (shown in Figure 2-12 on the next page) will appear to take you through the post-installation process. Fortunately, there are very few steps here, so you needn't worry much at this stage of the game.

1. **Welcome** Just click **Next** to proceed.

2. **License agreement** Give the agreement a read-through, and then select **Yes, I agree to the License Agreement** and click **Next**.

3. **Date and time** The defaults should be correct here, so, assuming they are, click **Next**. If not, you can adjust them now.

4. **User account** Just type the username you've decided upon (with no spaces and no caps), your real name (both first and last), and then whatever you decided upon for your user password in the two bottom boxes. Once you have done all this, click **Next**.

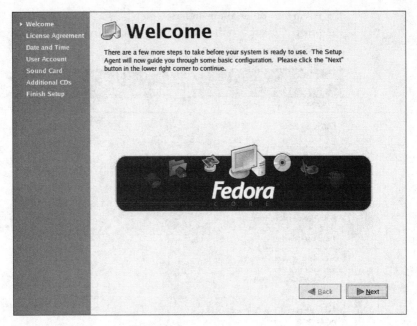

Figure 2-12: The post-installation Welcome screen

5. **Sound card**   Here you can test your sound card by clicking the **Test Sound** button. You will hear three sounds (one from each speaker individually and then one from both speakers in unison). After that, a window will pop up asking you if you heard the sound. Click **Yes,** and the window will disappear. Now click **Next**.

6. **Additional CDs**   You probably don't have any, so click **Next**.

7. **Finish setup**   The only thing for you to do now is click **Next**.

Now you have done it all, and your new Linux system is installed on your machine. After a few moments, you will see the login screen, so to find out what to do after that, go on to the next chapter. See you there. Aloha.

3

A NEW PLACE TO CALL HOME

Getting to Know the Desktop

So now you have Fedora installed on your machine and are ready and raring to go. The login screen that will appear every time you boot up Fedora Core is there waiting for you (see Figure 3-1 on the next page).

There's no need to keep the login screen waiting, so just type your username and press ENTER. After that, you will be prompted for your user password in the same screen. Type it in and press ENTER again. Now, within moments, you will have your first glimpse of your new desktop within Fedora.

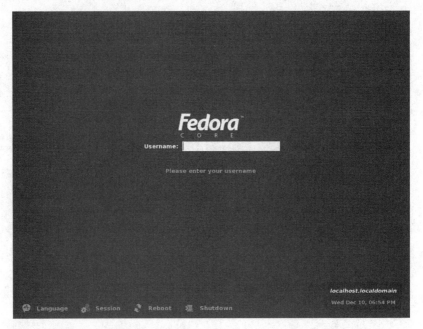

Figure 3-1: The Fedora Core login screen

Welcome to the GNOME Desktop

As I mentioned earlier, your Fedora distribution comes with two graphical desktop environments: GNOME and KDE. Both have their own strengths and weaknesses, and, as such, both have their fans and detractors. However, as GNOME is the default environment in Fedora Core, and because I think it is much easier for new Linux users to deal with, we will focus on it almost exclusively in this book.

In case you're wondering whether or not you're missing out on anything by using GNOME, let me assure you that you are not. You can run any KDE application from within GNOME, and vice versa. In fact, once you have a look at the Main menu, you will see that there are many KDE applications (*apps,* for short) listed in the various submenus. Most apps beginning with a *K* are KDE apps, such as the KAtomic and KBounce games, and the KPPP Internet dialer, which I will discuss in Chapter 4. If you followed my directions in Chapter 2, KDE is also installed on your machine, and you are free to use it on your own once you're finished with this book.

The GNOME desktop is shown in Figure 3-2, and as you can see, it isn't all that different from what you might be used to in a Windows environment. But don't be completely fooled; despite the similarities, things are different enough to be interesting. There are three main elements that you will probably notice right off the bat: the desktop icons, the GNOME Panel at the bottom of the screen, and the Main menu button at the far left corner of the GNOME Panel. I will focus on these elements in this chapter.

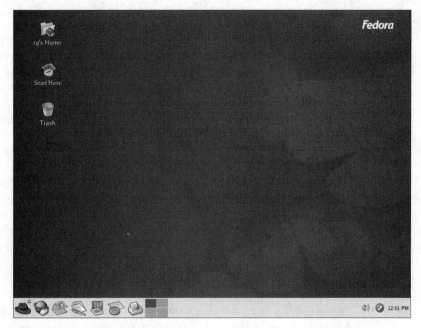

Figure 3-2: The GNOME desktop

Desktop Icons

As you can see, there are three icons on the desktop: *user's Home, Start Here,* and *Trash.* To makes things simple, we'll start with the easiest and, no doubt, most familiar of these: Trash.

Trash

There is nothing mysterious about Trash . . . at least nothing mysterious about the desktop Trash icon. It functions just as it does in other operating systems. Drag a file you no longer need or want to the Trash icon, and the can will fill up. If you want to empty the Trash, just right-click the Trash icon and, from the pop-up menu, select **Empty Trash**. If you drag something into the Trash that you are not supposed to, you will be informed that you can't do that. All very simple and familiar, no matter from whence you came.

Start Here

Despite the name of this icon, you needn't start with it. In fact, you can completely ignore it, as it is merely a collection of system preference links that can be more easily selected from the Main menu, but more on that later.

user's Home

The user's Home icon on your own desktop will not say "user's." It will instead be labeled with whatever your username happens to be. For example, my username is "rg," so my desktop icon says "rg's Home." If you are logged in as malachi, it will say "malachi's Home," and so on. All quite logical. Of course, I can't possibly guess the username of every person reading this book, so I will stick to the more generic "user's Home," or just "Home," when referring to this icon, and, as you will soon find out, I will do so very often.

As you will notice, the Home icon is the image of a house (home) on a folder. This should tell you that it is your home folder — something like the My Documents folder in a Windows system. This is where all your files will be saved to, all your downloads will be downloaded to, and all your music will be ripped to. It is your territory and, even if you are on a multi-user machine, nobody except you (assuming you are the only one who knows the root password) will be able to nose around in there.

Nautilus

If you double-click your user's Home icon, a window will open up showing you the contents of the folder — it serves as a shortcut to your user's folder on the hard disk. The program that creates this file-viewing and file-organizing system is called Nautilus. You may not have thought of an operating system's file manager as a program before, but, in fact, that is what it is.

Nautilus has a lot of interesting features that deserve mention. For example, Nautilus has a very cool feature that no doubt was inspired by Mac OS 9's WindowShade feature: Double-clicking the title bar of any Nautilus window causes the window to roll up, so to speak, into the title bar — a useful feature when trying to get one window out of the way for a moment or two. There are many more such features, so I will point out a few now, and more will appear in later chapters.

Nautilus as an Image Viewer

One of the very handy things about Nautilus is that it acts as a sort of picture viewer and previewer. When you view the contents of a folder that contains graphics files, Nautilus displays thumbnails of the files (as shown in Figure 3-3) along with the filenames. This lets you see your graphics files without having to use any other special imaging software. Admittedly, this feature is no longer unique in the world of operating systems, but it is handy nonetheless.

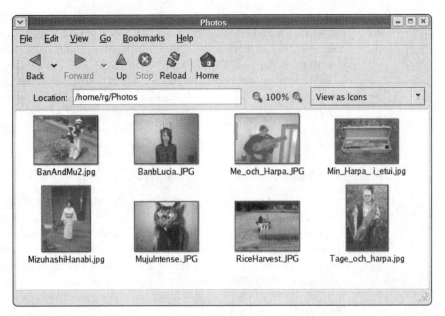

Figure 3-3: Viewing thumbnails in a Nautilus window

What is unique in Nautilus, however, is that when you double-click one of your thumbnails, the image will open in the same window at a larger size, as shown in Figure 3-4. In addition to that, you can zoom in to and out of the enlarged image by manipulating the + and − magnifying glass buttons or by right-clicking that general button area and selecting the desired percentage of zoom directly from the pop-up menu.

Figure 3-4: Viewing an enlarged image in a Nautilus window

You cannot manipulate the image in any way while viewing it in Nautilus, but if you want to make any changes to the image, all you have to do is right-click it and then select **Open With > The Gimp** in the pop-up menu, which opens the file in the GIMP — the Linux world's answer to Photoshop (more about using the GIMP later in this chapter and in Chapter 14). With the GIMP, you can, among other things, change the size of the image, adjust the color balance, brightness, and contrast, convert the image from one format to another (from .jpg to .png, for example), airbrush in a beauty mark on your cheek, and even stamp little green peppers all over your head. All very cool indeed.

Using Nautilus to View Text and PDF Files

In addition to letting you view graphics files, Nautilus also allows you to read the contents of text files (those saved with a .txt file format), again without the need for any other software. If, for example, you have some notes that you jotted down and saved as a text file, you can simply double-click the file's icon in Nautilus, and its contents will be displayed in the Nautilus window. Nautilus can even do the same for PDF files, acting as a simple PDF previewer.

The Nautilus Side Pane

Nautilus also has a side-pane feature that opens up a variety of options. To see the side pane, go to the **View** menu at the top of a Nautilus window and select **Side Pane**. Your Nautilus window will now show a mostly empty pane on its left side, with your username emblazoned upon it. In addition to your username, the side pane also shows how many files and subfolders you have in the folder you are currently viewing, and when you last added or deleted any files or subfolders in that folder. If that isn't enough to get your blood flowing, there's more.

Figure 3-5: Using the Tree view in the Nautilus side pane

If you click the **Information** menu within the side pane, you can see other options. Perhaps the most useful of these, and one that a Windows user should feel quite at home with, is the tree option. If you select **Tree** from the **Information** menu, a folder tree of your entire hard-disk layout will appear within the pane (see Figure 3-5). You can click on any folder in the tree, and its contents will be displayed in the main portion of the Nautilus window. This is very handy when you are busily searching for something within the various subfolders you will eventually create.

Bookmarks Within Nautilus

Another very handy feature of Nautilus is that it lets you create bookmarks. You are no doubt familiar with creating bookmarks for Web pages that you frequent, but why on earth would you want to create bookmarks within your file system? Well, imagine that you have a folder that you need to use often, but it takes an excessive number of mouse clicks to get to that folder, and all that clicking is giving you a bad case of carpal tunnel syndrome. Instead of maiming yourself in that way, you could click your way to that folder once, and then, in the **Bookmarks** menu of the Nautilus window, select **Add Bookmark**. After that, whenever you want to get back to that well-buried folder, you can just click the Bookmarks menu, and that folder will be right there waiting for you in the drop-down list (see Figure 3-6).

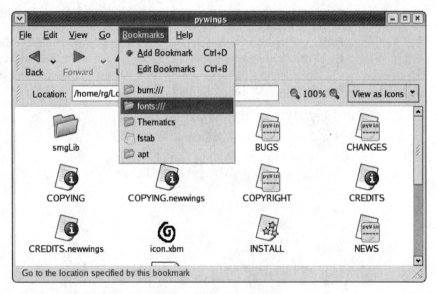

Figure 3-6: Using the Nautilus Bookmarks menu

Changing File and Folder Permissions Within Nautilus

You will find, as you make your way along in the Linux world, that occasionally you come across a file or folder that has a red, slashed circle symbol on it, as you can see in Figure 3-7 on the next page. I refer to this as the *verboten* (meaning *forbidden,* in German) symbol. This symbol can appear within an oval (meaning that you don't have permission to read that file), or with a pencil in the middle of it (meaning that you do not have permission to alter that file). This is another way that Linux tries to protect you, though in the case of copied CD files, it may not be clear as to how it's doing so.

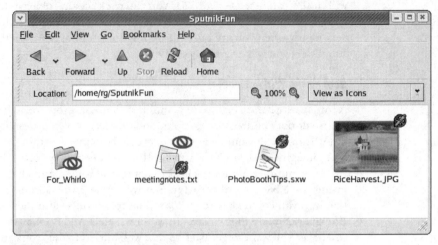

Figure 3-7: Files and folders with the verboten symbol

If you want to alter a file or gain access to a folder that has the *verboten* symbol, it is possible to do so in the Nautilus window, provided that you are listed as the owner of that file or folder. To change file or folder permissions, just right-click the file or folder in question, and then select **Properties** from the pop-up menu. Once the Properties window opens, click the **Permissions** tab, and you will see who the owner of the file or folder is and what you are allowed or not allowed to do with it (see Figure 3-8).

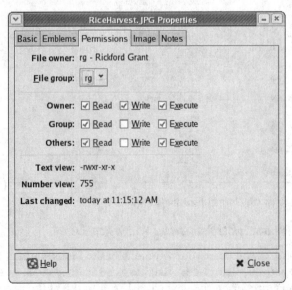

Figure 3-8: Changing permissions in the Nautilus Properties window

You might find this permissions business a bit confusing, but it is really quite simple to understand. As you can see in Figure 3-8, permissions can be granted or denied to the *owner* of the file or folder (you), to a specified *group*, or to *others* (everybody else). These permissions are:

Read   Permission to view the contents of a file or folder.

Write   Permission to alter the contents of a file or folder.

Execute   Permission to run a program or script.

In general, you needn't worry all that much about setting permissions for your own files, as you are really the only one who has access to your user account. The main exception to this is when you transfer files from CD to your hard disk. In this case, the files will be write-protected, meaning that you cannot alter the files until you change the permissions for them. You will also eventually find, especially when you try to change system settings or install additional program packages, that there are a good number of files and folders that are protected by root permissions, but you will learn how to deal with that in Chapter 9.

If you are dealing with a folder or file that you have transferred from CD and that, thus, has the red *verboten* symbol with a pencil in it, you can change the permissions to allow you to alter that file by clicking the checkbox in the **Owner** row next to the word **Write**. Once you are done, click the **Close** button, and you'll be on your way.

The Main Menu

At the very bottom left corner of your screen is an icon of a red hat. This is the Main menu, which is your access point to the majority of the applications and utilities included on your system. In a sense, the Main menu is very much like the Start menu in a Windows system, although it is not exactly the same. When you click the Main menu icon, all of the applications and utilities available to you are exposed.

Despite the importance of this menu, there is really very little to explain about it, although a complete explanation of each item in the menu wouldn't fit in this book. My personal feeling is that it is fun to just browse through the various items in the menu in order to see what you have to work or play with. It's sort of like digging down to the bottom of a Christmas stocking. I will also discuss some of these menu items in other chapters of this book, so if you're not the treasure-hunting type, just hang in there.

For the time being, however, I will give a brief explanation of the bottom eight items in the menu, because many of these are of considerable importance:

Help   Starts a viewer for GNOME help files.

Home Folder   Opens your user's Home folder.

Network Servers   Allows you to view the other computers connected to your local network.

Run Program   Allows you to launch a program by typing the run command for that program. After selecting **Run Program**, a dialog box will open (see Figure 3-9). Type glines to give it a try (the application's icon will almost immediately appear on the left), and then click **Run**. The game, Lines, will then start. Of course, we are too busy right now to be playing games, so just quit the program for now.

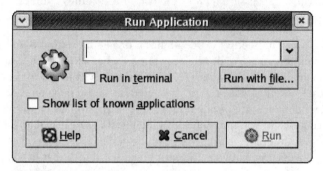

Figure 3-9: The Run Application dialog box

Search for Files   Helps you find files on your system. To give it a spin, select **Search for Files**. The search window will open. In the **Look in folder** field, your home folder will be the default search location. However, if you want to search the entire system and not just your home folder, delete everything in that box except the slash (/). Now, give it a try by trying to locate one of the icons we will be using in Project 3A-8. In the **File is named** field, type kolf.png, and then click **Find**. Your results should look like those in Figure 3-10.

Open Recent   Shows a submenu of recently opened files.

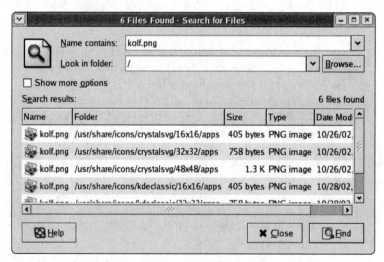

Figure 3-10: Search results for kolf.png in the Search for Files window

Lock Screen   Activates your screensaver and locks the screen so that no one can use your computer without typing your user password first. This is very handy when you are going to be away from your computer for a few minutes and don't want anyone messing around with things. You can give it a try right now if you like.

Log Out   Opens a window asking you whether you want to log out, shut down, or restart — just like Windows XP. I'll mention a bit more on this at the end of the chapter.

The GNOME Panel

As you have seen, the Main menu is located in the panel at the bottom of the screen. This panel is a separate application, or program, called the GNOME Panel (see Figure 3-11). In operation, it is sort of a cross between the Windows taskbar and the Mac OS X dock; and like both of those panel-like applications, it can be moved, hidden, resized, and customized to an even greater extent than with either of those two.

Figure 3-11: The GNOME Panel

When you first set eyes on the GNOME Panel, you will notice that it has a default set of icons on it. Some of these are program launchers, which allow you to start up a program with a single mouse click, while others are utilities of one sort or another. Here they are, from left to right:

Main menu   The access point to the majority of your applications, preferences, settings, and other configuration tools.

Mozilla   Your Web browser. Essentially, it's Netscape with a difference or two.

Ximian Evolution   The very popular Linux email program, scheduler, and task manager.

OpenOffice.org Writer   A Microsoft Word–compatible word processor.

OpenOffice.org Calc   A Microsoft Excel–compatible spreadsheet application.

OpenOffice.org Impress   A Microsoft PowerPoint–compatible presentation application.

GNOME Print Manager   An application that provides access to your print queues, settings, and print jobs.

Workspace Switcher   An application that allows you to switch between virtual desktops (I'll talk about this more in Project 3A-4).

Window List   A list of windows or applications you have open (very Windows-like). In Figure 3-11, there are no applications open, and thus no windows are shown in the list.

Volume Control   A control that allows you to adjust the overall volume of your system (Red Hat 9 users will have to add this themselves).

Red Hat Network Alert Notification Tool   A launcher for Up2date, which is a tool that allows you to update your Fedora Core or Red Hat Linux system directly via the Red Hat Network. You will learn more about Up2date in Chapter 19 and about APT, a handy alternative to Up2date, in Chapter 10.

Clock   The obligatory desktop clock and calendar.

Project 3A: Customizing the GNOME Panel

The GNOME Panel is not a static thing. You can add launchers (program shortcuts or aliases), utilities, and even amusements to make it do almost anything you want it to, within limits, of course. In the various stages of this project, you will customize your Panel to make things more convenient for you as you make your way through the rest of this book. You are, of course, free to change any of the customizations I ask you to make, but I'd suggest holding off on that until you finish the rest of the book — if you change things now, my instructions may not match what you see on your screen. Once you've finished the book, you can do whatever you like.

Each of the following subprojects in this project is very simple. Most are only two-step point-and-click procedures that you should be able to handle without any difficulty.

3A-1: Adding a Show Desktop Button to the Panel

One item not initially displayed in the GNOME Panel is the Show Desktop button. This is a handy utility that, when clicked, hides all the open windows so that you can see your previously obscured desktop. You may doubt whether you really need this, but trust me — you will eventually come to need and love this little button.

To add the button, here is all you have to do:

1. Right-click the GNOME Panel in an empty space to the left of the Volume Controller.
2. In the pop-up menu, select **Add to Panel > Actions > Show Desktop Button**.

3A-2: Adding a Home Folder Launcher to the Panel

Even if I weren't going to ask you to open your user's Home folder a million times throughout this book, you would still find a launcher that opens up your Home folder in Nautilus to be of great convenience. Once you've added this launcher to your Panel, you will always be able to open up a Home folder window even if you have a slew of other windows open and cannot see any of your desktop.

Here's how to add the launcher:

1. Right-click any open space to the left of the Show Desktop icon toward the right end of the Panel.

2. From the pop-up menu, select **Add to Panel > Launcher from menu > Home Folder**.

3A-3: Deleting a Program Launcher from the Panel

Let's say that you have a launcher on the Panel that you don't particularly need. How can you get rid of it? As an example, let's remove the launcher for OpenOffice.org Impress (don't worry, you can always put it back later).

Here's what you do:

1. Right-click the OpenOffice.org Impress icon.

2. From the pop-up menu, select **Remove from Panel**.

3A-4: Adding a Program Launcher to the Panel

Now that you've created some extra Panel space to play with, let's add a new program launcher. Because I will be asking you to use the Linux Command Terminal quite a bit in later chapters, that is the program you will add for now. To keep things tight and snappy, I'll just refer to it as the Terminal from here forward.

Here's what you do:

1. Right-click the open space to the right of the Workspace Switcher.

2. From the pop-up menu, select **Add to Panel > Launcher from menu > System Tools > Terminal**.

3A-5: Moving Icons on the Panel

You will notice that your new Terminal launcher seems stuck out there on its own, far from the other application launchers. This doesn't seem like a logical arrangement, so why don't you move it.

Here's how:

1. Right-click the Terminal launcher that you just added in the previous section.

2. From the pop-up menu, select **Move**. Your cursor should now look like a crosshair.

3. Drag the Terminal launcher to a point just left of the GNOME Print Manager icon. The other launchers should automatically make room for the move.

3A-6: Reducing the Number of Desktops on the Workspace Switcher

One of the really cool features of Linux is that it allows you to work with virtual desktops. Instead of viewing just one desktop, as in most operating systems, you can view and work in up to 100 discrete desktops, and you can switch between them with the Workspace Switcher. As things are, your Workspace Switcher should show four squares, each representing one desktop. This makes the icon a bit wide, and it takes up a bit too much space on your Panel. Because you are most likely new to the idea of virtual desktops, I think that two should be enough to play with for now — at least until you find out a bit more about them later in the chapter.

Here's how to reduce the number of desktops shown on the Workspace Switcher:

1. Right-click the Workspace Switcher icon.
2. From the pop-up menu, select **Preferences**.
3. On the right of the Preferences window, where it says **Number of workspaces**, select **2**, and then click the **Close** button.

3A-7: Adding a Drawer to the Panel

One of the features that I quite like about the GNOME Panel is the drawer. The drawer is a little pop-up panel that acts as the perfect location to place launchers that you do not want to place in your GNOME Panel because of space considerations and that do not appear in the Main menu and therefore must be run by command. Launchers of this sort are useful for quickly opening most of the programs that you compile from source code and also for several KDE programs. Of course, you can put anything you want there, including frequently used files.

Adding a drawer to your Panel is very easy:

1. Right-click any open space to the left of the Home Folder launcher.
2. In the pop-up menu, select **Add to Panel > Drawer**.

3A-8: Adding Program Launchers to the Drawer

The drawer you've just added is, of course, empty at this stage, so let's put it to good use by adding launchers for a couple of KDE games that do not appear in the Main menu. One such game is KBattleship, which is a clone of the well-known Battleship game. Another is a miniature golf game (and one of my personal faves), Kolf.

Here's what you do:

1. A little tab with an arrow pointing downward should be visible above the drawer in your Panel. If the arrow isn't visible, click once on the drawer, and it will be.
2. Right-click the tab and, from the pop-up menu, select **Add to Panel > Launcher**. A Create Launcher window will open (see Figure 3-12).

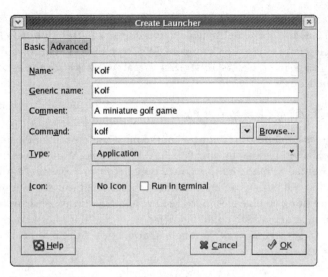

Figure 3-12: Creating a launcher in a drawer

3. For both the **Name** and **Generic Name**, type Kolf.

4. In the **Comment** field, type: A miniature golf game.

5. In the **Command** field, type: kolf (no capitals).

6. Click the big square button that says **No Icon**. The Browse Icons window will then open (see Figure 3-13).

Figure 3-13: Choosing an icon for an application

7. At the top of the icons window, you should see **/usr/share/pixmaps**. Delete that, and type in /usr/share/icons/crystalsvg/48x48/apps/kolf.png, and then press ENTER. The Kolf icon should now appear in the Create Launcher window.

8. Finally, click **OK**, and the launcher will appear in the drawer.

To add a launcher for Battleship, follow the same steps as above, but in the **Name** and **Generic Name** fields, type KBattleship; in the **Description** field, type A KDE Battleship clone; in the **Command** field, type kbattleship (no capitals); and type /usr/share/icons/kdeclassic/32x32/apps/kbattleship.png for the location of the game icon.

3A-9: Adding a Fish to Your Panel

Now we come to what might seem the most useless part of this project: adding a fish, named Wanda, to your Panel. At first glance, Wanda does little more than bat her tail around and spurt out a bubble or two. However, if you click on her, a window will pop up telling you what Linux kernel you are running, what time it is, how long you have been logged on, and how many users are currently using your machine, which could be useful.

To get a glimpse of Wanda in action, limited though that action may be, follow these steps:

1. Right-click an empty space to the left of the drawer.
2. From the pop-up menu, select **Add to Panel > Amusements > Fish**.

3A-10: Adding a Force Quit Button to Your Panel

Finally, to round things out, let's get back to the realm of the clearly useful and add a **Force Quit** button to the Panel. The **Force Quit** button is a very handy utility that lets you quickly and easily deal with non-responding windows. Yes, it does happen on occasion: A window suddenly refuses to do anything. Regardless of what you want it to do or what it is supposed to be doing, it just sits there as if it is on strike (maybe it is). With just one click of the **Force Quit** button, your cursor becomes a powerful surgical instrument that will kill the window you click on. You needn't worry, however, because you can immediately run such apps again, though in some cases you will have to reboot first.

You definitely don't want to be without this button, so here's how to add it to the Panel:

1. Right-click the empty Panel space to the left of Wanda.
2. From the pop-up menu, select **Add to Panel > Actions > Force Quit**.

You are now done with this rather simple project. You have more or less learned the basics of Panel customization and, in the process, created a very useful Panel configuration. If you did everything the way I told you to, your Panel should now look like the one in Figure 3-14.

Figure 3-14: Your newly customized GNOME Panel

More Panel Fun

In addition to the basic customization you've just done in the previous project, you can do a lot more to change the look and feel of your Panel. Most of these options are available by right-clicking any open space in the panel and then selecting **Properties**, which will bring up the Panel Properties window (see Figure 3-15).

Figure 3-15: The GNOME Panel Properties window

From this window you can change the position of the Panel, alter its size, change its color, or make it (but not the launchers on it) invisible — very cool. You can also set the Panel so that it will automatically disappear when you are not using it, and have it reappear when you bring your mouse cursor into the area where the panel normally resides. Don't feel afraid to play around and give things a try — that's half the fun!

Mac Users Can Feel Right at Home

Another cool feature of the GNOME Panel program is that you can add additional panels to other parts of the screen. Former Macintosh users can create a fairly Mac-like desktop by right-clicking any open Panel space and selecting **Add Panel**, which will cause a new panel to appear at the top of the screen. As is, the new panel will be a bit too fat to look like a Mac menu bar, but you can reduce its size in the Panel Properties window (a size of 29 or 30 pixels should do the trick).

To further Mac-ify things, you can right-click the panel to add a Menu Bar in the left corner (select **Add to Panel > Add Menu Bar**), a Window Menu to the far right corner (select **Add to Panel > Utility > Window Menu**), a Clock (select **Add to Panel > Accessories > Clock**), a pair of Eyes next to that (select **Add to Panel >**

Amusements > Eyes), and a Sticky Notes utility (select **Add to Panel > Accessories > Sticky Notes**) to the left of that. This will give you a sort of hybrid Mac OS 9/X menu bar. With a few more touches here and there, Mac emigrants can quite easily create a desktop environment that looks very much like that in Mac OS X (see Figure 3-16).

Figure 3-16: A Mac OS X–like desktop with panels at the top and right side of the screen

If you are curious how to get the Aqua-like window borders and controls shown in Figure 3-16, flip to Chapter 5.

Virtual Desktops

It is now time to discuss a rather unique and convenient feature of Linux: virtual desktops. And the best way to understand what this virtual-desktop business is all about is to just give it a try.

In your GNOME Panel, click on Wanda, your Home folder, and Mozilla. You will then have three windows open in your present desktop, or workspace. Now look at the Workspace Switcher icon on your panel. The top half of the icon should be blue; this is your present workspace. Click the bottom half of the icon, the gray half, and all your open windows will suddenly disappear.

Actually, nothing has really disappeared — you are just viewing a new desktop. All your other windows are still open and running in the previous desktop. In this second desktop you can open something else: Go to the Main menu and select **Games > AisleRiot**. The AisleRiot solitaire card game will soon appear.

You now have windows open in two different desktops, and you can switch back and forth between them. To do so, just go to the Workplace Switcher in your Panel and click the top gray box, which will take you to your original desktop. Once you've done that, the bottom box will become gray, and you can then click that one to go back to your game desktop.

As you can imagine, this feature has some potential benefits for you, in addition to helping you avoid clutter. Just imagine that you are at work typing up some long document in OpenOffice.org Writer. Eventually, you get a bit tired and decide to goof off a bit by playing GNOME Mines for a while. To do this, you switch to another desktop where you open and play the game. A bit later, when you notice your boss making the rounds of the office, you simply switch back to the first desktop so that you look busy when he walks by and says, "Keeping yourself busy, Boaz?"

Phew!

Project 3B: Screenshots

It wouldn't be fair to end this chapter without telling you how to take part in what seems to be the average Linux user's greatest passion: screenshots. I don't know why Penguinistas are so obsessed with screenshots; perhaps it is the fact that they can customize their system so much, or perhaps it's just that screenshots can be taken so easily from within Linux. Whatever the reason, chances are that any personal Linux Web page you come across will have at least a few screenshots of that user's desktop.

Now that you've joined the waddling masses, you can join in the fun too, and in the process, show your friends and colleagues images of cool apps you have found, show your mother by email where such-and-such a menu selection is (as I have often done), or just show off the cool customizations you've done to your system after you've completed Chapter 5.

3B-1: Full-Screen Screenshots

Taking screenshots from within GNOME is pretty easy, and there are a few ways to go about it. To take a shot of your whole desktop, just press the PRTSCN (Print Screen) or PRTSCN-SYSRQ keys on your keyboard. A Save Screenshot window (shown in Figure 3-17 on the next page) will then open and, by default, will ask you to save your screenshot to your Home folder. If you want to save the screenshot to another folder, simply choose a different folder before you click the **Save** button.

Instead of using the PRTSCN key on your keyboard, you can add a screenshot button to your Panel that will do the same thing, though I don't see much advantage in doing that, unless you want the I'm-taking-a-picture feeling that a button provides. Anyway, to add the button, just right-click any empty space on the Panel and select **Add to Panel > Button > Screenshot**. Then, when you want to take a screenshot, all you have to do is click the button. *Kachunk!*

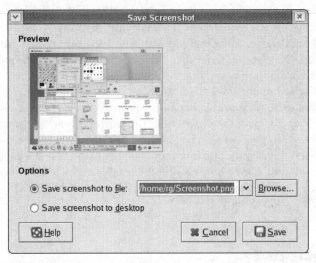

Figure 3-17: Saving a screenshot

3B-2: Taking Screenshots of a Single Window

If you only want to take a screenshot of a single window, rather than of the entire screen, the process is almost as easy. First, make sure your mouse cursor is hovering within the boundaries of the window that you want to take the shot of, and then just hold down the ALT key with one finger and press the PRTSCN key with another. The Save Screenshot window will open.

3B-3: Taking Screenshots with the GIMP

These methods of taking screenshots are simple, fun, and easy, but they do have one limitation: They do not let you take screenshots while you have a menu open. If you want to take a screenshot of the desktop or any window with an open menu, you will need to use the GIMP.

Fortunately, taking a screenshot with the GIMP is also a very, very simple procedure. First, start up the GIMP by going to the Main menu and selecting **Graphics > The GIMP**. Once the ol' GIMPster is open, go to the **File** menu at the top of the main GIMP window (that's the one with all the tools in it), and select **Acquire > Screenshot**.

The Screen Shot window will open shortly (see Figure 3-18). Once it is open, select **Whole Screen** and adjust the numbers in the **Seconds Delay** field at the bottom of the window in order to give yourself enough time to get to the menu you want open by the time the screenshot is taken.

When you're ready, click **OK**, rush to open whatever menu it is you want to take a shot of, and voilà, it will be done. The screenshot will soon open right there within the GIMP, and you can do with it as you will.

Figure 3-18: Taking a screenshot with the GIMP

Shutting Down

Well, now that you know your desktop environment so well, you may feel like calling it a day and shutting down your machine. To do so, just go to the Main menu and select **Log Out**. A small window will appear with three choices to choose from: *Log out* (default), *Shut down*, and *Restart the computer*. Select **Shut down** and then click **OK,** and the shutdown process will begin. If, however, nothing seems to happen after clicking **OK**, press CTRL + ALT + BACKSPACE in unison, which will bring you to the login screen (Figure 3-1 on page 32). Once there, click **Shutdown** at the bottom of the screen. This will bring up a small window asking you if you are sure you want to shut down. Just click **OK**, and shutdown will commence.

During the shutdown process, your screen will go back to text mode and you will see a string of white text and green Oks on a black screen as the system shuts down its various components. When it is all done, the system will most likely power down your computer as well, in which case you are done. On a few machines, however, the system cannot power down your machine. You will know if this is so in your case because the flow of text on the screen will stop at the words **Power down**. If you see those words on the screen and nothing else happens for 15 seconds or so, then just power down the machine manually by pressing the power button. It is completely safe to do so at that point.

4

MORE THAN WEBBED FEET

Doing the Net with Linux

These days, a computer that isn't hooked up to the Internet is like an aluminum espresso maker without water in it cooking away on the front burner of your stove. Fortunately, your Fedora system is well equipped to handle the many Internet tasks that you no doubt have in store for it.

Getting the Hardware Connected

In order to get connected to the Internet, you have to have the hardware to do it. There are a number of possible ways to do this, ranging from the higher-speed local area networks (LANs), cable modems, and ADSL connections from phone companies. Most computers also have internal 56 Kbps modems or can connect to external modems for slower dial-up connections over regular phone lines.

Higher-Speed Connections

If you have a high-speed Internet connection from your cable television or phone company, or if you are connected to the Net by a LAN system at your office, you are really in luck, as these setups are probably the easiest to deal with. Most likely, all you have to do is connect the Ethernet cable from the wall (if you are using a LAN), or from your cable modem, to the port of the network card on your machine. After that, once you start up your machine you will be ready to go.

NOTE *In case you're not sure what an Ethernet cable looks like, it is a round cable, about an eighth of an inch thick, with a plug at the end that looks like an oversized phone plug, as you can see in Figure 4-1.*

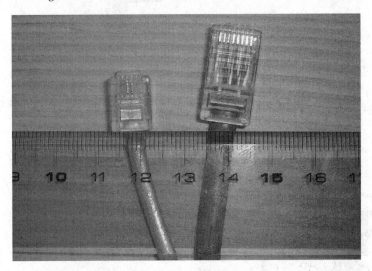

Figure 4-1: Standard telephone and Ethernet connectors compared

If you have a problem getting online, and you are trying to connect to the Net via a LAN or cable modem, the problem could very likely be that your network card is not supported by your system. This is easily remedied (by replacing it) and, fortunately, is relatively rare.

However, the problem could also be that your network or service provider does not automatically assign addresses via Dynamic Host Configuration Protocol (DHCP). DHCP is a means by which your Internet provider can automatically (dynamically) provide your system with the configuration information it needs in order to connect to the Internet. If your provider does not utilize DHCP, you will have to get the necessary information about settings from the network administrator or service provider and enter them yourself.

If this happens to be the boat you are in, you will enter them into the Network Configuration window. To access this window, go to the Main menu and select **System Settings > Network**. After you provide the requested root password, the configuration window will open. Your Ethernet or network card should already be highlighted, so just click **Edit**. This will bring up the Ethernet Device window, and this is where you will input all the settings, as instructed.

Wireless Network Connections

Recently, many offices, universities, and even homes with a high-speed Internet connection from their cable television company have gone wireless. In most cases, setup is quite similar to the process for connecting via a wired Network, as just described. Of course, there are some differences worth noting. If you are using a wireless network to connect to the Internet, or are just curious as to what this *wireless* thing is all about, check out Chapter 18. In most cases, you should be able to set things up quite easily with the skills you have so far.

Internal Modems

Many, if not most, of you are still using dial-up Internet connections, which means that you need to have a traditional dial-up modem to reach beyond your box to the outside world. These modems, in case you've forgotten, are those wonderful machines that whistle, chime, screech, and spit whenever you dial up your Internet provider. I suppose you could think of them as noisy telephones in need of a good burp.

The biggest drawback to dealing with modems in Linux is that very few modems are supported by Linux. On the positive side of things, though, once you do find a modem that works, it is relatively easy to set up. The main culprit in the compatibility problem is a beast called the Winmodem. As hardware makers try to bring you cheaper and cheaper machines, they inevitably try to cut costs here and there. The Winmodem is one of these cost-cutting developments.

Although a Winmodem is, technically speaking, a piece of hardware, it is a far cry from what is known as a hardware modem. A hardware modem is, to oversimplify things a bit, a telephone without a handset and dial that plugs in to your computer somewhere. It is a fully functioning machine that only needs your system for dial-up and connection information. A Winmodem, on the other hand, is totally system dependent. It is a faux modem that has more in common with a lamprey than a telephone, in that it must utilize the Windows system in order to do its chores. As you are not using a Windows system when you are using Linux, you are sort of sunk, as the Winmodem has nothing to utilize. The fact that most of a Winmodem's work is done by the system itself means that it is a very simple piece of hardware. This means, of course, that Winmodems are much cheaper to produce than true hardware modems. That being the case, you can be fairly sure that if you have a built-in modem in your machine, it is a Winmodem.

Of course, the Linux community has been working on ways to deal with these Winmodem beasts so that they will work with Linux systems. When they do work, Winmodems are called Linmodems, but support for the wide variety of modem models is still rather spotty. If you are not sure what kind of modem you have installed, my advice would be to go through the Internet connection setup process to see if your modem works or not. If it doesn't, you can replace the modem with one that is known to work, preferably a true hardware modem.

Probably the best way to find out what modems do work with Linux is to go to one of the online forums, such as Linux Questions (www.linuxquestions.org) or JustLinux (www.justlinux.com), and ask for suggestions. The US Robotics models 56K V.92 Performance Pro Modem (internal slot) and 56 PC Card

Modem (PC Card slot, for notebooks) are both true hardware modems that are easily available and said to work, though I must admit that I haven't tried these myself. You can check out the US Robotics site for more information on these models (www.usr.com).

WARNING *When purchasing a modem, beware of generic, no-name internal modems that say they are Linux compatible. Check out the Internet first to verify such a claim. Sometimes, such modems are only compatible after you do all sorts of dreadful things to your system that even a hard-core Linux geek wouldn't want to bother with. A cute little Tux icon on the box doesn't necessarily mean that the modem is Tux-friendly. It might just be that the poor bird was hoodwinked.*

External Modems

The best solution if you are going to use a modem with your Linux system is to use an external serial modem. An external modem sits in a box outside your computer, and it connects to the serial port in the back of the computer, which is the one that looks like a hole with little prongs in it (see Figure 4-2). Because the modem doesn't use your operating system to operate, it does not tie up system resources while it's busy, which may result in a possible pickup in computer speed.

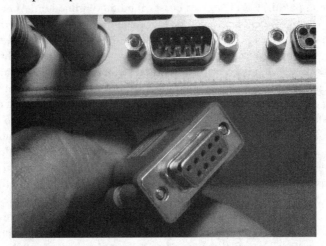

Figure 4-2: Serial port and connector

Most external serial modems should work with your system, or at least that is what most people will tell you. If you are worried and are looking for a sure thing, Zoom Telephonics (www.zoom.com) makes an external serial modem that is compatible with Linux, and they say so right on their site. The US Robotics 56K V.92 External Faxmodem is also said to work, though I haven't tried this model out myself.

If you find another model that you think will do the trick, before you commit to it by slapping down the cash, do a Yahoo or Google search with that modem's make and model number, along with the word "Linux," and see what search results you get. Of course, you can also try out one of the Linux forums and ask about the modem make and model there. There are a lot of people in the same boat as you, so you are sure to get plenty of opinions and advice.

Making Sure All Is Well with Your Modem

So let's say that you finally get a modem that is supposed to work with your Linux system. What you have to do now is make sure that your system recognizes it. To set it up, connect your modem to the computer and to the telephone jack in the wall. Turn the modem on (if it's an external modem) and then start up your machine. If all is as it should be, Fedora will automatically find and configure your modem.

However, you may first have to go through a couple of very simple steps to configure your modem soon after you start up your machine. If so, you will see a semi-graphical screen telling you that Kudzu (the Red Hat hardware browser) has found a new piece of hardware. To configure the new device, just press any key to continue and then press ENTER to configure it. That's all there is to it.

Setting Up KPPP as Your Internet Dialer

Your modem is now all set up and ready to go, but before it can actually go anywhere, virtually speaking, you will have to set things up so that it can dial up your Internet provider. This is pretty easy to do, and through this process you can also make sure that your modem actually works with your system.

There is a way to set this up via GNOME, it isn't really as smooth or satisfactory as using KPPP, which is the KDE Internet dialer. KDE applications will work within GNOME, so don't worry about that point.

To get to KPPP, go to the Main menu and select **Internet > More Internet Applications > KPPP**. After that, you will be prompted for your root password, so type that in and click **OK**; the KPPP window will soon appear (see Figure 4-3).

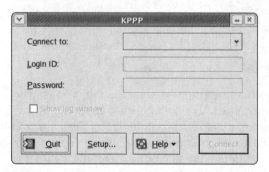

Figure 4-3: Using KPPP to enter your Internet settings

Click the **Setup** button. The KPPP Configuration window will open, and once it does, click the **Modem** tab, and then in the Modem page, test your modem by clicking the **Query Modem** button. KPPP will search for your modem and, if it finds it, will display the results of its query (see Figure 4-4 on the following page).

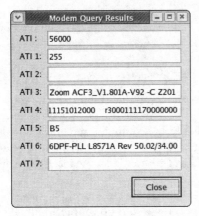

Figure 4-4: KPPP displaying the results from a successful modem query

If KPPP cannot find your modem, it will tell you so in a message window (see Figure 4-5). If this is the case, click **Cancel** to dismiss that window, and then click the **Device** tab in the main Configuration window. In the Device page (shown in Figure 4-6), look at the **Modem Device** drop-down menu, which will most likely have /**dev/modem** listed as the default location; select the next device location in that menu, /**dev/ttyS0**. Once you've done that, return to the **Modem** tab and try the new settings by clicking **Query Modem** again. If that doesn't work either, just keep repeating this process of select the next device and querying the modem again and again until you find the right device location. If KPPP never finds your modem, it is time to replace it with one that is known to be compatible with Linux.

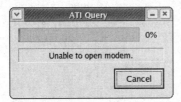

Figure 4-5: KPPP's "can't find modem" message

Once KPPP does find your modem, you can set up a dial-up account. (You will need the appropriate configuration details as supplied by your Internet service provider.) Click the **Accounts** tab and then click **New**. A small window will immediately pop up asking whether you want to use a setup wizard or a standard dialog-based setup. Ignore the fine print, forget the wizard, and just click **Dialog Setup**, which will bring up the New Account window (see Figure 4-7).

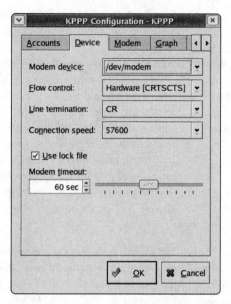

Figure 4-6: Selecting another device location in the KPPP Configuration window

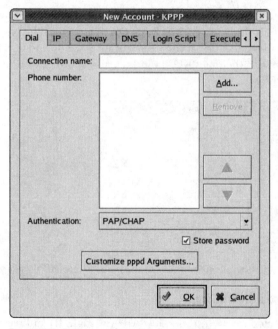

Figure 4-7: Setting up a new account in KPPP

Near the top of the **Dial** tab in the New Account window, you can give your connection account a name; you can decide what to call it on your own, but most people use something related to the name of their provider. Next, you have to add some dial-up numbers, which you should have received from your service provider. To add a number, just click **Add**, type the number in the pop-up window, and click **OK**. If your provider gave you more than one number, add each number in the same way.

If you're really lucky, you are all done. However, if you're slightly less lucky, your provider might require you to input some other information manually. The only other thing you will probably have to do in that case is click the **IP** (Internet Protocol) or **DNS** (Domain Name System) tabs and add the information specified by your provider. See what your provider has to say about what to type in where. If they give you some hogwash about their not supporting Linux, just take screenshots of each of the first four tabbed pages in this New Account window, fax or mail the screenshots to your provider, and then demand that they tell you what to type in. There is no reason that things should not work if they give you the right information. Anyway, you probably won't have to go through such a confrontational scenario.

NOTE   *If you are wondering what IP and DNS are all about, you can simply think of them in this way: The DNS translates the easy-to-remember URLs that you have come to know, such as www.yahoo.com, into numerical, or IP, addresses that the Internet can understand. The address http://www.yahoo.com, thus becomes http://216.109.118.68/. You can type the numerical version into your browser later to see for yourself.*

Once you are all done setting up your modem and inputting any necessary settings, the only thing left to do is click **OK** to get rid of the New Account window, and then click OK in the Configuration window to lose it as well. You should be left with the main KPPP window, now showing your new account information (Figure 4-8).

Figure 4-8: Your new account information as shown in the main KPPP window

Connecting and Disconnecting

To get connected to the Internet, just type the login ID and password that your provider gave you into the KPPP window, and then, after double-checking that your modem is on (if it is an external modem), click **Connect**. In a moment or two, your modem should start making its dreadful spitting, hissing, and churning noises, and you will be up and running. You will know that you have established an Internet connection when your KPPP window automatically minimizes, though it will continue to be accessible in the GNOME Panel.

Once you are done surfing around, you can disconnect from the Internet quite easily by clicking on the minimized KPPP window in the Panel and then, when the window bloats back up to its original size (see Figure 4-9), clicking **Disconnect**. You can then click **Quit** to exit KPPP. The next time you open up KPPP, you shouldn't have to type in your login ID or password.

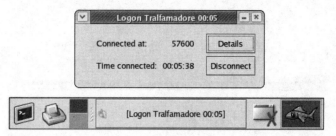

Figure 4-9: The maximized and minimized (Panel) views of the KPPP logged-on window

It is very likely that you will be using your KPPP dialer quite often. Therefore, it would probably be good, and definitely exceedingly convenient, to add a launcher to your GNOME Panel. You should know how to do this now, but just in case, here are the steps:

1. Right-click an empty space in the GNOME Panel.
2. From the pop-up menu, select **Add to Panel > Launcher from menu > Internet > More Internet Applications > KPPP**.

Mozilla — Your Internet Browser

If you have ever used Netscape, then you essentially know Mozilla, as Netscape is based on the Mozilla design. If you are coming from the Internet Explorer or Apple Safari worlds, there shouldn't really be anything to stump you in any way, either. Things work more or less the same in all of these browsers. That being the case, you should be able to use Mozilla's basic features without any instruction.

Tabbed Browsing in Mozilla

There is, however, one point unique to Mozilla (and, consequently, Netscape) that warrants special mention; this is the very useful feature known as tabs.

Usually when you click a link in a Web page, the new page opens in the same window. On some pages, links are coded so that the new page opens in a new, separate window, or maybe you occasionally opt for opening a link in a new window by right-clicking the link and then selecting the **Open Link in New Window** option. This can be very useful; however, once you have more than a few browser windows open, it gets sort of hard to find what you're looking for in all those open windows. It can also slow things down a bit as well.

This is where the tab feature comes in handy. To see how it works, try it out yourself right here and now. Open your Mozilla browser by clicking the Mozilla launcher on the GNOME Panel; then go to www.google.com and do a search for metro boiling frogs, for a fun example. Once the results are shown, right-click on the top link, and in the pop-up menu select **Open Link in New Tab** (see Figure 4-10).

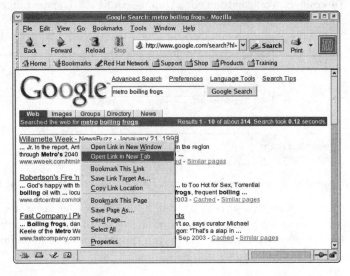

Figure 4-10: Opening a link in a new tab in Mozilla

Once you have done this, the new page will appear in a new tab, and your original page of search results is still there, ready and waiting in the other tab (see Figure 4-11). I am pretty confident in saying that, once you get used to this feature, you will never miss your old Internet Explorer again.

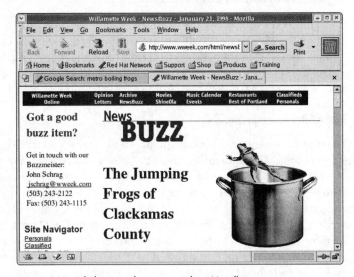

Figure 4-11: A link opened in a new tab in Mozilla

You can also set up Mozilla to open pages in a new tab when you type in a URL. Just go to the **Edit** menu and select **Preferences**. In the Preferences window, click **Tabbed Browsing** in the pane on the left side of the window, and then check the checkbox next to **Control+Enter in the Location Bar**. While you are there, you might as well also check the box next to **Middle-click or Control-click of links in a Web page**. Once you have done that, just click **OK**.

Now when you type in a URL and then simultaneously press the CTRL and ENTER keys, the new page will open up in a new tab rather than the same window. Also, if you press the CTRL key while clicking a link, it too will open up in a new tab (or if you have a three-button mouse, clicking the middle button alone will do the same trick) — a variation on the right-click method.

Mozilla Popup Manager

The more recent versions of Mozilla, which come with Fedora Core, have a handy new feature called the Popup Manager. When you first come to a Web page that shoots out one of those annoying pop-up windows, Mozilla will bring up a dialog box to ask you if you want to set up your preferences to suppress the appearance of such windows. If you opt to use this feature, the Preferences will open to the Popup Windows section where you can do away with most of those pesky nuisances (see Figure 4-12). You can still allow pop-ups for sites that you specify by clicking the **Allowed Sites** button. Needless to say, this is an extremely useful, effective, and welcome feature.

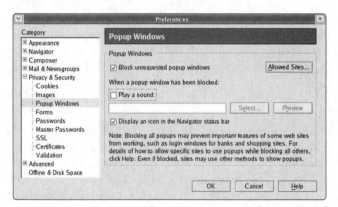

Figure 4-12: Blocking pop-up windows in the Mozilla Preferences window

Using Mozilla to Create Web Pages

Mozilla not only lets you view Web pages, it lets you make them as well. Mozilla Composer (shown in Figure 4-13 on the next page) is a rather simple, but powerful enough, HTML editor. It is a WYSIWYG (what you see is what you get, pronounced *wiz-ee-wig*) editor, which means that you can see what your page will look like as you build it — you don't have to learn or deal with HTML coding (unless you want to, of course). If you want to take it out for a spin, click the **File** menu of your Mozilla browser and select **New > Composer Page**.

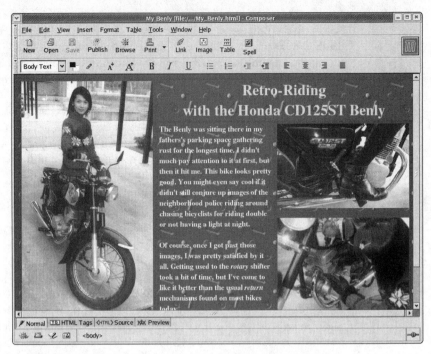

Figure 4-13: Using Mozilla Composer to create Web pages

If you need a little help getting started with Mozilla Composer, take a look at the brief, but useful, tutorial at http://thelinuxapprentice.com/designwebsitemozcomp.html. You can also find more information by going to the **Help** menu of a Composer window and selecting **Help Contents**.

Email

Evolution is the default email program in Fedora Core, and it could probably best be described as a better-groomed, spunkier clone of Outlook (see Figure 4-14). It allows you to send and receive mail, make appointments, and keep a list of tasks. It can also display weather conditions for a wide variety of cities around the world and news headlines from a variety of sources, all of which is customizable in the program settings. By providing direct access to information of this kind, it does Outlook one better. It is also a much more handsome program to look at than Outlook, and the more recent versions, which ship with Fedora Core, look even better than their predecessors.

To use Evolution, just click the email launcher on the GNOME Panel or go to the Main menu and select **Internet > Evolution Email**. When you first run Evolution, you will be greeted by a setup wizard, so have the account details you received from your Internet service provider handy. These should consist of your POP host address (for receiving mail), your SMTP host address (for sending mail), and your mail password, which is very often different from your Internet logon password. Your mail password is not actually entered during the various wizard steps, so check the **Remember this password** checkbox when filling in the

POP details. When you first connect to your mail server, you will be prompted for your mail password, so you can type it in at that time and you won't have to deal with it again.

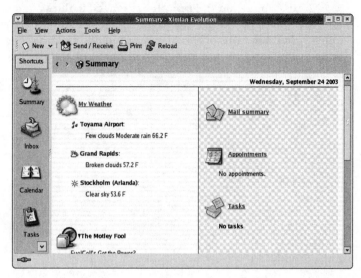

Figure 4-14: Using Evolution for email, appointments, tasks, and weather reports

Evolution is, without a doubt, the most popular email software in the Linux world, but despite its obvious attractions and popularity, I prefer the more straightforward Mozilla Mail for my email chores. In contrast to the multi-functional Evolution, Mozilla Mail is a mail-only program that is very straight-forward to use. It is also the program you want to use if you have to deal with mail in multiple character sets (English and Japanese, for example), as Evolution seems weaker in this area. Mozilla Mail also has a handy and effective Junk Mail Control feature to help you deal with junk email (spam). If you would like to try out Mozilla Mail, you can run it from the Main menu by selecting **Internet > More Internet Applications > Mozilla Mail**. Try both Evolution and Mozilla Mail and use whichever you like better. That's one of the great things about Linux: choices.

If you find that you prefer Mozilla Mail to Evolution, you can change the mail launcher in your GNOME Panel to launch Mozilla Mail to make things easier on yourself. Just right-click the email icon in the panel, and then in the Properties window, change the name "Evolution Email" to Mozilla Mail and the command "evolution" to /usr/bin/mozilla -mail.

Instant Messaging with Gaim

Fedora Core allows you to do instant messaging too. It doesn't matter if you usually use MSN/Windows Instant Messenger, Yahoo Messenger, AOL Instant Messenger (AIM), or ICQ; you can set up Gaim, a single application, to check *all* of these messaging accounts. The question most people had in the past, however, was *how* to set up Gaim to do this — it was, shall we say, less than intuitive. In the new version of Gaim that ships with Fedora Core, however, things have gotten much easier, so you are really in luck.

To get Gaim set up and ready for action, go to the Main menu and select **Internet > Instant Messenger**. Click the **Accounts** button, and in the Accounts window click **Add**. This will bring up the Add Account window shown in Figure 4-15.

Figure 4-15: Adding instant messaging accounts to Gaim

From this point on, setting up Gaim is easy enough to do. First, select the appropriate protocol for your messaging service in the drop-down menu. Then type in your screen name (usually the email address under which your messaging account is registered), your password (your messaging password, that is), and finally, your alias (the nickname that other people see when you are in their buddy's list). Once you've done all this, click **Save**, and then close the other Gaim windows, including the main one. Now run Gaim again, and your new account will appear in the main Gaim window (see Figure 4-16). All you have to do now is click **Sign On**, and you will be blabbing in no time.

Other Internet Applications

In addition to the programs I've already discussed, there are many other Internet applications included in your Fedora distribution. You have the Konqueror Web browser, which is useful if you want to save Web pages as PDF files, and, as I will discuss in Chapter 8, yet another Web browser called Epiphany. However, there are other applications included for different Internet tasks, and I will briefly mention a few of these now.

Figure 4-16: Signing on with Gaim

Dictionary

While not usually thought of as an Internet application, the GNOME Dictionary is in fact just that. To open it, in the Main menu select **Accessories > Dictionary**. Type a word in the Dictionary input box, click the **Look Up Word** button, and the dictionary will search a variety of online databases and then provide a definition for that word (see Figure 4-17).

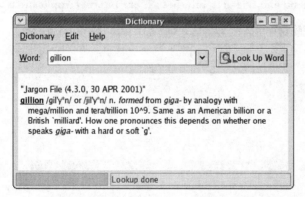

Figure 4-17: Looking up words with the GNOME Dictionary

gFTP

If you do a lot of downloading from the Internet via File Transfer Protocol (FTP), then the GNOME application gFTP is what you will be using. If you are familiar with FTP applications already, you should feel right at home with the very traditional layout of gFTP (see Figure 4-18 on the following page). You can run gFTP by going to the Main menu and selecting **Internet > More Internet Applications > gFTP**.

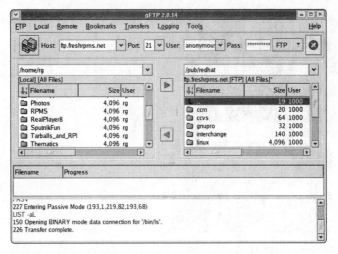

Figure 4-18: Using gFTP to download via FTP

X-Chat

Finally, chat-room lovers need not despair; Fedora Core comes with the chat
client X-Chat (see Figure 4-19). X-Chat is a very robust and highly customizable
piece of software that should be readily usable by those who have used similar
software under different operating systems. You can run X-Chat by going to the
Main menu and selecting **Internet > More Internet Applications > IRC Client**.

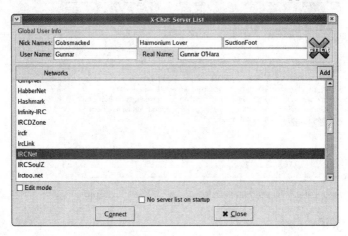

Figure 4-19: Chatting with X-Chat

5

DRESSING UP THE BIRD

Customizing the Look, Feel, and Sound of Your System

Before entering the world of Linux, I had used just about every desktop operating system around. Despite the differences among them all, however, one thing that I eventually suffered from in each case was a kind of visual boredom. I suppose you might call it GUI fatigue. It wasn't that I was tired of using a graphical interface; it was just that I couldn't help but get sick of looking at the same old icons, window borders, and color schemes. Of course, there were some changes that could be made, but it just wasn't possible to get around the basic look and feel without add-ons that demanded a price in terms of performance.

One of the features of Linux that pleased me to no end, and continues to do so, is that users can drastically change the look of things. I don't mean just the icons and backgrounds, but everything, including the actual window borders and controls. Add to that the variety of GUIs available for Linux that can be milked for all their graphical worth, and you have a totally customizable system. Is it any wonder that there are so many more Linux desktop screenshots out there on the Web than for any other system?

You may not be as fickle as I am in terms of the look and feel of your system, but you can learn to use and enjoy all the graphical customization power that Linux offers you as you work through this chapter.

Experimenting with a New User Account

If you are reluctant to alter the look of your present setup, you can set up a new user account and experiment with making the changes in this chapter when logged in to the new account. If you opt to go this route, your regular home environment will remain untouched because look-and-feel customizations that are performed in one user account do not affect other user accounts. When you are all done with the project, you can then simply delete the new user account. Either way, it's up to you.

To set up a new user account, follow these steps:

1. Go to the Main menu and select **System Settings > Users and Groups**.

2. When prompted for your root password, type it in, and then click **OK**. The User Manager window will open.

3. In the User Manager window, click the **Add User** button, which will bring up a Create New User window.

4. Type in a new username, such as graphika. In the **Full Name** field, you can type in whatever you like; I used Graphics Lover in the example. Then type in an easy-to-remember user password in the two password boxes; the one you're using for your present account will do just fine. Once you've done all this, your window should look more or less like that in Figure 5-1.

5. If everything looks fine and dandy, click **OK** to close the window and get back to the main User Manager window. The User Manager will now list your new user account right below your current one (see Figure 5-2).

To use this new account, go to the Main menu and select **Log Out**. In the small window that pops up saying "Are you sure you want to log out," accept the default selection, **Log Out**, by clicking **OK**. In a few seconds, you will be at the Login Screen where you need only type in the username for your new account, press ENTER, and then type in the user password for that account, followed by another tap on ENTER.

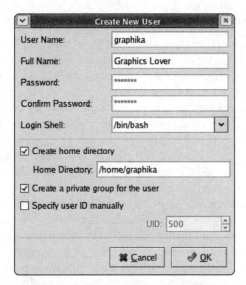

Figure 5-1: Creating a new user account

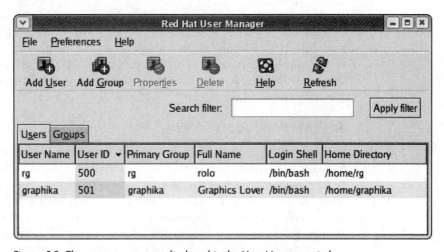

Figure 5-2: The new user account displayed in the User Manager window

Project 5A: Customizing Your Desktop Environment

Whichever user account you've decided to play with, you are now ready for action. We are going to start off easy by just creating folders, but by the time we get to the end of the process, you will have created a much wilder, and, depending on how you look at things, gaudier desktop environment than you've ever seen before. All of this is in good fun, of course, and when you are done, you should be able to completely and confidently customize things the way you want on your own. So let's go.

5A-1: Creating Folders

To get started, open your user's Home folder by clicking the Panel icon that you created in Chapter 3. Once you have done that, you will see that there is nothing at all inside the Home folder except for a folder called Desktop, which basically contains any files, folders, and shortcuts to programs that you have put on your desktop. If you are anything like me, you will want to put an end to this rather empty state of affairs by creating some folders in which you can organize your files in the future.

The first folder you will create will be for your writings, which you'll call "Documentia," though you can, of course, change the name later if you like. You can create a folder quite easily, much in the way you do in Windows, by either clicking on the **File** menu and then selecting **Create Folder**, or by right-clicking in an empty space within the Nautilus window and then selecting **Create Folder** from the pop-up menu. An untitled folder will appear in the window.

Having a folder titled "untitled" is, of course, a tad goofy, so you will want to change that. The text in the box below the folder will already be highlighted, so just type Documentia and press ENTER. Once you have done that, the folder will show its new name.

Now you can repeat the process and create four more folders: **Photos** (for your photos, of course), **Tarballs_and_RPMs** (where you can dump all the used files you will install along the way in this book), **Thematics** (for files you will use in customizing the look of your system), and **ogg** (the default directory for music files you rip from music CDs with the program Grip). Once you have done all this, your Home folder window should look like that in Figure 5-3.

5A-2: Adding Emblems to Folders

You must admit, things do indeed look a bit better than before, but this is just the beginning. To graphically remind yourself what each folder is for, you can add little folder-top icons called *emblems*. These can be added to any folder or file. For now, let's add one to the Documentia folder by right-clicking it, and then, in the pop-up menu, selecting **Properties**. When the Properties window shown in Figure 5-4 opens, click the **Emblems** tab and then scroll down until you see the emblem called **documents**. Click the checkbox next to **documents** and then click the **Close** button. The emblem should now appear on your folder.

Now, for additional practice, try adding the **sound** emblem to your **ogg** folder. Just use the same steps as before, and substitute the appropriate items and entries.

5A-3: Setting Window Backgrounds (and Emblems Again)

Once you've added those two emblems, your folders should look a bit spunkier. Nevertheless, the background of the Nautilus window is still white. You need not stand for that if you don't want to; you can change that as well. To do so, just go to the menu bar of your Home window, click the **Edit** menu, and select **Backgrounds and Emblems**. The Backgrounds and Emblems window will then appear (see Figure 5-5 on page 74).

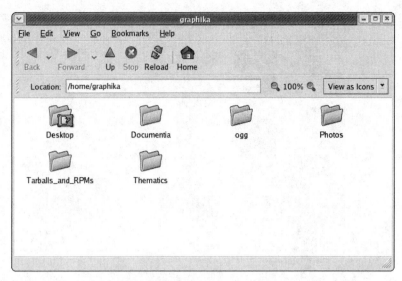

Figure 5-3: Adding folders to your Home folder

From this window, you can drag any pattern into your Home window, or into any other Nautilus window for that matter, and the pattern will then become the background for all your Nautilus windows. So, for experience's sake, scroll down to find the pattern swatch called **Manila Paper**, and then drag it to the white space of your Home window. Once you're done, the previously white window area will look like the wallpaper in a lawyer's office. Very nice, if you like that sort of thing. You can change it to a different background in the same way, of course, or you can go back to the default white by dragging the **Reset** swatch into the window.

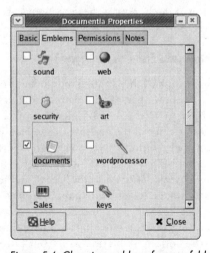

Figure 5-4: Choosing emblems for your folders

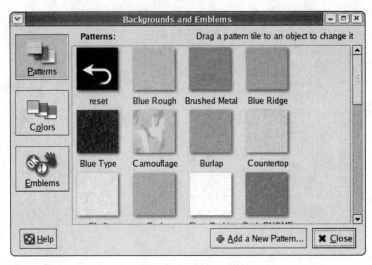

Figure 5-5: Choosing a background for your Nautilus window

Apart from the buttons for pattern and color swatches, there is a third button in the Backgrounds and Emblems window called **Emblems**. As you know, you've already added emblems to a couple of your folders by right-clicking the folders and selecting **Properties** in the pop-up menu. The **Emblems** button provides another way to do the same thing, but this method is far handier when adding emblems to several folders or files in the same go.

To see how this works, click the **Emblems** button if you haven't already done so. Then drag the emblem named **Camera** onto your Photos folder, **Cool** onto your Thematics folder, and **package** onto your Tarballs_and_RPMs folder. The selected emblems will then immediately appear on those folders. (And in case you are wondering why some of the names of these emblems are capitalized and some are not, I have no idea. Sorry.)

5A-4: Dolling Up the Side Pane (and Emblems Yet Again)

Now let's go on to change the look of the Nautilus side pane. Keeping the Backgrounds and Emblems window open (and if you already closed it, open it again), go to your user's Home window, click the **View** menu, and select **Side Pane**. The side pane will now appear in the left side of the Nautilus window.

You can add a different background pattern to the side pane as well, but for practice let's add a color instead. To do this, click the **Colors** button in the Backgrounds and Emblems window. The window will now be filled with swatches of color. Drag the **Grapefruit** swatch to your side pane, and it will turn from gray to, of all things, grapefruit (albeit a very dark and unusually colored grapefruit). You can also create a two-color-gradation effect by adding yet another color. Drag the **Mango** swatch to the bottom of the side pane (but still within the pane) and you should have a grapefruit-to-mango, top-to-bottom gradation within the pane. Of course, if you are not pleased with this tropical color set, you can get back to your original default gray panel by dragging the **Reset** swatch onto the area. When you're done, you can close the Backgrounds and Emblems window.

The side panel of your Nautilus window provides yet a third way to work with emblems. But before I let you in on this third, and last, way, you will need to add two more folders to your Home folder. Create one folder and name it "Finances," which you can use to store files dealing with your relative worth in the modern scheme of things, and then create another and call it "MyFaves," where you can place . . . well, your favorite files.

After you've created the new folders, go over to the side pane, click the drop-down menu that says **Information**, and select **Emblems**. A list of emblems will appear within the side panel (see Figure 5-6). Find the emblem named **Money**, and drag it onto your **Finances** folder. Next, find the **favorite** emblem and drag it onto your **MyFaves** folder. Once you are done, go back to the drop-down menu and select **Information** to get everything back to relative normalcy again.

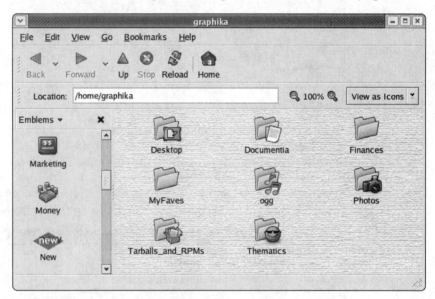

Figure 5-6: Selecting emblems from the Nautilus side pane

Even if it's not your cup of tea, you have to admit that your Nautilus window is definitely more colorful now. You can, of course, change it to look however you want it to, but I'll ask you to hold off on that a little while longer because you are going to be doing a little more playing around with it shortly.

5A-5: Changing the Desktop Background

Now that your Home folder window is all gussied up, or gaudied up (depending on your aesthetic sense of things), you may feel that your desktop looks rather drab in comparison.

Changing the desktop background (often called *wallpaper*) is easy, and your system comes with several alternative wallpapers preinstalled. You might as well start off by trying out one of these, so right-click any open space on the desktop, and select **Change Desktop Background** in the pop-up menu. This will bring up the Background Preferences window (see Figure 5-7 on the next page).

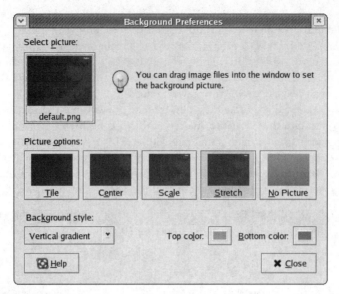

Figure 5-7: Changing your desktop background

To select a new background from this window, click the button that should read **default.png** below the words **Select picture**. This will bring up a window (shown in Figure 5-8) in which you can select from a number of alternative images that come with your system. To have a look at what's there for you, click one of the filenames within the right pane of the window, and a thumbnail preview will appear to the right of that pane. You can preview all of the images this way.

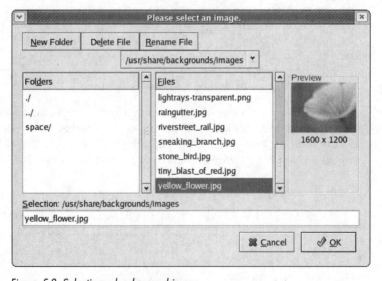

Figure 5-8: Selecting a background image

You will also notice that there is another folder in the left pane called **space**, which contains images of space-related themes. If you'd like to have a look at what's in there, just double-click that folder, and the files within it will be listed in the right pane. Once you're done browsing through those files, you can get back to the first folder by double-clicking ../ in the left pane.

Now that you've looked at all of the background images available within your system, select one that you wouldn't mind using for a minute or two, and then click **OK**. The selection window will now disappear, and the wallpaper you selected will appear on the desktop. You can then close the Background Preferences window.

Getting Some Wallpaper of Your Own

You've seen what your system has available to you, but I am sure that you will want to use a few background images of your own. Of course, to use your own images, you first have to get them, so let's get cracking by downloading one off the Net. The Internet has plenty of sites with downloadable wallpaper, but for this project I will point you to one site in particular: http://art.gnome.org. The art.gnome site has all the files you'll need for the steps in this chapter, and lots of others you can use later, on your own.

Connect to the Internet, if you haven't already, and then, in your Mozilla browser, type in the address http://art.gnome.org and press ENTER.

Once you get there, look for the heading **BACKGROUNDS** on the left side of the page, and then click the **GNOME** link beneath it. Once the backgrounds list opens, look for a background image of your liking. If you want to use the same image that I will be using for this particular task, look for the image called GNOME-Orange.

When you find an image, click its thumbnail, which will take you to the information and download page for that file. Download it by right-clicking the link under the word **Resolutions** (**png-1280x1024** in the case of GNOME-Orange) and then selecting **Save Link Target As** in the pop-up menu. A Save As window will pop open, and you can select the folder you would like to download the file to (see Figure 5-9 on the next page). In this case, scroll down in the Save As window to the Thematics folder, double-click to open it, and then click the **Save** button. Your new wallpaper will soon be saved in your Thematics folder.

Installing Your New Wallpaper

Once the download is done, open up the Background Preferences window again by right-clicking an empty area on your desktop and selecting **Change Desktop Background**. As before, click the button under the words **Select picture**. In the input box at the bottom of the selection window, type /home/username/Thematics/background_image_name.png and then click **OK**. Your newly downloaded background image will now appear as your desktop wallpaper (as shown in Figure 5-10 on the next page). Once that's done, you can close the Background Preferences window.

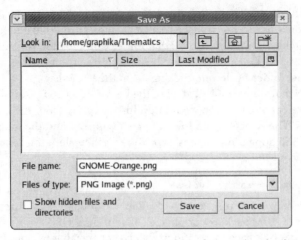

Figure 5-9: Selecting the destination folder for your download

If you wish to get back to the default wallpaper you started with, just right-click the desktop and select **Use Default Background**.

Figure 5-10: Your newly wallpapered desktop

By the way, you may have noticed that you cannot see the Panel at the bottom of the screen in Figure 5-10. This is because the Panel obscured the bottom of the new wallpaper, which somehow irritated me. I went to the GNOME Panel preferences window by right-clicking an empty space in the Panel and selecting **Properties** in the pop-up menu. In the Preferences window, I clicked the checkbox next to the word **Autohide** and then clicked **Close**. The autohide function works just like it does in Windows or Mac OS X — the Panel stays out of view until you move your mouse into the general vicinity of where it should be. You can make the same change if you like, but that is an aesthetic matter that I will leave up to you. Ah, the sweet taste of artistic freedom.

5A-6: Changing Window Borders, Controls, and Icon Sets

Now we get to my favorite part of this journey through the world of digital cosmetic surgery — changing the way window borders and controls look in GNOME. Let's set about doing just that.

The procedure is really quite easy. Go to the Main menu and select **Preferences > Theme**. The Theme Preferences window will open up and show you a list of the themes that are installed on your system (see Figure 5-11). The default theme in Fedora Core is called Bluecurve, but, as you can see, there are many others as well.

To get the hang of things, have a look at each of the themes listed by clicking them one by one. The changes will take effect immediately. Just clicking on a theme will change your window borders, controls, and even, if you take a peek in your user's Home folder, the icons. This is especially noticeable when you click Crux or Grand Canyon.

Each theme consists of a window border, a set of controls, and a collection of icons. This being the case, it is possible to mix and match these elements on your own. For example, let's say that you like the look and color the of bubbly controls in Grand Canyon, but you prefer the window borders in Mist and the icons in Ocean Dream. Well, you needn't despair, because you can create a custom theme consisting of these three different elements.

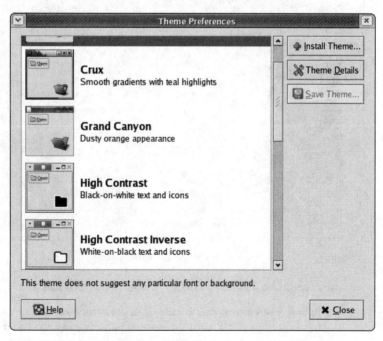

Figure 5-11: Selecting a theme in GNOME

To create your own mix-and-match theme, just click the **Theme Details** button in the Theme Preferences window. A new window will open, and you will find three tabs: Controls, Borders, and Icons. From within each of these tabs you can select the components you prefer. First click the **Controls** tab and select **Grand Canyon**. Then click the **Window Border** tab and select **Mist**. Finally, click the **Icons** tab and select **Sandy**, which is the icon set for the Ocean Dream theme.

Now take a look at what you've done. Hmm . . . not bad. But, on second thought, you don't really like the look of those Mist window borders all that much. To find something that suits you better, click the **Window Border** tab again and scroll down until you see **Metabox**, and click that. Yes, that's better. Now that you are satisfied, you can click the **Close** button.

You will now be back at the Theme Preferences window, where you will notice that at the top of the list there is a new theme entry called Custom Theme. If you want to save this combination that you've just created for later use, click the **Save Theme** button. Doing so will open a dialog box in which you can name your theme and write a brief comment about it. So, name your theme, write a comment if you like, and then click **Save**. Your new theme will now appear in alphabetical order within the theme list under the name you chose.

Once that's all done, your Home folder window should look like that in Figure 5-12 (and take a look at your Panel and Main menu while you're at it). Ah, trés cool!

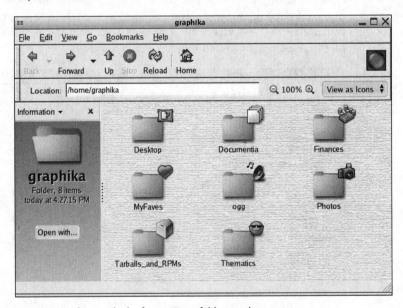

Figure 5-12: The new look of your Home folder window

5A-7: Installing Additional Window Borders, Controls, and Icons

If you have gotten hot on this customization thing and are not satisfied with the theme choices included with the system, you can download and install still other window borders, controls, and icons. To show you how to do this, I will walk you through creating a faux Mac theme, which will look fairly similar to the standard

Aqua theme of Mac OS X. If you still have some of the Mac-hating, Windows user in you, don't get too bent out of shape. Windows-like themes are already available in Fedora's default theme collection. Anyway, you're just learning right now, so drown out your passions for the time being.

Getting the Files You'll Need

To get the files you'll need to do this, make another trip to this URL: http://art.gnome.org. Once there, click the **Applications** link under the **Desktop Themes** heading, and look for a theme called **Aquativo**. Once you find it, click it to get to the information and download page. Download it by right-clicking the filename, **GTK2-Aquativo-1.5.tar.gz**, and selecting **Save Link Target As** in the pop-up menu. Be sure to download it to your Thematics folder.

You will have to download a window border theme too. On the left side of the art.gnome home page, click the **Window Borders** link under the **Desktop Themes** heading, and, when the page opens, look for a file called **Metativo**. Click the filename, once you find it, and then, from the information and download page, download it to your Thematics folder by right-clicking the filename, **MCity-Metativo.tar.gz**, and selecting **Save Link Target As** in the pop-up menu.

Finally, you will want to download a new set of icons as well. The icons you will be downloading are a sort of Mac-meets-Tux collection, which, while not truly Mac-like in flavor, look pretty cool. Anyway, to download them, just click the **Icon** link under the **Desktop Themes** heading, and then click the link **Tux n Tosh 0.2** in the new window. Once you arrive at the information and download page for that file, download it to your Thematics folder by right-clicking the link for that file, **ICON-Tux-n-Tosh-0.1.tar.bz2**, and selecting **Save Link Target As** in the pop-up menu.

Installing Your New Theme Files

Now that you have some new theme files, installing them is a breeze. First, open your **Thematics** folder in Nautilus, and then drag the window to the right side of your screen so that it is readily accessible. Then, open your Theme Preferences window, if it isn't still open, and click the **Theme Details** button, and, in the Theme Details window, click the **Window Border** tab.

Instead of using the **Install Theme** button, simply drag the **MCity-Metativo.tar.gz** file from your Thematics folder window and drop it into the list of borders on the left side of the Window Border tab in the Theme Details window. A small window like that in Figure 5-13 on the next page will then open. Just click the **Install** button in that window, and the theme will then be added to the list of borders as **MetaTivo**. Once you see it in the list, you can click on it and the theme will immediately take effect.

Now you can add the control theme in essentially the same way. Click the **Controls** tab in the Theme Details window, and then drag the file **GTK2-Aquativo-1.5.tar.gz** from your Thematics folder window to the list of controls on the left side of the Controls tab in the Theme Details window. Once again, a small Install New Theme dialog box will appear, and, as before, just click **Install**. The new control set will immediately appear in the controls list as **Aquativo-1.5**. Click that name in the list, and the changes will immediately take effect.

Figure 5-13: Installing a new theme

Finally, you need to install the new icon theme. Click the **Icons** tab in the Theme Details window, and then drag the file **ICON-Tux-n-Tosh-0.1.tar.bz2** to the Icons list in the left side of the Icons tab in the Theme Details window. The Install New Theme dialog box will appear, and you just need to click **Install**. Once you've done that, scroll down the Icons list in the Theme Details window, and click on **Tux 'n' Tosh**. The changes will take effect immediately.

NOTE   *If, after following the procedure for installing your new icon theme, you find that your icons do not change, and the name **Tux ' n' Tosh** does not appear in the list of icon themes in the Theme Details window, you will have to do things a bit differently. See Chapter 20 to find out how to do it.*

Your windows, menus, icons, and Panel should now have a more Aqua-esque look to them, though the folder and Nautilus backgrounds could use a tweak or two. In any case, you are now free to do whatever you like. You can continue the aquaization process with the skills you have acquired, you can leave things as they are, or you can switch to whatever theme you like. For consistency's sake, I will switch back to Bluecurve now.

Changing Your Login Screen

On the art.gnome site, you may have noticed that there is a link for something called *Login Manager*. The Login Manager is your login screen, also known as a *greeter* — the screen where you type in your username and user password when you first log in to your system. The Login Manager is another thing that you can customize, but you have to have root privileges in order to do so. In addition, any changes you make will be system-wide, not just for you, so whatever Login Manager theme you install and choose will be the Login Manager theme that everyone else using your computer will see when they use the machine. Of course, if you are the only one using your machine, this point is moot.

Downloading a Login Manager Theme

In order to try customizing the Login Manager, go to the http://art.gnome.org site and click the **Login Manager** link. Once you've done this, browse through the various themes and download one or two that you want; I'm giving you free rein this time around. As with the other files you've downloaded thus far, be sure to download these to your Thematics folder.

Installing Your New Login Manager Theme

Once you've downloaded a theme or two of your liking, you need to open the Login Screen Setup window. To do this, go to the Main menu and then select **System Settings > Login Screen**. A dialog box asking for your root password will then open. Type in your root password, click **OK**, and the Login Screen Setup window will then soon appear (see Figure 5-14).

Click the **Graphical greeter** tab at the top of the window. You will then see a list of the greeters that are included by default in your system, and you can click each one to see a thumbnail preview.

You can add the greeters you just downloaded to this list, but, unfortunately, you cannot install them by just dragging them here. Instead, you have to click the **Install new theme** button, but that is hardly a gargantuan task.

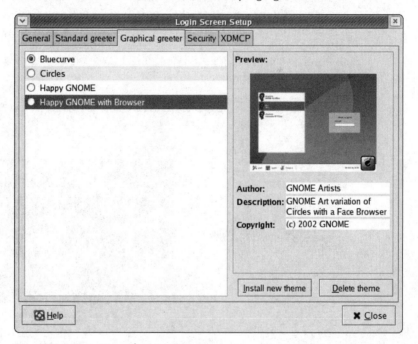

Figure 5-14: Customizing the Login Manager

Once you click **Install new theme**, a window will open up from which you can locate your new file. Remember, the file should be located in **/home/username/Thematics**. After you've selected your file, click **OK**, and it will immediately appear in the list of greeters.

To select the greeter you wish to use, just click its name in the list in the Login Screen Setup window, and then click the **Close** button. Of course, to see your greeter in action, you will have to log out first so you can log back in, but you needn't restart or shut down the machine.

Choosing a Screensaver

Used to be that screensavers were a must-have (and must-use) item for computer users so as to prevent damage (burn-in) to your monitor. Video display technology, however, has now advanced to the point that screensavers are no longer necessary. Nevertheless, screensavers are cool to look at, and one very nice thing about Fedora is that it comes with an unusually extensive collection of screensaver modules — nearly 200 of them! There are so many that you are sure to find at least a few you like. The screensaver settings are preconfigured to switch between modules randomly, changing the current module every few minutes. You can change these settings by going to your Main menu and selecting **Preferences > Screensaver**.

The Screensaver Preferences window, shown in Figure 5-15, allows you to do a variety of things, such as set the length of time between module changes and the length of idle time before the screensaver starts up. You can also opt to use only one screensaver module or no screensaver at all. In random mode, you can also omit the modules that you don't like by unchecking the boxes next to the undesired modules' names.

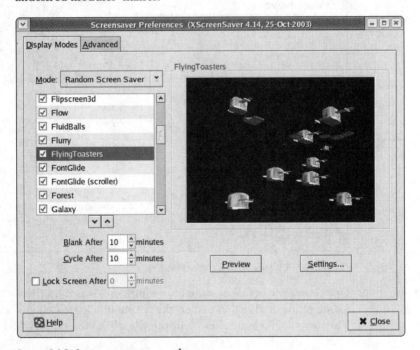

Figure 5-15: Setting screensaver preferences

Setting System Sounds

A friend of mine once said, "What fun is a painting if you can't hear the music?" He was obviously talking about something else, and no doubt acting a bit pretentious, but his words apply to this business of customization as well. If you're going to gussy up your system so as to make it scream out at you visually, why not make it do so audibly too?

I won't insist that you do anything here, because not everyone is keen on system sounds, but you should at least know that you can set up your system to play sounds for various system events. In the default system setup, sound events are inactive, so if you want sounds, you will have to enable them and set up these events yourself. This is, fortunately, quite easily done.

To enable system sounds, go to your Main menu and select **Preferences > Sound**. Once you've done this, the Sound Preferences window will appear in all its simplicity: two tabs, two checkboxes, two buttons. To enable system sounds, you should first click the two checkboxes in the General tab: **Enable sound server startup** and **Sounds for events**. You must select both of them.

After that, click the **Sound Events** tab, which will provide you with a listing of events and preconfigured sounds for said events (see Figure 5-16 on the next page). You can preview any sound in the list by selecting the event or sound and then clicking the **Play** button.

The list of events and sounds is for the GNOME Environment and several GNOME games, and you will notice that several events have no sound associated with them. By using the **Browse** button, you can add sounds from any appropriate (in genre and length) sound files that you might have or might download in the future.

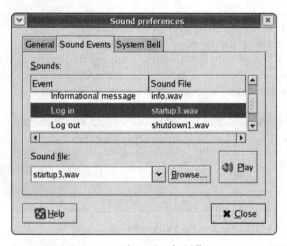

Figure 5-16: Setting sounds to play for different events in GNOME

Mozilla Themes

In addition to all the system customization you can do in GNOME, Mozilla allows you to customize its interface through the use of skins designed specifically for Mozilla. You can try this out, if you like. To start, open your Mozilla browser. It should look pretty much as it always has.

Trying Out the Preinstalled Themes

Mozilla comes with two preinstalled themes right out of the box: Classic (the default) and Modern. To try this out, let's try changing to the Modern theme. Go to the Mozilla **View** menu and select **Apply Theme > Modern**. Then exit Mozilla and run it again.

When it appears this time, the Modern theme will be in place, which you should recognize if you've been using recent versions of Netscape. This change will affect not only your Mozilla Web browser, but also Mozilla Composer and Mail.

Installing New Themes

If you are not satisfied with the themes that come preinstalled with Mozilla, you can download and install more. To do this, go back to the **View** menu, and this time select **Apply Theme > Get New Themes**. A new window should now open, and there will be a choice of two links to click: themes.mozdev.org and theme.freshmeat.net. For sake of convenience, click the **mozdev.org** link, and that page will load in yet another new window. Once it has loaded, scroll down the page until you find a link for **Skypilot Classic** on the right side. Once you find the link, click it.

After the new page loads, you will see a sample of the Sky Pilot Classic theme and, a bit further down the page, a link that says **Install It!** Click that link.

A dialog box (Figure 5-17) will then appear to confirm that you want to install and use the theme in question. Click the **OK** button, which will then bring up a window showing the progress of your download and installation.

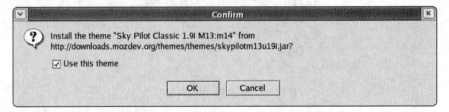

Figure 5-17: Mozilla makes sure that you want to go on with the installation

After the download is complete, the word *success* will replace the progress bar. Click **OK** to close the window.

Now, select your new theme by going back to the Mozilla **View** menu and selecting **Apply Themes > Skypilot Classic**. Quit Mozilla and then run it again, and you should see the new theme (see Figure 5-18).

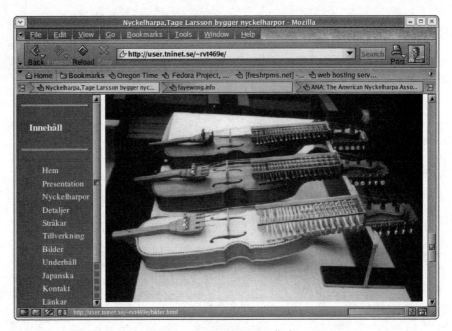

Figure 5-18: Mozilla with the Sky Pilot Classic theme installed

You can, of course, download and install other themes in the same manner from
either site. Just be sure to download versions that are appropriate for your
browser, though both sites should automatically direct you to the correct version.
You can find out what version of Mozilla you are running by going to the **Help**
menu in Mozilla and selecting **About Mozilla**.

6

GUTENBIRD

Setting Up and Using Your Printer

Unless the only thing you use your computer for is playing games, listening to MP3s, or stopping doors on hot, windy days, you will no doubt want to hook up your machine to a printer. It just seems to be one of those innate characteristics of human beings that makes us want to see our words in print. If print you must, and print you want, then print you shall . . .

Is My Printer Supported?

Setting up a printer to work with your new system is a pretty easy task, but you do have to make sure that your printer is supported. Fortunately, it seems that printer support in the Linux world is getting much, much better than it once was. In general, support for Epson and Hewlett-Packard inkjet printers is pretty good, while support for other makers and other printer types is a bit spottier.

If you really want to make sure whether or not your printer is supported (and why wouldn't you?), the best thing to do is probably to go to www.linuxprinting.org. On that site, you can check out the online database to see if your printer is currently supported and, if so, to what degree. Listings for supported printers also include information on what drivers are best for your purposes. If you're thinking of buying a printer, there is also a page of suggested makes and models.

Setting Things Up

To get started, you will have to turn your computer off, connect your printer to the computer, turn on the printer, and then restart your computer. Of course, if your printer was connected and on during installation, you can skip this step. Either way, if your printer is supported, the system will find it and automatically configure it.

Sometimes, things can be a tad less automatic: When your system starts up, it will, upon finding your printer, shoot up a blue and red Kudzu (hardware-probing utility) screen, which will tell you that it has found some new hardware. On that screen, you then press any key to proceed, and on the following screen you tell it to configure your printer by hitting ENTER.

That's it, as far as printer hardware goes. After that, you still might have to set it up so that the operating system knows how to communicate with that particular printer.

To see whether or not you will have to do this, go to the GNOME Panel and click the GNOME Print Manager icon (the one that looks like a printer). If a printer icon appears in the window that pops up, you are all set.

If not, follow these steps:

1. In the GNOME Main menu, select **System Settings > Printing**. You will be prompted for your root password, so type it in and then click **OK**. After doing this, the Printer Configuration window (shown in Figure 6-1) will appear, and it will be as empty as my head in the early morning.

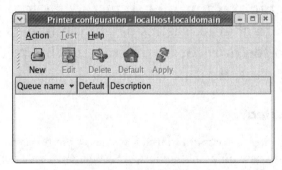

Figure 6-1: The empty Printer Configuration window

2. To remedy this emptiness, you will need to create a new print queue — a *print queue* is more than just where your documents line up for the next crack at the printer — it is a *virtual* printer, but you will learn more about that further on in the chapter. For now, just click on the **New** button to get started. This will start up the Print Queue wizard (see Figure 6-2).

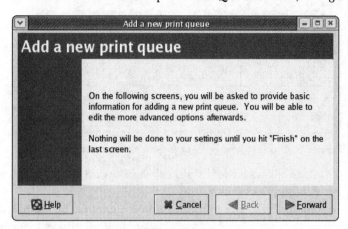

Figure 6-2: Starting up the Print Queue wizard

3. Click the **Forward** button to get to the next page of the wizard. In this page, you will give your printer a name and, if you like, write a comment about it. Because my printer is a Hewlett-Packard, I'll call it "Hewie," but you are free to name yours whatever you like. You needn't worry too much at this point; you can always change the name later. You can also leave the comment section empty for now — you can fill it in later when you find out how to use it best for your purposes. Once you are done bestowing a name upon your printer, click the **Forward** button.

4. The next wizard page is quite important, as it will show you whether or not your printer was configured properly (see Figure 6-3 on the next page). If it was, the name of the printer should appear here as **/dev/lp0** *yourprintername* or **/dev/usb/lp0** *yourprintername*, depending on whether your printer is connected to a parallel/printer port or a USB port. (The *yourprintername* part will be the name you gave your printer in the previous step, of course.) If your printer appears here, then you can proceed by clicking **Forward**.

5. In the next page of the wizard, it is likely that your printer will already be selected. If it is, then just go on to the next step. If it is not, and the dropdown menu says **Generic**, click the menu and scroll down to find and select your printer's manufacturer. Once you do that, a list of all the supported models for that manufacturer will appear in the bottom portion of the wizard page. Scroll through that list to find and select your model. When you are all done, the wizard page should look something like that in Figure 6-4 on the next page, although yours will differ depending on the printer you have.

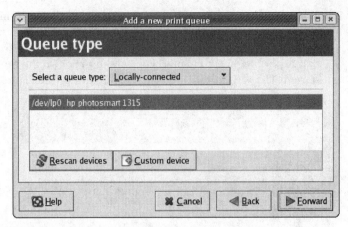

Figure 6-3: Checking the queue type for your new printer queue

6. Once all is as it should be, click the **Forward** button, which will take you to the last page of the wizard.

7. This last page is merely an announcement that the wizard is about to create a new queue. Click **Apply,** and a small window will open asking if you want to print out a test page. Doing so isn't a bad idea, so click **Yes** and you will soon find out if all is working as it should. If your test page looks okay, you've done well, and you now have yourself a print queue. You can start committing your words to paper.

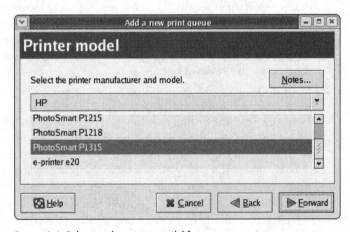

Figure 6-4: Selecting the printer model for your new printer queue

NOTE *If your test page didn't come out the way it should, or if your printer wasn't configured automatically or correctly by the system, check out www.linuxprinting.org and see if there are any special requirements or caveats for your model.*

Printing with the Printer

Now that your printer is set up, you will no doubt want to start printing. This is an easy task and not much different how it works in the Windows and Mac worlds, so you will need little explanation in this regard. There is, however, one simple point that might confuse you at first, so I'll cover it now.

When you first print from OpenOffice or other programs, you will notice that the print dialog box will have **Generic Printer**, **Default**, or **Postscript/Default** listed as the selected printer. The print queue you created just moments ago is the default printer, so any of those more generic selections also refer to your printer. However, if you prefer seeing the name of your printer listed, as I prefer seeing my Hewie, click the button at the right edge of the drop-down menu next to the word **Name** in the print dialog box, and you will find your printer by name. Again, it doesn't matter which of these printers you select, as they are all one and the same.

Printing to PDF

While you were looking at the print dialog box discussed in the previous section, you may have noticed that there was another choice in the list: **PDF Converter**. When you are printing from other programs, it might be listed as **Print to PDF** or something to that effect, but the purpose is the same: You can save your document as a PDF file. You probably have read documents in PDF format, so you most likely know what they are, but now you can create them too.

This is very handy, as it allows you to create documents that cannot be altered by others and yet can easily be read regardless of what word processor program or computer platform another person is using. It also makes for smaller files that can more easily and quickly be sent as email attachments. Chapter 2 of this book, for example, was a 5.5MB OpenOffice document, but when I printed it to PDF, it became a 770KB PDF file. All in all, this is a very handy feature that you would have to pay a pretty penny for in the Windows world.

NOTE   *Printing to PDF is also a very handy way of saving a Web page that you would like to keep on hand in its graphical entirety for future reference. At this time, Mozilla does not support this feature, so if there is a page you would like to save in this way, try punching it up in the Konquerer Web browser (in the Main menu select **Internet > More Internet Applications > Konquerer Web Browser**).*

Changing Printer Settings

As you print various things, it is inevitable that, for some reason or another, you will want to change your printer settings. For example, let's say that you are running low on color ink and want to keep everything in black or shades of gray for a while. Or maybe you want to print a particular photo at a higher resolution than the default resolution setting of your current printer driver. Doing all this is pretty easy, and there are a couple of methods — one very temporary and the other a little more permanent.

Changing Settings Temporarily

Let's say you want to print an OpenOffice document that contains a variety of colors, but you want to print it out in grayscale. Just go to the **File** menu and select **Print** as you normally would. When the Print dialog box opens, click the **Properties** button. After the Properties window appears, click the **Device** tab, and from the **Color** drop-down menu select **Grayscale** (see Figure 6-5). Once you've done that, just click **OK** to close the Properties window, and then click **OK** to print the document. These settings will remain until you have finished and closed the document that you are printing.

Although this method seems straightforward enough, it can be quirky at times. If you find that it doesn't work well for you, try the more permanent method in the following section.

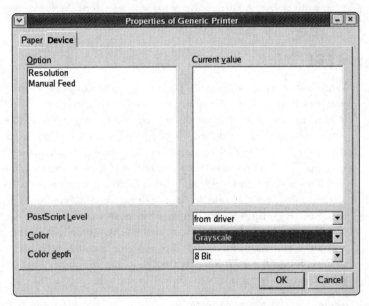

Figure 6-5: Making temporary printing changes in the print Properties window

Changing Settings More Permanently

The second method of changing printer settings is best used if the first method does not work for you, if you are going to be preparing a lot of documents that require the identical setting changes, or if you want to make changes to the resolution setting. This method is also pretty easy, though it may be a bit more indirect than you are used to. Just go to your Main menu and select **System Settings > Printing**. You will be prompted for your root password, so type it in and click **OK**. After doing this, you will see the Printer Configuration window. Click the name of your printer, and then click the **Edit** button.

Once the Edit a Print Queue window appears, click the **Driver Options** tab and you will see a screen very much like that in Figure 6-6, though yours might be slightly different depending on the make and model of your printer.

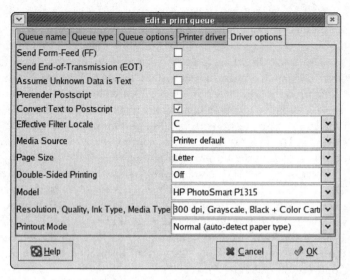

Figure 6-6: Setting driver options in the Edit a Print Queue window

Now that you are where you're supposed to be, just go to the **Resolution, Quality, Ink Type, Media Type** drop-down menu and select the color configuration and print quality that you want or need. Once you are finished, click **OK**.

After this window closes, you will be back at the Printer Configuration window, so in that window click the **Apply** button. Then you are done, and you can close these windows. If you later wish to go back to your old settings, just follow the same steps and select your old settings. This is, after all, the *more permanent* method.

Adding Another Print Queue (and Why You Might Want to Do So)

Well, changing the printer settings was all easy enough, but if you have to make changes like this often, you will end up getting pretty annoyed. Let's say that you make changes of this sort often because you write up a lot of black and white draft documents that you only need to print at a 300 dpi resolution, but once you are done fixing them up, you want to print and send them to other people at a higher quality, such as 600 dpi. And when you aren't writing up business documents, you love to print out high-quality photos that you took on your digital camera, but before printing out the final version, you like to preview them at a lower, and faster-printing, resolution. Satisfying all these needs would require a lot of trips to the Edit window, and that just will not do.

This is where having multiple print queues comes in handy. Although you have only one printer, you can create a variety of print queues, each with its own set of driver preferences. These function like a series of virtual printers, from which you can freely choose. The original queue you created is most likely a 300 dpi, color and B/W cartridge, letter-page-size setup. You can, however, add other queues that have different configurations in terms of color choice, print resolution, and even paper size.

To show you how this is done, I will use myself as an example. Let's say that I am satisfied with my 300 dpi, color and B/W setup, but I also often print out high-quality color photos. I will create a new queue for that purpose.

Just as you did when you created your original queue, I will go to the GNOME Main menu and select **System Settings > Printing**. Now when the Printer Configuration window opens, I will click the **New** button, and I will go through the wizard pages, this time naming my queue Color1200 (no spaces are allowed in the name). In the Comments box I write: High quality color printing and cocktails. Then I go through the remaining wizard steps, as before, until I am done and back at the Printer Configuration window.

I can now see my original Hewie, and there below it is my new Color_1200. The next thing I have to do is change my driver settings for the new queue, so I select Color_1200 by clicking it, and then I click the **Edit** button. In the Edit window, I click the **Driver Options** tab and then in the **Resolution, Quality, Ink Type, Media Type** drop-down menu, I select **1200 dpi, Photo, Black + Color Cartridge** and then click the **OK** button. To apply my new changes, I click the **Apply** button and I am done.

Because I sometimes prefer to create documents in grayscale only, I will create yet another queue called Grayscale300 and follow the same steps, except for the Comments box (where I will enter General grayscale printing) and the selection of the driver options.

Now that I'm all done with that, I think I should change the name of my original Hewie so that I won't get confused in the future. To do this, I click **Hewie** in the Printer Configuration window and then click **Edit**. In the Edit window, I change Hewie's name to Color300, and in the Comment box I write: General color printing. Then I click **OK**, and back in the Printer Configuration window I click the **Apply** button to apply my changes. That is all there is to it. My Printer Configuration window now looks like the one in Figure 6-7.

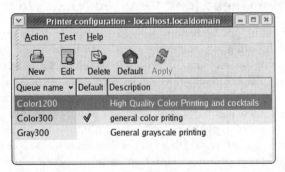

Figure 6-7: Print queues listed in the Printer Configuration window

Of course, if you decide to take an approach similar to this, make sure you exit from and restart any program you were in when you made the changes, or your new print queues will not show up within the Print dialog box for that program.

Selecting Print Queues

Now that I have all these print queues, you might be wondering how I can switch among them when printing. If I am switching a lot, it is probably easiest to just select the queue I want to use from the print dialog box of a program like OpenOffice. If, however, I am going to print several documents in succession requiring the same queue, I might just want to make that queue the default printer, if it is not already.

Changing the default printer is a no-sweat operation. There are a couple of ways to do it, but I will tell you the easiest one. Once you create a few queues of your own, all you need to do is open the Print Manager by clicking the printer icon in the left portion of the GNOME Panel. When you do this, you will be able to see your print queues, each shown in the form of a printer icon in the GNOME Print Manager window. In my case, my present default is Color300, but I am going to change the default to Gray300. To do this, I simply right-click **Gray300** and select **Set as Default** in the pop-up menu. Gray300 now has a check mark on it to indicate that it is the default print queue, as you can see in Figure 6-8.

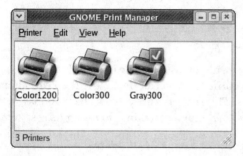

Figure 6-8: Setting a default print queue in the GNOME Print Manager

The approach you take to printer queues depends on you and your needs. You might not need anything more than a single print queue, but at least you now know how it all can be done. Whatever you eventually choose to do, you needn't worry at every point along the way, because you can undo anything you have done in one way or another. Just have fun with it. Feel empowered. Move on.

Canceling a Print Job

It happens to all of us. You wanted to print just 1 page of a 57-page document, but by accident you started printing the whole thing. What can you do to save your ink and 56 sheets of paper? Fortunately, the solution is simple.

Once you've clicked the **Print** button and the print job is sent to your printer, a small printer icon will appear at the right end of your GNOME Panel, as you can see in Figure 6-9 on the next page.

Figure 6-9: A print queue icon in the GNOME Panel

Just click that icon once, and two windows will appear: a GNOME Print Manager window, which shows what print queues you have created, and a window for your current print jobs (shown in Figure 6-10). Your errant print job will be listed in that window, so click the name of the job to select it, and then, in the **Edit** menu, select **Cancel Documents**.

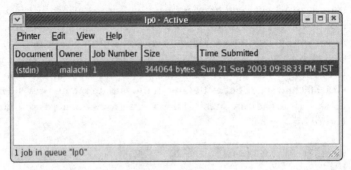

Figure 6-10: Canceling a print job

After you do this, the print job listed in the queue window will disappear, and your printer will stop printing. You can then close the Print Manager and the print queue windows. This is a very easy process that you may well find is more effective than what you've experienced in other operating systems.

NOTE *After canceling a print job, you may need to switch your printer off and on in order to be able to print again.*

7

PUTTING YOUR DATA ON ICE

Working with Floppies and CDs

As you no doubt know from experience, the longer you work on your computer, the more and more files you will have on your hard disk. Many of these you will have created yourself, others you will have downloaded off the Net, and others you will have gotten from other people on CD or floppy.

Being able to use floppies and CDs is essential when using your computer. Whether it be for sending photos to your relatives, listening to music on your computer, or just backing up all the valuable items you have stored on your hard disk, you will eventually want or have to turn to disk.

Floppies

When the original Macintosh first came out, one of the coolest things about it was that it used 3.5-inch floppy disks (aka floppies). At the time, I thought that those disks, with their hard casing and sliding metal doors protecting the media itself, were the incarnation of high-tech cool. Times change, of course, and there are fewer and fewer people using floppies these days. The reason for this change is simple: Files have just gotten too big for floppies and their very limited 1.4MB capacity. The audio, video, and image files most people deal with these days are gigantic. You'd be lucky, for example, to fit more than three digital photos on one floppy disk. Compared to the other removable storage media popular today, such as CDs, Zip disks, memory cards, and the like, floppies are also too slow. You could practically feed the cat, make a cup of coffee, and read the first three pages of the newspaper in the time it takes to write a good number of files to a floppy. (Well, okay, that's an exaggeration, but floppies are slow compared to the alternatives.)

Despite being small and slow, floppies are still used by a dwindling number of people who have no other way of transferring files to removable media, or who just want to hand over one or two small word-processing documents to another person who can read no other type of media. You may be one of these people, or you may have to send files to or receive them from someone in this situation.

Using floppies on your system is easy enough, though it is probably not as straightforward a task as you are familiar with, especially if you are a Mac emigrant. Let's say you have a floppy that you made with your old system, and you want to copy the files on it to your new system. As you might imagine, you first need to put the floppy into the disk drive. So far, so good. In order to see what's on the floppy, though, you have to *mount* the disk. To put it simply, mounting a disk is sort of like telling your system, "Hey, I've just stuck a disk in the drive, so wake up and deal with it." If your system isn't aware that your floppy is in there, it can't very well show you what's on it, right? While Fedora, like most operating systems these days, automatically mounts CDs, it does not extend the courtesy to floppies.

The easiest way to mount the floppy is to right-click anywhere on your desktop, and then in the pop-up menu select **Disks > Floppy**. Fedora will then mount your floppy and place a small floppy disk icon on your desktop to let you know it's done the job. Now double-click that icon, and a new Nautilus window will appear, displaying the contents of that disk.

Writing to and Copying from Disk

Copying files from your floppy to your hard disk involves the same drag-and-drop procedure that you used in your previous operating system, and as such, it requires no special explanation. However, things are a little different when it comes to writing to the floppy — when you drag a file to the Nautilus window with the list of your floppy disk's contents, your system doesn't actually write anything to the disk at that time. You can confirm this by looking at the activity light on your floppy disk drive.

When you first put your disk in the drive, you will see that the light stays off. Mount the drive by right-clicking the desktop and selecting **Disks > Floppy**, and the drive light comes on. Drag a file from the floppy to the trash, and the drive light will come on. Drag a file from the floppy to the desktop or your Home folder, and the light will come on. However, drag a file from your Home folder, or anywhere else on your hard disk, to the floppy, and the light will stay off. The file will appear in the floppy's Nautilus window, but the drive light will not come on because the files have not yet been written to disk.

The actual writing takes place when you are all done. Once you have dragged whatever it is that you want to copy to the floppy and are ready to eject it, you have to *unmount* the floppy first. To do this, close the floppy's Nautilus window, right-click the desktop floppy disk's icon, and in the pop-up menu, select **Eject**. At that time, the light on your floppy drive will come on as your system writes the files to disk. Once it is done, the floppy disk icon will disappear from your desktop and you can remove the disk from the drive. As you can see, this is a bit different, but not at all difficult.

After you have gone through the unmounting process I have just mentioned, you may sometimes still get a window telling you that the system cannot unmount your floppy disk, when in fact it has just done so or is in the process of doing so. You will know that this is the case if the floppy's icon on the desktop disappears while you are in the midst of reading the no-can-do message. If you come across this scenario, it is all because your floppy is just too slow to keep up with the system. You can safely ignore the warning by clicking **OK**. If the floppy disk icon disappears, you know that it has been unmounted.

NOTE *As data is written to a floppy disk when the disk is ejected, things can get confusing if you want to directly transfer data from another form of removable data to floppy. I would strongly recommend creating a folder on your hard disk called **data_transfer** (or something to that effect), which you can use as a staging area of sorts. Just copy the data from one removable source (such as a CD), and then copy the data from there to your floppy. I would also recommend this approach for files that you want to transfer from floppy to CD.*

Formatting Floppies

Before you can actually write anything to a disk, that disk has to have been formatted. This is true of any kind of storage media, whether it be your hard disk, CDs, storage cards in your digital camera, or floppy disks, though it is sometimes done before you buy the media. By formatting a disk, your system (at your request) lays down a sort of map on the disk to specify where data can be stored. Because there are, and have been, many operating systems, there are many such formats. Linux can read both Linux-native *ext2*-formatted disks and Windows/ DOS *FAT*-formatted disks. It can also create either format.

To format an unformatted floppy disk, place the disk in the drive, and then, in the Main menu, select **System Tools > Floppy Formatter**. This will bring up the Floppy Formatter window (see Figure 7-1 on the next page).

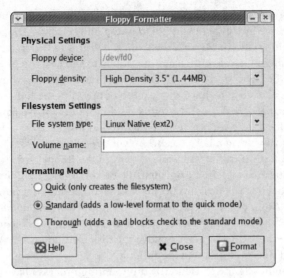

Figure 7-1: Formatting a floppy disk

In this window, you can specify the information density of the floppy (1.44MB or 720KB), the file-system type (ext2 or FAT), and the name for the disk. Once you have done that, you can begin formatting the floppy by clicking **Format**. Very simple.

If you want to reformat an already formatted floppy in order to erase it or change the format (from ext2 to FAT, for example), you can get to the Floppy Formatter in the way just mentioned, or you can first mount the floppy and then right-click the floppy disk icon that appears on the desktop, and select **Format** from the pop-up window.

Reading Data CDs

Dealing with CDs is much easier than dealing with floppies, as everything is quite automatic. To read a CD with data on it, rather than music, place the CD in your CD drive, and a CD icon will automatically appear on the desktop. Double-clicking that icon will bring up a Nautilus window displaying the CD's contents, and copying files from that window to your Home folder is a standard drag-and-drop procedure. Remember, as I mentioned in Chapter 3, any file that you copy from CD to your hard disk will be write protected, as indicated by a red *verboten* symbol with a pencil through it. In order to be able to write to that file, you will have to change its permissions. These are accessible by right-clicking the file, selecting **Properties** in the pop-up window, and then clicking the **Permissions** tab in the Properites window.

When you want to remove the CD, just close its Nautilus window, right-click the desktop CD icon, and in the pop-up menu select **Eject**. The CD will be ejected automatically. Now that really is easy, even for Mac emigrants.

Playing Music CDs

Playing music CDs is equally automatic. Place a music CD in your drive, and the GNOME CD Player (shown in Figure 7-2) will open automatically and begin playing the CD. To eject the CD, just click the eject button at the bottom-right of the CD Player window.

Figure 7-2: Playing CDs with the GNOME CD Player

The GNOME CD Player automatically queries the Internet to get the title of your CD and a playlist of the songs on it, but the CD Player also allows you to input this information manually in the CDDB Track Editor. This is useful if the online database information is wrong or if you don't have an Internet connection.

To open the CDDB Track Editor, click the Track Editor button in the CD Player window (near the bottom-left corner, showing the hand on the list). When the Track Editor window opens, you can input or modify the title of the CD, the name of the artist, and all the song titles (see Figure 7-3).

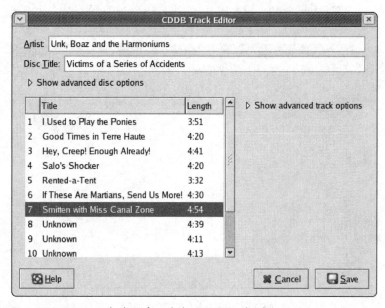

Figure 7-3: Entering playlist info with the CDDB Track Editor

If you click the arrow next to the words **Show advanced track options**, you can also write comments about each song, if you like doing that sort of thing. All of this information is then saved to your hard disk, where it will be available next time you insert that CD into your machine. If, of course, you place the same CD in another machine, the information that you manually inputted will not appear.

CD-RW Drives

These days it seems that almost all computers have built-in CD-RW (CD-Rewritable) drives, so much so that I would call them a near necessity. CD-RW drives, in case you're wondering, work just like CD-ROM drives in that they allow you to read data or play music from CDs. They also, however, allow you to burn data to blank CDs. If you don't have a CD-RW drive in your machine, I would strongly recommend your getting one. Drives for desktop machines are relatively cheap (around $40 or less from Amazon.com), and are easily installed. If you would like a little help with doing it, check out my Web page for this book (www.edgy-penguins.org/non-geeks). You'll even find a set of instructions I created in PDF format that you can download.

Burning Data CDs

Burning data CDs in GNOME has become extremely easy since the appearance of the Nautilus CD Creator in Red Hat Linux 9. It is one of the many reasons I prefer GNOME to KDE. To burn a data CD, just place a blank CD-R (CD-Recordable) disk in your drive, and an empty Nautilus CD Creator window will open (see Figure 7-4).

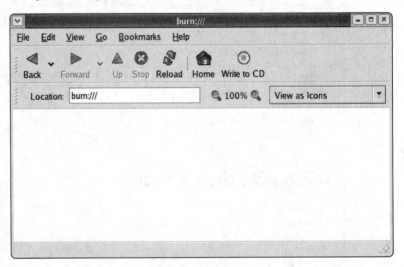

Figure 7-4: An empty Nautilus CD Creator window

After that, things are just as simple. Drag all of the files you want to burn to CD to the CD Creator window. Remember that once you've written those files to a CD-R disk, the files are there to stay; you cannot add or remove files from that disk later, so make sure you've got everything you want to burn ready to go before you commit. Once your list of files is complete, click the **Write to CD** button.

The window shown in Figure 7-5 will then appear, telling you how many megabytes of files you have selected to write to CD. In this window, you can adjust the write speed and give your CD a title; you can also just accept the defaults that CD Creator automatically selected. You should uncheck the **Reuse these files for another CD** checkbox unless you are planning to burn more than one CD of the same data.

Once you are ready to burn the CD, just click the **Write files to CD** button, and CD Creator will do its work. When it is done burning your CD, it will even automatically eject it for you. Very, very simple. And yes, the CDs you create in Linux *will* be readable in other operating systems.

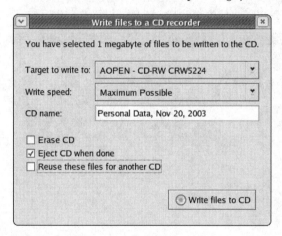

Figure 7-5: Setting options before writing a CD

Dealing with CD-RW Disks

CD-RW disks are pretty much like CD-R disks except that they can be erased and then written to again. They are also quite a bit more expensive than CD-R disks.

Using CD-RW disks is much like working with CD-R disks. If the disk is blank, there is no difference in the process at all, which makes things quite simple. If, however, the CD-RW disk already has data on it that you wish to replace with something else, the process is only slightly different.

One of these differences is that Nautilus will treat your CD-RW disk as a regular data disk rather than a blank one. This means that when you pop your disk into the drive, a regular Nautilus window will automatically open, rather than a CD Creator window.

To write to the disk, you will need to switch from the Nautilus window to a CD Creator window manually, which is easily done by selecting **CD Creator** in the **Go** menu of the Nautilus window (or by replacing the **/mnt/cdrom** text in the **Location** box of that Nautilus window with burn:/// and pressing ENTER). Once you've done this, the window will become a CD Creator window. Now drag the files you want to burn to CD to that window, and, once you are ready to burn, click the **Write to CD** button.

Now comes the only other difference: In the Nautilus CD Creator dialog window (shown in Figure 7-5 on the previous page), click the **Erase CD** checkbox. Once you have done that, just click the **Write files to CD** button, and CD Creator will erase the files already on the CD-RW and replace them with the new ones that you dragged to the CD Creator window. Not bad at all, eh?

Duplicating Audio and Data CDs

Duplicating audio and data CDs is also easily accomplished in Fedora. Rather than using the Nautilus CD Creator, however, you can do this with X-CD-Roast. To get started, go to the Main menu and select **System Tools > CD Writer**. You will be prompted for your root password, so type it in and click **OK**. This will bring up the main X-CD-Roast window (see Figure 7-6).

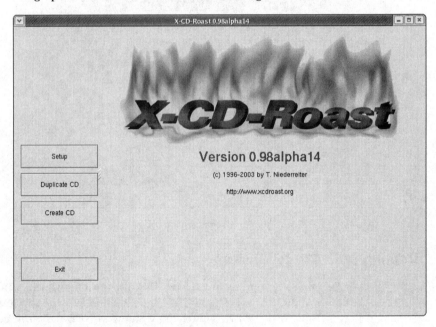

Figure 7-6: X-CD-Roast copies audio and data CDs

Setting Up X-CD-Roast

The first time you use X-CD-Roast, you will most likely be told that you need to set things up before you go on, so click the **Setup** button, and in the Setup window, click the **CD Settings** tab. Your CD drive should be listed as the **CD Writer Device** and **Primary Read Device**. If not, make it so in both cases. Then click the **HD Settings** tab. In this page you must designate a folder in which X-CD-Roast will look for disk images to copy, and in which it can write and store files during the CD duplication process.

If you are going to be doing a lot of CD copying, it would probably behoove you to create a new folder within your Home folder for this purpose to keep things tidy. You could name the folder something like "CD_stuff." If you aren't going to be doing a lot of CD copying, you can probably get away without creating any new folders.

At the bottom of the Setup window, where it says **Path**, type /home/username/CD_stuff if you created a CD_stuff subfolder (of course, you should replace *username* with your actual username), or you can just type in /home/username if you did not create a CD_stuff subfolder. Then click **Add**.

Once you've done all this, click the **Save Configuration** button. A little window will then pop open telling you that the configuration has been saved; click **OK** in that window, and then click **OK** on the left side of the Setup window. You will be returned to the main X-CD-Roast window where you started off.

Reading the CD You Want to Duplicate

To get started with the duplication process, click the **Duplicate CD** button on the left side of the main X-CD-Roast window (shown earlier in Figure 7-6). In order for X-CD-Roast to duplicate a CD, it must first read that CD and temporarily store its data in the folder you specified during setup, so put the CD that you want to duplicate in your CD drive. Of course, GNOME CD Player will automatically start up if you put in an audio CD, so you will have to quit the player before going on.

Once you have done that, click the **Read CD** button in the Duplicate CD window (see Figure 7-7 on the next page). The type of CD you have in your drive, as well as the number of tracks on it, should then be listed in the CD-Information frame in the window. If everything looks right, adjust the read/write speed in the **Speed** box to the highest speed your drive allows, or maybe a little slower for safety; the default speed setting is 1, which will cause the process to take forever and a day if you don't change it. Next, click the **Read all tracks** button, and the read process will begin. The progress of the read process will be shown in a read-progress window, and when the process is complete, that window will tell you so. Click **OK** when it says it's done.

Writing the Files to the New CD

Once the CD has been read, you will want to write a new CD. Remove the source CD from your drive, and then click the **Write CD** button on the left side of the Duplicate CD window. If all the data looks correct, adjust the drive speed so that it is somewhat lower than the highest write speed of your drive, and then click the **Write CD** button at the bottom of the window (not the big one on the left). A small window will then pop up telling you to insert a blank CD in your drive. Do what it says, and then click **OK**.

X-CD-Roast will then begin burning your duplicate CD, and it will show its progress in a progress window. When the writing is all done, X-CD-Roast will automatically eject your CD and tell you it is done. At that point, you can close the progress window by clicking **OK**.

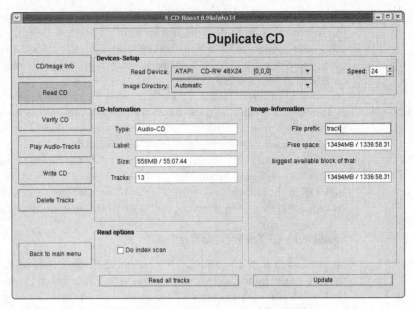

Figure 7-7: Setting up X-CD-Roast to read a CD you want to duplicate

Deleting Tracks

The steps in the preceding sections will cause X-CD-Roast to write all the files from your source CD to your Home folder (or to your CD_stuff folder if you created one) during the read process, and then to transfer all those files to the new CD. However, you probably do not want the copied versions of these files taking up space on your computer long after the new CD is burned, so you should delete them.

To do this, click the **Delete Tracks** button on the left side of the Duplicate CD window (shown in Figure 7-7). You should now see a list of all the tracks it created. Click **Select All**, and then click **Delete Selected Tracks**. A small window will then pop up asking you if you want to delete the number of tracks you have selected; click **Yes**, and the files will be deleted. When the process is finished, the progress window will say so, and you can click **OK**.

Burning ISO Images to Disk

When you download Fedora Core or other Linux distributions from the Internet, you usually download them in the form of one or more disk images, which are commonly referred to as ISOs because such files end in the .iso extension. An *ISO* is an image of a CD's file contents, which means that it is the CD minus the media itself. To put it another way, if CDs had souls, the ISO would be the soul of a CD; take away the CD's metal and plastic, and the remaining data would be an ISO.

As it is impossible to physically download a CD over the Net, the bodyless ISOs are the next best thing. For example, to get a working copy of Fedora Core from the Net, you need to download three ISOs, each which you can then burn onto a blank CD in order to give the images their bodies back, so to speak. In the process you thus create the three working installation disks that you need to install Fedora.

X-CD-Roast is the program of choice, my choice anyway, for burning (or duplicating) ISOs. The process is similar to that for duplicating CDs, albeit a bit simpler, as you already have a virtual CD, the ISO you downloaded, on your hard disk.

To start off, run X-CD-Roast as in the previous section and, assuming you have already gone through the setup process, click the **Create CD** button in the main window (shown in Figure 7-6 on page 106).

Once in the Create CD window, click the **Write Tracks** button, and you will be in the Write Tracks page of the Create CD window (see Figure 7-8). Click the **Layout tracks** tab, and in the Image Information pane you will see a list of all of the ISOs that are present in your CD_stuff folder (or whatever other folder you specified during setup). Click the ISO that you want to copy to disk, and then click **Add**. The ISO you selected will then appear in the Tracks to Write pane, and you can click the **Accept Track Layout** button at the bottom of the page. Then click the **Write Tracks** tab.

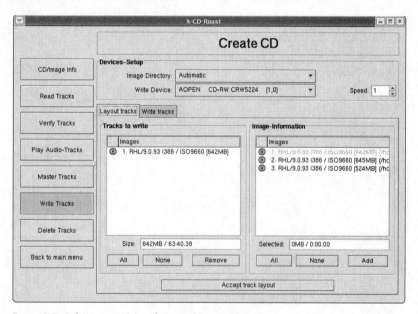

Figure 7-8: Selecting an ISO to burn to CD in X-CD-Roast

In the Write Tracks tab, the ISO that you selected should appear in the white pane. If so, adjust the write speed in the **Speed** box so that it is less than the maximum write speed for your drive; I personally find it better to limit the speed to about 8 when creating Linux installation CDs, as CDs written at faster speeds sometimes create installation headaches.

Once you've done that, click the **Write Tracks** button at the bottom of the page, and you will be prompted to put a blank CD in your drive. Do that, and then click **OK**. The write process will then begin.

As ISOs are usually quite large, the process will take a bit of time, so you will have to be a little patient. When it is all finished, X-CD-Roast will automatically eject your CD, and you can then close the remaining windows.

Burning ISOs an Easier Way

If you really don't feel like bothering with X-CD-Roast for your ISO-burning chores, I am glad to inform you that there is a much easier way of going about things. Just open a Nautilus window and locate the icon for the ISO file you want to burn to CD. Right-click the ISO file, and in the pop-up menu that appears, select **Write to CD**. Once you do this, the Write Files to a CD Recorder window will appear; just click the **Write Files to CD** button and you'll be on your way.

8

RPM ISN'T A 1980s ATLANTA-BASED BAND

Installing Programs with RPM

Well, now that you know what RPM isn't, you are no doubt wondering what it is. *RPM* stands for Red Hat Package Manager, and it is a very handy system that Red Hat came up with to allow users to install and remove packages easily. Of course, at this point you may be wondering what a package is.

At the most basic level, a *package* is simply an archived file or an archived collection of files, like the ZIP (.zip) or StuffIt (.sit) files you may already know. Packages designed to be used with the RPM system, however, are slightly different. Such packages are usually called RPM packages, RPM files, or just RPMs, and they are easily recognizable by the .rpm extension at the end of the filename. An RPM package consists of an archived file or set of files, along with a set of installation instructions telling the system's package manager where in the system to install the package files.

Usually these RPM packages are applications, though they could be other things too, such as fonts or documents. The Package Manager automatically installs each of the components that are in the package in the proper place on your system, making it all very easy on you. All in all, using RPM is very similar to installing Windows programs with an installer.

Fedora (and its Red Hat Linux predecessors) is not, of course, the only distribution that is RPM based — other distributions, most notably Mandrake and SuSE, are also RPM based. However, because different distros place various system files in different places, and because they are compiled differently, RPM packages are often distro specific. Thus, an RPM package for any popular application will most likely come in many different flavors, so to speak, to go with the various Linux distros. As if that weren't enough, there may also be different RPM packages for the different versions of a particular distro. For example, in the case of Red Hat Linux, you may find RPMs specifically designed for versions 7.3, 8, 9, and so on.

As you will come to notice, RPM filenames also specify a CPU architecture before the .rpm extension. You will thus see RPM files ending with *i386.rpm* (386 class CPU or better), *i586.rpm* (Pentium class CPU or better), *i686.rpm* (Pentium II class CPU or better), and even *ppc.rpm* (Motorola/IBM Power PC CPU, as used in modern Macintosh computers). Those packages labeled *noarch.rpm* (no architecture) can be used with any CPU.

Project 8A: Working Directly with RPM Packages

If all that information I just gave you about RPMs seems a bit much, don't worry. Installing RPM packages is quite an easy task. Usually, you can install an RPM package simply by double-clicking the RPM package file. In this project, you will get a chance to install four RPM packages in this manner.

8A-1: Installing Skoosh

Let's start out this project by installing a simple little sliding-tile puzzle game called Skoosh (Figure 8-1). Skoosh is not included with Fedora Core, so you will have to download it yourself. You can do this by going to http://dag.wieers.com/packages/skoosh. Once there, download the most recent file appropriate for the version of Linux you are running (e.g., *rh90 for Red Hat Linux 9.0* or *rhfc1* for Fedora Core 1, and so on) by simply clicking on the file name. The Skoosh file only weighs in at about 150KB, so the entire download process should be over very quickly.

Once the Skoosh RPM file is on your hard disk, you are ready to install it. To do this, just double-click the Skoosh file. You will then be prompted for your root password, so type that in and click **OK**. A completed System Preparation window will then appear, telling you how many packages will be installed and how much disk space will be used when the installation is completed (Figure 8-2). To continue, click **Continue**.

Figure 8-1: The sliding-tile puzzle game, Skoosh

A progress bar will show how things are coming along during the rather short installation period, and when it's all over. . . pffftt, the progress window will disappear, and all will be right with the world. Pretty easy, isn't it!

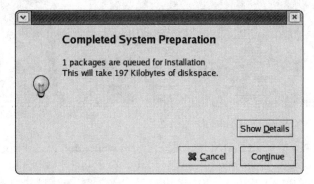

Figure 8-2: Preparing to install Skoosh

Once Skoosh is installed, you can run it by going to the Main menu and selecting **Games > Skoosh Tile Puzzle**. By the way, if you prefer using an image of your own to the one that comes with Skoosh, you can do so by going to the **Settings** menu and selecting **Preferences**. Once in the Skoosh Preferences window, click the **Browse** button to navigate to the location of the image you wish to use.

8A-2: Installing Frozen-Bubble

So far everything has been quite easy. Unfortunately, this isn't always the case; sometimes you will find that the RPM package you are trying to install contains system dependencies that your system is not set up to handle. To illustrate this point, let's look at the Frozen-Bubble game.

Frozen-Bubble (see Figure 8-3) started out as a standard game in the Mandrake Linux distribution, but because of its popularity it made its way to SuSE and even Windows. It is a pleasant game with cool graphics and music. It is also very attractive, in that you just can't lose. Unlike other arcade-style games, Frozen-Bubble lets you do a game level over and over and over and over until you get it right.

Figure 8-3: Playing Frozen-Bubble

Frozen-Bubble and Perl-SDL can both be downloaded from http://freshrpms. net/packages. When you go to that page, locate and click the link for the version of Linux you are using. Once on the package page, look at the list on the left of the page and click the **frozen-bubble** link. This will bring you to the download page. To download the file, right-click the tiny floppy disk icon near the top of the page, and select **Save Link Target As** in the pop-up menu. Once you've done that, look at the list on the left side of the page again, and download the file perl-SDL using the same procedure.

Installing Frozen-Bubble and Perl-SDL

Installing the two files is very simple. However, if you install Frozen-Bubble before Perl-SDL, you will experience what is often referred to as "dependency hell."

To see what I mean (don't worry, nothing bad will happen), double-click the Frozen-Bubble RPM file, and the Package Manager will do its usual dependency search. In this case, it will find that your system is lacking the Perl-SDL package, and it throws up a window telling you so (see Figure 8-4). In order to get around this problem, close the warning window by clicking **OK**, and then just double-click the Perl-SDL file and install it. Once Perl-SDL is installed, go on and install Frozen-Bubble in the same manner.

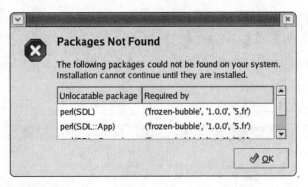

Figure 8-4: The Package Not Found warning window

In the case of Frozen-Bubble, there is only one extra file needed, but sometimes there are more. Worse yet, sometimes some of those required files that you download and try to install have dependencies of their own — the truly hellish scenario. Of course, as these dependency files might be required by other RPM packages you try to install in the future, you may well find that this dependency problem will gradually lessen for you over time.

Running Frozen-Bubble

Once you have installed the two files, you can play Frozen-Bubble by going to the Main menu and selecting **Games > More Games > Frozen Bubble**. That's all there is to it; unless you end up playing the game until the middle of the night (and coming in to work late as a result), you will be more than pleased with the results of this project.

I should mention here that you cannot use your mouse in Frozen-Bubble. Once the game starts, you can begin playing a game by pressing ENTER. After that, use the left and right cursor keys to aim your ball, and then use the up cursor key to shoot it. To quit the game, press the ESC key once, which will bring you to the high scores window where you can input your initials. Once you are done with that, press ENTER (or press the ESC key again to skip over it), which will bring you back to the opening screen. Finally, hit ESC again, and the game will close.

Project 8B: Adding and Removing RPM Packages via the Package Management Window

Your entire Fedora system (like previous versions of Red Hat Linux) is RPM based. This means that all of the applications and support files were originally stored in RPM packages that were installed one by one during the installation process. This means that installing additional packages from your installation

CDs is a very simple process. Most of these RPM packages can be accessed, installed, and even uninstalled via the Package Management window (shown in Figure 8-5).

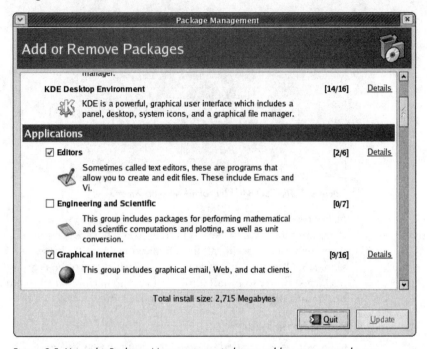

Figure 8-5: Using the Package Management window to add or remove packages

8B-1: Fixing the Package Manager Bug (Fedora Core 1 Users Only)

If you are using Fedora Core 1, there is a small matter that you must first attend to before you can proceed with this project. You see, the Fedora Core 1 Package Manager has a bug that prohibits you from reading data on the installation disks it asks you to insert. This problem can be easily remedied by installing a single RPM update file, **redhat-config-packages-1.2.7-1.noarch.rpm**, via the double-click method you've just learned. The file is available from http://ayo.freshrpms.net/fedora/linux/1/i386/RPMS.updates.

If your system does not permit you to update the file via the double-click method, hold off on this final project until you have completed Chapter 10, and then update **redhat-config-packages** using the APT/Synaptic package application duo that you will learn about in that chapter.

8B-2: Installing Epiphany or GnuCash

Now that you have fixed the bug, you can have a go with the Package Management window. The two packages we are going to try installing are Epiphany (an alternative GNOME Web browser that is sort of a light version of Mozilla) and the home finance software package GnuCash.

Epiphany (shown in Figure 8-6) made its debut in Fedora Core, and thus is not present on the Red Hat Linux 9 installation disks. In many ways, it is very similar to Mozilla, as it is based on the same rendering engine. Unlike Mozilla, however, Epiphany is designed to be integrated into the GNOME desktop environment and to follow GNOME's interface features. This is good news for customization freaks, as any customization features you apply to GNOME will also take effect in Epiphany.

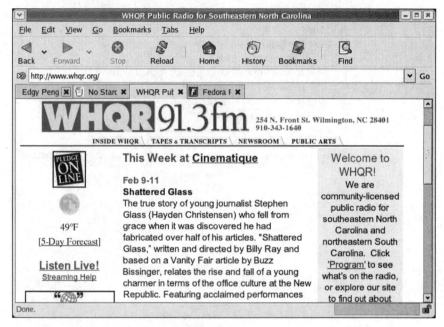

Figure 8-6: Using Epiphany to browse the Web

GnuCash is essentially the Linux answer to Quicken — it is a home finance manager that you can use to do your budgeting, balance your checkbook, and amortize your home and car loans. If you have been a Quicken user up to now, you can take heart, as GnuCash can even read Quicken files.

To install these two programs, here is all you have to do:

1. Go to the Main menu and select **System Settings > Add/Remove Applications**. Type in your root password when prompted to do so, and click **OK**.

2. The Package Management window will then appear. In that window, scroll a short way down to the **Applications** section, and then click the **Details** link to the right of the **Graphical Internet** category. (If you are a Epiphany-less Red Hat Linux 9 user, just skip down to step 4 instead.)

3. The Graphical Internet Package Details window will then open (see Figure 8-7 on the next page). In that window, select **Epiphany** by clicking the checkbox next to its name — leave everything else as is! Once you've done that, click **Close**.

4. Now you will be back in the main Package Management window, so scroll down in the **Applications** section to the **Office/Productivity** subcategory and click the **Details** link.

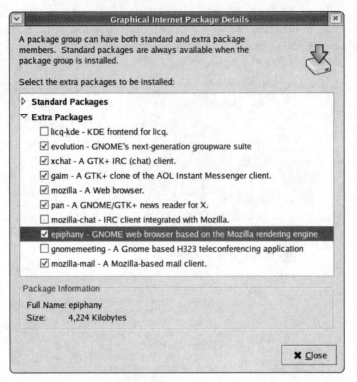

Figure 8-7: Selecting Epiphany to be installed

5. In the Package Details window for that group, select **GnuCash** by clicking the checkbox next to it. Once you're done, click **Close**, which will close the Package Details window, and return you to the main Package Management window.

6. Now that you have selected the software you wish to install, just click the **Update** button at the bottom of the window.

7. The Preparing System Update window will then appear while the system checks to see what you already have installed. Once it has done its business, a Completed System Preparation window will be displayed (as was shown in Figure 8-2 on page 113). Click the **Continue** button.

8. A new window will appear asking you to insert one of the installation disks. Insert the appropriate disk in your CD drive, and when your drive light stops blinking, click **OK**.

The installation process will then commence, and that is essentially that. If you're using Fedora, you can go have a look at your new Web browser when the installation process is done. Go to the Main menu and select **Internet > More Internet Applications > Web Browser**. To use GnuCash, just go to the Main menu and select **Office > More Office Applications > GnuCash**.

By using the method you've just learned, you can install any of the additional packages listed in the Details windows. For example, if you installed your system in Chapter 2 without following my special package-customization steps, this is how you can get in sync. Just refer to that chapter and then install the packages or package groups specified there. Who says there are no second chances in life?

Uninstalling Packages

Another good thing about RPM packages is that they are easily uninstalled, which is very handy if you are tight on disk space and want to rid your disk of anything you aren't using or aren't likely to use. Quite conveniently, you can use the Package Management window to do this chore; however, this will only work for those RPMs which you installed via the Package Management window or which were installed during the initial system installation.

Whenever you are ready to take the ax to one or more of these RPMs, here's all you need to do:

1. Go to the Main menu and select **System Settings > Add/Remove Applications**. Type your root password when prompted to do so, and click **OK**.

2. In the Package Management window, scroll down to the section containing the files you wish to remove, and then click **Details**.

3. When the Package Details window opens, uncheck the checkboxes next to the packages you wish to remove. Once you are done, click the **Close** button.

4. Once you are back in the Package Management window, click **Update** to begin the removal process.

5. The system will check things for a second or so before popping up a Completed System Preparation window (just like that in Figure 8-2 on page 113). In this window, you can see how many packages are queued for removal. If the number listed is greater than the number you remember selecting for removal when you unchecked the boxes next to the program names, you'd better click the **Show Details** button to make sure all is hunky dory. If it isn't, just **Cancel** and **Quit** your way out of things, and start all over from scratch. If everything is as it should be, just click **Continue**.

6. The system will then remove the packages you specified, and it will tell you when it's done, at which point you need only click **OK**.

9

SIMPLE KITTEN WAYS
Getting to Know the Linux Terminal and Command Line

Many people shy away from Linux because they envision it as a system for compu-geeks: an environment in which you do everything the hard way by command line. In this era of graphical interfaces, the idea of typing commands to get things done seems a dreadful throwback to the days of DOS, and that puts many people off — especially those who remember what it was like in those "old days."

This reaction is fair enough, but it is not really an accurate reflection of the reality of the Linux world. After all, most Linux users today utilize some sort of graphical interface. They can, and often do, achieve all that they hope to achieve through drop-down menus and mouse clicks alone. Many are able to survive quite happily without ever once opening their Terminal. The same could be true of you.

Be that as it may, there is still much to be said for the power and convenience of the command line. The fact that the command line can now be utilized within a graphical environment provided by the Terminal application also makes it much less forbidding. The Terminal is just a tiny text-based island in a sea of graphical bodies (see Figure 9-1). Using the command line can be as harmless as anything else you do on your system, and it can actually provide you with a little fun if you are willing to give it a try.

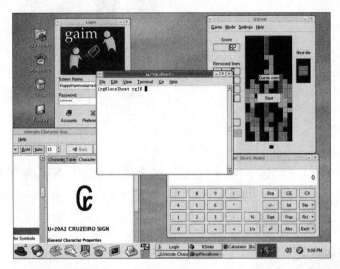

Figure 9-1: Putting the Terminal in perspective

Unfortunately, many guides to using the command line are written by hard-core command-line junkies, whose enthusiasm for what they see as a really good thing inadvertently makes what they write seem even more off-putting than it already seems to the recent Linux immigrant or wannabe.

For your sake, I will try to curb my own enthusiasm so as not to scare you right back to Chapter 8 and the seemingly safe world of RPMs. I will also try to help you keep things in perspective by teaching you, whenever possible, to use the command line as a complement to the various graphical tools that you have at your disposal, rather than presenting it as the sole way of going about things. Of course, I am not going to cover every possible angle in this regard — just enough to give you some exposure and experience and, hopefully, make you feel at least a little more at ease with the command line. Who knows; you might actually come to think of using the command line as . . . fun? Well, I won't get too carried away.

Meet the Terminal

The Linux Command Terminal application in your Fedora system can be run by going to the Main menu and selecting **System Tools > Terminal**. However, you should have already added a launcher for the Terminal to your GNOME Panel in Chapter 3, so you might as well click that instead. When the Terminal opens, it will, in all its simplicity, look much like Figure 9-2.

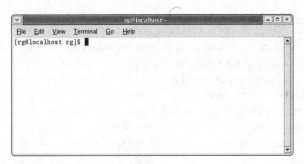

Figure 9-2: The Terminal application

As you can see, all it says is **[rg@localhost rg]$**. In this case, the first **rg** is my username, **localhost** is the default name of my computer, and the second **rg** is the directory I am currently in, my user's Home directory, which is the default location of the Terminal application. In your case, the username and default directory will all be different. If your username is frog, for example, the command line will say **[frog@localhost frog]$**. If all this is sounding rather obtuse to you, just think of it this way: **[username@localhost username]$** in the Command Terminal is the equivalent of your user's Home folder in Nautilus.

Typing in the Terminal is straightforward enough; you just type as you usually do. You can also delete and insert letters or phrases by using the DELETE and BACKSPACE keys and the cursor keys. For practice, try the following:

1. Type: I like strawberries so very much.

2. Now, change strawberries to cherries (because cherries are, in fact, so much better). Just use your left cursor key to move the cursor in front of the first *s* in strawberries.

3. Next, tap on your DELETE key as many times as necessary to erase the word strawberries (uh, that would be 12 times, methinks).

4. Finally, just type cherry and then use your right cursor key to move the cursor back to the end of this meaningful sentence.

Now that you've completed this fascinating bit of typing practice, press the ENTER key. As you will almost immediately see, the Terminal's response to your efforts thus far is merely a dismissive: **bash: I: command not found**. Although you've typed a string of text that has meaning to you, it means absolutely nothing to your system. In fact, the system was so shortsighted that it could see nothing other than the first word you typed in the Terminal (I); and because *I* is not a valid command, the system had no idea what do to with it.

Nontoxic Commands

As you now know, all of this typing is easy enough, but in order to actually do something useful with your Terminal, you need to type commands, and there are more of them than you could ever hope or need to know. To get you started, we will begin with some commands that are easy to understand, nontoxic, and completely child-friendly.

$ whoami

There is no command as easy, safe, and even as seemingly useless, as **whoami**. Rather than help those with multiple-personality disorders discover who they are at any given moment, the **whoami** command simply tells you what user is currently logged in. Try it out by typing whoami after the **$** and then pressing the ENTER key. Remember that commands are case sensitive, so type accordingly. The Terminal will now tell you the username of the person currently logged in. If you are logged in as frog, you should get **frog** as the answer to your command.

$ pwd

If you essentially know who you are but aren't exactly sure where you are, the **pwd** command (print working directory) should come in handy. The **pwd** command tells you exactly where the Terminal is in your directory tree.

Let's say, for example, that my Terminal is in my rg Home directory when I use the **pwd** command; I would, after pressing the ENTER key, get **/home/rg** printed to my Terminal. You should get similar results if you try it out.

NOTE   *The word* print, *in this case, has nothing to do with your printer; it merely means that the response will be printed to, or displayed in, the Terminal.*

$ df

Another safe and easy, but much more useful, command is **df** (disk filesystem). The **df** command tells you how much disk space you have used, as well as how much space you still have available, on each of the partitions on your various mounted disks. Try it out by typing df and then pressing ENTER. Your output should look something like that shown in Figure 9-3 (depending, of course, on the size of your mounted disks and how they are set up).

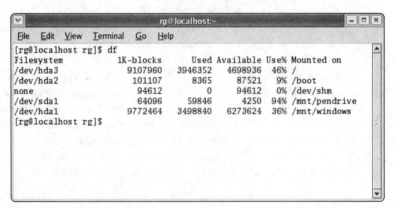

Figure 9-3: Output from the **df** command

As you will notice, the sizes are given in kilobytes (KB) rather than the GB (gigabytes) and MB (megabytes) you are probably more used to, but there is a way around this. Many commands accept a *flag*, or *option*, to further instruct the command how to perform. These flags are written directly after the main command and are preceded by a space and a hyphen.

In this case, you can try using the **-h** (human readable) flag to have your figures come out in the way you are most familiar with. Try this out by typing df -h on the command line and pressing ENTER. The output should now appear in a more familiar format (see Figure 9-4).

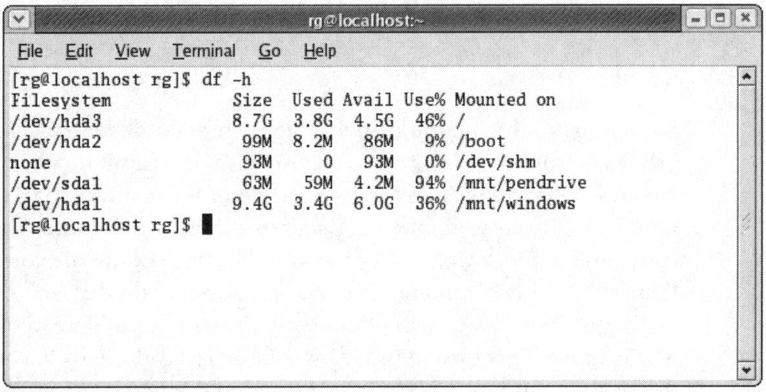

```
[rg@localhost rg]$ df -h
Filesystem          Size  Used Avail Use% Mounted on
/dev/hda3           8.7G  3.8G  4.5G  46% /
/dev/hda2            99M  8.2M   86M   9% /boot
none                93M     0   93M   0% /dev/shm
/dev/sda1           63M   59M  4.2M  94% /mnt/pendrive
/dev/hda1           9.4G  3.4G  6.0G  36% /mnt/windows
[rg@localhost rg]$
```

*Figure 9-4: Output from the **df** command with the **-h** flag*

$ ls

Another harmless but handy command is **ls** (list directory contents). The **ls** command shows you what is in your current directory. This is the non-graphical equivalent of double-clicking a folder in Nautilus to see what is inside. Try it out by typing ls and then pressing the ENTER key.

If you've been following *my* commands so far, your results should list all of the folders in your Home directory. You can also use the **-R** flag to show not only the list of files in the folder, but also what is within the subfolders. Of course, you should have no subfolders in any of the folders you created in Chapter 5, so you can hold off experimenting with this for a while. Instead, try typing ls -a to see your *invisible*, or *hidden*, files.

$ su

When you have to change from being a normal user to being the root user, there are two simple and straightforward steps involved. Open a new Terminal window by clicking the Terminal launcher in your Panel, and then type su and press ENTER; you will be asked for your root password. As you type your password, the password itself will not appear in the Terminal, but that is how things are supposed to be, so don't panic. When you are done, press the ENTER key and the prompt you usually see in your Terminal, **[username@localhost username]$**, will be replaced by your root prompt: **[root@localhost username]#**. Notice that instead of a **$** at the end of the prompt, you now have a **#** instead, which indicates that you are in root mode.

As you can see, you are now root, but you are still in your Home folder. If you change to root while in a different folder, such as **[username@localhost multimedia]$**, the prompt will similarly be in a different folder: **[root@localhost multimedia]#**.

exit

You can get out of root and back to your normal user mode by using the **exit** command. Just type exit and press ENTER and you will become your old self in user mode again. Very simple and handy. If you use the **exit** command while in user mode, you will exit the Terminal window.

$ locate

In contrast to the seemingly lightweight commands you have learned so far, the **locate** command is really quite useful. In fact, you might well find it a much easier, faster, and more effective method of finding files than the graphical search tool in the Main menu. Using the command is quite easy: You simply type the command followed by a space and the name of the file you are searching for. You can use this command in either root or user mode.

Before you can use this command, though, you will need to create a database of filenames for **locate** to use. This is quite easily done by becoming root using the **su** command, which you just learned in the previous section, and then typing in updatedb (Whoa, Nellie! Yet another command!), followed by a tap on the ENTER key. It will seem that nothing is happening for a while, but don't worry. As long as the cursor in your Terminal is blinking, progress is being made, and when your root prompt returns, you will have successfully created the database file. After that, you can go on and use the **locate** command.

To take this new command out for a test-drive, let's look for the **kolf.png** file that we searched for via the graphical search tool in Chapter 3. Just type in locate kolf.png and press ENTER. Your results should look like those in Figure 9-5.

*Figure 9-5: Results of your **locate** search*

Commands with Some Teeth

The simple commands you have tried so far are all of the safe-and-sane, fire marshal–approved variety; they merely print out information to your Terminal. Now you are going to try to get some real tangible results from the commands you use. These commands are also essentially safe and sane if you follow my instructions.

$ mkdir

You have already learned how to create folders by means of menus and your mouse, but you can also do this using the command line. The command is **mkdir** (make directory), and it is easy as punch to use (though I've never been quite sure how punch is easy).

To see how this command works, and to work with the commands that follow, use the **mkdir** command now to create a folder called **command_exp** (for command experiments). All you have to do is type mkdir command_exp and then press ENTER. The new folder should appear in your Home folder, so go ahead and check to see if it is there by clicking the user's Home icon on your desktop.

OK, good, *bra, bueno!* Now let's create another new folder within that new folder — a *subfolder*, if you will. We'll call this one **sub**. So, just type mkdir command_exp/sub and then press ENTER. You can now go take a peek and see if the subfolder appears within the command_exp folder, if you like.

$ mv

The next command is the **mv** (move) command, but before we experiment with it, we need to create a dummy file — we need something to move, after all. Go to the Main menu and select **Accessories > Text Editor**. This will bring up the text editor program called Gedit. All you are going to do with Gedit is click the **Save** button; you don't have to write anything in the document itself. A **Save As** window should then appear, and in the box near the bottom of that window (just under the words **Selection: /home/username**), type expfile and then click **OK**. The new file, named expfile, should appear in your Home directory.

To move the file that you've just created, you will use the **mv** command, of course. Just type mv expfile command_exp/sub (this tells the system which file to move and where to move it to) and then press ENTER. The file will now be in your sub folder.

$ cd

Until now, you have been using the command line from your Home folder. With the **cd** command, you can change your Terminal's location to another folder. This is a very handy command that you will be using quite a lot when doing the other projects in this book. To take it out for a spin, let's get inside the **command_exp** folder by typing cd command_exp and pressing ENTER. If you've done this correctly, the prompt in your Terminal should now read **[username@localhost command_exp]**. If so, you can pat yourself on the back.

While you are there, you might as well try out the **ls** command with **-R** flag to see how that works. Just type ls -R and press ENTER. Your Terminal should now show that you have a subfolder there called **sub** and a file inside that subfolder called **expfile**.

That is all you really want to do in there for now, so to get back to your Home directory, just type cd and press ENTER, which will take you back home, so to speak.

$ cp

Being fickle, as humans by nature are, you have now decided that you not only want your **expfile** in the **sub** folder, but that you also want a copy in your Home directory, where it was in the first place. To copy **expfile**, you can use the **cp** (copy) command.

To do this, the command needs to know where the file you want to copy is, what it is called, and where you want to copy it to. In this case, type the following command (replacing *username* with your actual username) and then press ENTER:

```
cp command_exp/sub/expfile /home/username
```

Be sure to put a space between the file you are copying and its destination (in this case, between the expfile and /home/username).

Once you've done this, you should have two copies of **expfile**, one in your Home folder and one in your **sub** folder. Go have a look to see the fruit of your endeavors.

$ rm

When you were a kid, you may well have experienced the joy of building a castle out of LEGO bricks and then the even greater joy of tearing the whole thing down (preferably with D-cell batteries). We will now embark on a similar move. The first tool in this nostalgic endeavor is the **rm** (remove) command, with which we can trash files.

The **rm** command, albeit very useful and easy to use, should be used with caution. Once you remove a file with this command, there is no going back — the file is gone for good.

To play it safe, let's try out the **rm** command by getting rid of that new copy of **expfile** that we just created in your Home folder. The basic **rm** command structure consists of the command itself, **rm**, followed by the name of the file that you wish to remove. In this case, you want to remove the file called **expfile** located in your Home folder. Assuming your Command Terminal shows you to be Home, you can remove the file by typing rm expfile followed by a tap on the ol' ENTER key. The file will then be gone, and gone for good.

Now, double your pleasure by getting rid of the version of **expfile** that is located in the subfolder **sub**. In this case, you need to specify where the file is because it isn't in the folder that the Terminal is in. Just type rm command_exp/sub/expfile and then press ENTER. Oooh, very cool. Brings ya back, doesn't it?

$ rmdir

You will now continue the fun with the **rmdir** (remove directory) command, which is a bigger and more powerful version of the **rm** command.

The **rmdir** command, like the **rm** command, should be used with caution. There are no do-overs with **rmdir**. Once you remove a directory or folder with this command, it is gone for good.

To try this command, you can get rid of that **sub** folder you created. Type `rmdir command_exp/sub` and press ENTER. The **sub** folder should now be gone. Finally, to round out the fun, use the **rmdir** command once more to get rid of the **command_exp** folder that we created earlier. You've probably got it down by now, but just in case you haven't, type `rmdir command_exp` and then press ENTER.

$ chmod

In Chapter 3, you learned how to change file permissions via the Nautilus interface. This is without a doubt the easiest way to go about such things, but when you have a folder full of files, perhaps copied to your hard disk from CD, that are emblazoned with the *verboten* symbol, it can prove quite tiring to change the permissions of such files one by one. In this case, the command-line approach proves to be much easier to deal with.

The command for changing file permissions is **chmod** (change mode). To use it, just type the command followed by the permissions you want to extend to a file, and then the location of the file itself. For example, let's say that you copied a JPEG file called mybirthday.jpg from CD to the personal subfolder within the Photos folder on your hard disk, and the file is write protected. To change the file so that you have write permissions (meaning that you can alter the file), you would type in the following and then press ENTER:

```
chmod 744 photos/personal/mybirthday.jpg
```

To change the permissions of all the files and subfolders (and all the files within those subfolders) in one fell swoop, you can add the **-R** (recursive) flag to the **chmod** command. The command would thus be as follows:

```
chmod -R 744 photos/personal
```

The number 744, by the way, extends read, write, and execute permissions to you, the owner, but gives read-only rights to everyone else — a pretty safe choice when in doubt. If you want to figure out permission numbers for yourself, it is pretty easy. You are basically dealing with three number positions, each of which has eight numerical possibilities (0–7). The left slot represents permissions for the owner; the center slot represents the permissions for the group; and the third slot represents permissions for others.

The meanings of the numbers themselves are as follows:

7 = Read, write, and execute permissions

6 = Read and write permissions

5 = Read and execute permissions

4 = Read-only permissions

3 = Write and execute permissions

2 = Write-only permissions

1 = Execute-only permissions

0 = No permissions

Figure 9-6 points out the meaning of each of these numbers and what each number slot represents — permissions aren't all that complicated.

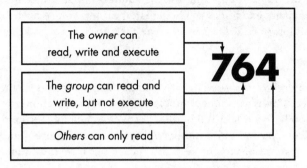

Figure 9-6: The meaning of permissions numbers

A Couple of Other Biters You'll Be Using Soon

This is as good a place as any to introduce yet two more commands that you will be called upon to use in this chapter and elsewhere in the book: **rpm** and **ln**. You needn't practice with these yet, as you will be using them very soon, but you might as well know what they are all about.

$ ln

The **ln** (link) command is used to create a link file that launches or activates another file located in a separate folder. This is very useful when trying to activate a file that is buried deep in the subfolder of a subfolder of a subfolder somewhere on your hard disk. The command is very often used with the **-s** (symbolic) flag, which provides essentially the same thing as the "shortcut" you've come to know in Windows, or the "alias" on the Mac.

The easiest way to use the **ln** command is to first use the **cd** command to change the Terminal's location to the folder where you want to place the link. Then you can type the *ln* command on the command line, followed by the path of the file you wish to link to. For example, let's say that you wanted to put a link in your Home folder for an OpenOffice.org Writer file of the autobiography you've been writing, called **myLife.sxw**. The file is pretty well buried in a nest of subfolders deep within your user's Home folder: /home/username/Documentia/personal/self/autobiography/myLife.sxw. To create the link, you would open a new Terminal window, type in the following command string, and then press ENTER:

```
ln -s Documentia/personal/self/autobiography/myLife.sxw
```

Once you are finished, the link will appear in your Home folder as an icon matching the original file in terms of appearances, albeit sporting a green arrow to signify that it is a link.

rpm

As you might have guessed on your own, the **rpm** command is used to install RPM files. Of course, you can do this through simple mouse clicks alone, but sometimes the command-line alternative can be quite useful. As the **rpm** command usually requires the system to write to files that can only be written to by root, you must first become root in order to use it for installation. That is why there is a # sign before the command in the heading.

As with most commands, **rpm** can be used in conjunction with flags. In fact, the most commonly used command and flag combination for this command is **rpm -Uvh**. There are actually three flags used together in this case: **U**, **v**, and **h**. When using more than one flag simultaneously, the flags are written together after the hyphen (**-Uvh**, not **-U -v -h**).

The **U** (update) flag either installs a file anew or updates a previously installed version of the same file, depending on whether or not a version of the file exists on the system. Thus, if you are trying to install a file called **dog-1.0.2**, and your system already has a file called **dog-1.0.1**, the **U** flag tells the **rpm** command to update that file. If there is no such **dog** file on your system, the **U** flag merely tells the **rpm** command to install it. The second flag, **v** (verbose), tells the **rpm** command to give you a progress report of what is going on. The last flag, **h** (hash), tells the command to use hash marks (###) as the means by which to indicate that progress — a sort of Terminal version of the progress bar.

Project 9A: Command Practice with pyWings

Now that you know a few commands, let's put them to good use. The program you will be installing in this project is a simple, and admittedly kind of silly, oracle program called pyWings (see Figure 9-7). pyWings will give you cryptic guidance in response to whatever questions you may ask it.

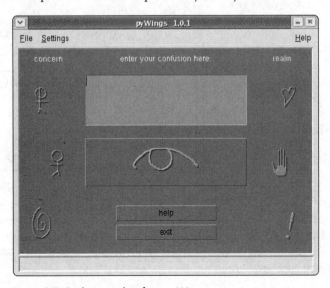

Figure 9-7: Seeking wisdom from pyWings

To use pyWings, you type whatever your *confusion* is in the input box, and then click one of the *concern* icons on the left (self, another, world), one of the *realm* icons on the right (love, work, truth), and then you hit the big button that looks like half an eye. The oracle will then tell you what it has to say. As an example, I asked the oracle if I am going to be rich, picked *self* as my concern and *truth* as the realm. Figure 9-8 shows the wisdom that was bestowed upon me.

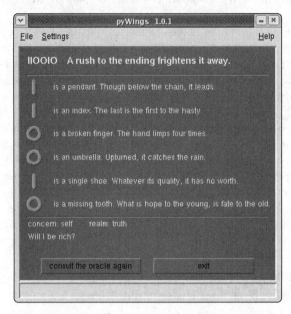

Figure 9-8: PyWings bestows its wisdom

As you can see, the oracle told me, "A rush to the ending frightens it away," which I will interpret as a call for patience — if I push too much, I will remain a paycheck-to-paycheck sort of guy.

pyWings is written in a programming language called Python, which actually creates scripts rather than true conventional programs. You will find out a little more about this distinction in Chapter 11. For now, one of the differences I can mention right off the bat is that you don't actually have to install pyWings; you are simply going to put it on your hard drive in your Home folder and run it from there, more or less as is.

9A-1: Getting the pyWings Files

OK, so now you are just about ready to begin installing pyWings, but before you do, you must get the files you need. First of all, you will need pyWings itself, which you can get from the project's home page at http://pywings.sourceforge. net/download.html. Just scroll down the page to the section that says **Unix/Linux/X11** and click the **HTTP** link, which will get you the file **pywings-1.0.1.tar.gz** (the .tar.gz ending tells you that this is a *tarball* — the Linux world's answer to ZIP files). Put the file in your Tarballs_and_RPMs folder, which is inside your Home folder.

PyWings requires that you have **tkinter**, one of the several graphical interface packages for Python scripts, installed on your system, and tkinter has three dependencies of its own that you must also install in order for it to work — this is your first real experience with dependency hell. Fortunately, this isn't all that hellish an endeavor, as all four files are available on your installation disks. Of course, you can simply copy these files to your hard disk via the familiar drag-and-drop method, but because you are learning about the command line, let's do it via the Terminal.

9A-2: Copying tkinter and Its Dependencies to Your Hard Disk

The files **tkinter**, **itcl**, and **tix** can all be found on the Fedora (or Red Hat) installation disks. Before you copy these files to your hard disk, first use the **mkdir** command to create a special folder inside your Home folder in which to place these RPM files:

1. Open a new Terminal window, type `mkdir expRPMS` and then press ENTER.

    Now that you have a folder in which to place these RPM files, it is time to copy them from the CD to the expRPMS folder you've just created. To do this, you will be using the **cd** (change directory) and **cp** (copy) commands.

2. Insert Install Disk 2 (or Disk 3 for Red Hat 9 folk or those of you using the three-CD edition of Fedora Core) into your CD drive and wait until it is automatically mounted.

3. In the Terminal window, **cd** to the RPMS folder on the installation disk by typing the following and pressing ENTER:
    `cd /mnt/cdrom/Fedora/RPMS/`
    (for Red Hat 9 users, that would be */mnt/cdrom/RedHat/RPMS/*, of course).

    Now copy each of the RPM files to the **expRPMS** folder on your hard disk by typing the following command strings and pressing ENTER after each one (be sure to use *your* username where it says **username**):
    `cp tkinter* /home/username/expRPMS/`
    `cp itcl* /home/username/expRPMS/`
    `cp tix* /home/username/expRPMS/`

NOTE   *In the preceding step you used the wildcard character, the asterisk (*), rather than typing in the full filename (for example, **tix*** instead of **tix-8.1.4-93.i386.rpm**) in order to save your fingers some wear and tear. The wildcard character (*) is a shortcut of sorts. When you typed in* tix*, *you were essentially telling your system to copy anything beginning with* tix. *If you had typed* *tix, *you would have been telling the system to copy anything ending in* tix. *As you can see, you should be careful when you do this on your own, because you might end up copying a lot of files you weren't counting on.*

4. In your Command Terminal, **cd** back to your home directory by typing `cd` and pressing ENTER.

5. The other required dependency file, **tk**, should already be installed on your system if you followed my system installation instructions in Chapter 2, but you can check it out for yourself using the **rpm** command with the **-q** (query) flag. Type in `rpm -q tk` and press ENTER. If the tk file is already installed, the Terminal will display the filename and version number: **tk-8.3.5-93**, or whatever the version installed in your system happens to be. Note that you do not have to become root in order to use the **rpm** command in this case because you are not installing anything and, therefore, you do not need to write anything to disk in root territory.

If your Terminal tells you that tk is already installed on your system, skip on down to section 9A-3. If the Terminal tells you, **package tk is not installed**, you have a little more work to do.

If you are using Fedora Core, unmount the disk you have in your drive now, and insert Install Disk 1. A small window should open, asking you if you want to run /mnt/cdrom/autorun. Just click **No**. Once the disk icon appears on your desktop, use the Terminal window to **cd** to the RPMS folder on that disk by typing `cd /mnt/cdrom/Fedora/RPMS/` and pressing ENTER.

If you are using Red Hat Linux 9, tk will be on Install Disk 3, so you do not have to change disks. Just follow the **cd** step above, substituting `RedHat` for `Fedora`.

6. Now copy the tk RPM package to your expRPMS folder by typing the following command and pressing ENTER:
```
cp tk* /home/username/expRPMS/
```

9A-3: Installing tkinter and Its Dependencies

As tkinter and its dependencies are all RPM files, you could install them one by one, using the double-click method you learned in Chapter 8. However, because I've just introduced the command-line way to do it, what fun would that be? You will also see that using the command-line alternative will allow you to install all four files simultaneously, killing, so to speak, four birds with one stone. This is a good example of how the command line can occasionally save you time.

So just suppress your natural inclinations for the time being and humor me by doing the following:

1. Open a new Terminal window, and become root by typing su and pressing ENTER.

2. Type your root password and press ENTER.

3. Type `cd expRPMS` and press ENTER. This will take you to your new expRPMS folder.

CAUTION   *In the following step, you are going to use the wildcard character (*) to tell the **rpm** command to install everything that ends in .rpm into the expRPMS folder. Before you do so, make sure that the only files in your expRPMS folder are the three or four RPM files you are trying to install.*

4. Type `rpm -Uvh *.rpm` and press ENTER.

The installation process will then begin, and you will see its progress in your Terminal window. When the progress bars in your Terminal have hit 100 percent and you are back at your root prompt, your Terminal should look like the one in Figure 9-9. If it does, then you've successfully installed tkinter and everything it needs to function properly.

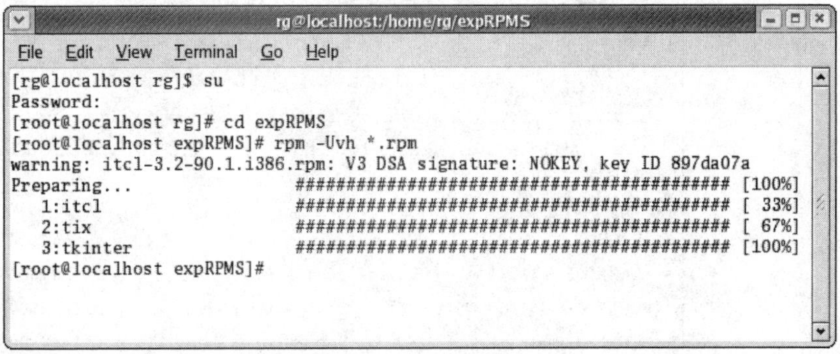

```
[rg@localhost rg]$ su
Password:
[root@localhost rg]# cd expRPMS
[root@localhost expRPMS]# rpm -Uvh *.rpm
warning: itcl-3.2-90.1.i386.rpm: V3 DSA signature: NOKEY, key ID 897da07a
Preparing...               ######################################### [100%]
   1:itcl                  ######################################### [ 33%]
   2:tix                   ######################################### [ 67%]
   3:tkinter               ######################################### [100%]
[root@localhost expRPMS]#
```

Figure 9-9: Installing RPMs with the **rpm** command

5.   Type exit and press ENTER to get out of root mode. You can also dump your expRPMS folder by dragging it to the Trash, by right-clicking it, and selecting **Move to Trash**, or via the command line by typing rm -r expRPMS and pressing ENTER.

9A-4: Creating a LocalApps Folder for pyWings

As I mentioned before, you will be installing the pyWings program locally in your Home folder. Installing a program *locally* means that you are installing the program and all its support and data files in your own Home folder. This makes things a bit easier, but it also means that the program will not be available to other users. It also means that, if you're not careful, you might inadvertently delete it.

To make things a bit easier and safer for you in the future, you are going to create another folder in your Home folder in which to place pyWings and all other applications that you install locally on your machine in the future. You will, logically enough, call the folder **LocalApps**. Let's make the folder by command in order to get some more practice. Here's what to do:

> In the Terminal, make sure you are in your Home directory and then type the following command and press ENTER:
> mkdir LocalApps

9A-5: Extracting the pyWings Tarball

Earlier you downloaded the pyWings tarball into the Tarballs_and_RPMs folder, and now it is time to extract the tarball. You can do this by using the command line, but that seems such a pain compared to the double-click method, which is so much more convenient and straightforward, so we will opt for the latter method instead.

1. In your Tarballs_and_RPMs window, double-click **pywings-1.0.1.tar.gz**. This will bring up the File Roller program (shown in Figure 9-10), which is used to extract archived files (and to create archives as well).

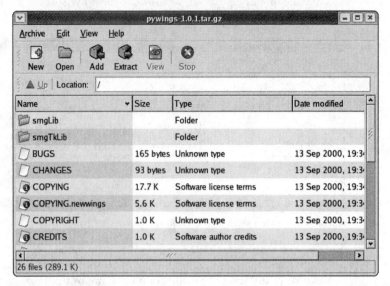

Figure 9-10: File Roller extracts and creates file archives

2. Click the **Extract** button in the main File Roller window. This will bring up the File Roller Extract window (Figure 9-11).

   The contents of most tarballs are grouped together in a single folder; however, in the case of pyWings, this is not the case, as you probably noticed in Figure 9-10. As a result, you will have to create a folder in which you can place all of the pyWings files.

3. In the **Destination folder** text box in the File Roller Extract window (shown in Figure 9-11), change the default location to /home/your_username/LocalApps/ pyWings/ (replacing your_username with your actual username, of course) and then click **OK**.

4. A small window will then pop open to tell you that the destination folder (pyWings) does not exist, and it will ask you if you want to create it. You do, so click **Create Folder**.

   If you take a look in your LocalApps folder now, you will see that you have a new subfolder inside called **pyWings**, and that all the pyWings files are in that folder.

5. Now go ahead and close the File Roller window.

Figure 9-11: Using File Roller to extract files from a tarball

9A-6: Running pyWings

You have now done all you really have to do to use pyWings, so let's start the great oracle up right now so that you can get a better perspective on how to deal with those problematic aspects of life that trouble you.

In the Terminal, make sure you are in your home directory and then type `LocalApps/pyWings/pywings.py` and press ENTER.

If all went according to plan, pyWings should be up and running and should soon be making you a wiser person.

9A-7: Creating a Launchable Link for pyWings

The method of running pyWings that you've just used works well enough, but it is a pain in the posterior to open your Terminal and type that somewhat lengthy string every time you want to find out what fate has in store for you. Let's find a way to make things easier in the future.

To run an application from the Terminal, you generally type the name of that application, or, to put it more precisely, the name of that program's executable file; the application's name thus acts as a sort of command. In order for your system to recognize that command, however, the command (the executable file, or a link to it) must be in a location where the system can find it. Whenever you run a command of any sort, your system checks a series of locations (all of which are **bin** folders, where executable files are located) to find that command.

You can easily find out where these locations are by typing echo $PATH in a new Terminal window and then pressing ENTER. As you will see, on your Fedora or Red Hat Linux system, these locations are:

- /usr/local/bin
- /usr/bin
- /bin
- /usr/X11R6/bin
- home/username/bin

(The last of these folders you create yourself if and when you need it.) If the command you typed is in one of those locations, the program, or script, will run. As you no doubt know, however, pyWings is not in any of those locations. It is in /home/username/LocalApps/pyWings and is thus, in a sense, out of your system's sight.

To remedy this situation, you could add the path of your pyWings script to the list of paths that the system checks for run commands, so as to make the system aware of your new application's existence. However, you will have the same problem later on in this book, and perhaps in your longer life as a Linux user. Instead, let's try another method that I think is easier. What you will do is create a link, a sort of launchable alias, in one of the locations your system does check for commands.

To create this link, you will be using three commands: **cd** (to change directories), **su** (to become root), and **ln -s** (to create the link).

1. In the Terminal, type cd /usr/local/bin and press ENTER. This puts you in one of the searchable bin folders.
2. Type su and press ENTER. You will then be prompted for your root password, so type it and then press ENTER again.
3. Type ln -s /home/username/LocalApps/pyWings/pywings.py pywings and press ENTER. (Note that there is a space between the words pywings.py and pywings at the end of that command string.) The pywings at the end of that command string is the name that you are giving the link; the name of the link thus becomes the command you will use to run the application. If you type nothing, the link will be called pywings.py, which would mean three more keystrokes for you every time you wanted to start the program.

9A-8: Running pyWings Again

Now that you have created the link, you should be able to run the pyWings program much more easily. Let's try it out.

1. Quit pyWings, if it is still running, and then open a new Terminal window.
2. In the new Terminal window, type pywings and press ENTER. Your friendly pyWings oracle should now open again.

You've managed to cut down on the number of keystrokes required to run pyWings from the Terminal. However, if you are really into this pyWings thing and want to use it often, it will probably be handiest to add a launcher to your Panel or drawer, as you learned to do in Chapter 3. Point-and-click still beats the Terminal for most everyday chores. Check out Appendix A for the launcher specs.

9A-9: Adding Emblems to Your LocalApps Folder

Now that pyWings is successfully installed and working, it is probably a good idea to add an emblem to your new LocalApps folder so that you don't inadvertently dump it in the trash someday. You have already learned how to do this in Chapter 5, so I won't give you the step-by-step instructions. I will suggest, however, that you select the **apps** emblem.

Project 9B: More Command Practice with pyChing (Optional)

If you just can't get enough of this oracle stuff, or, more importantly, if you just want to get a little more practice with the command line, there is a companion program to pyWings called pyChing (see Figure 9-12). The concept is essentially the same as pyWings, but it is based on the Chinese Taoist *I Ching*, so it is a bit more cultural and educational. pyChing is, to be sure, equally fun and ultimately as useless as pyWings, though it is perhaps a bit cooler and more cryptic in its advice.

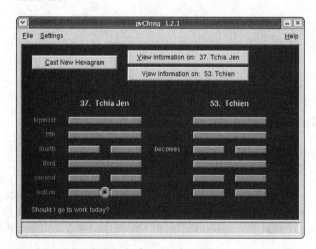

Figure 9-12: Predicting the future with pyChing

9B-1: Getting the pyChing Files

To get pyChing, go to the project home page at http://pyching.sourceforge.net/download.html. Once there, scroll down to the **Unix/Linux/X11** section and click the link that says **pyChing's sourceforge download page**. This will take you to the download page, where you should download the latest tarball version. At the time of this writing, that would be **pyching-1.2.1.tar.gz**.

Installation Tips

pyChing is also a Python script, and it is created by the same person as pyWings, so the process of installing it will be exactly the same. The only difference is that you will type pyching in every place that you typed pywings earlier, and pyching-1.2.1.tar.gz instead of pywings-1.0.1.tar.gz. You also do not need to install tkinter and its dependencies again.

Project 9C: The Mozilla Flash Plug-In

Now that you've had some fun using the command line, let's fill in one of the missing pieces in your system — the Macromedia Flash plug-in for your Mozilla browser. As you might know, several Web sites have been written using Macromedia's Flash. To view the Flash content of such sites, you must have the Flash player plug-in installed for your browser.

If you go to the Macromedia plug-in test page at http://www.macromedia.com/shockwave/welcome, you will see what I mean. Without the Flash plug-in installed, any Flash content in a Web page merely appears as a plug-in icon, which looks like a blue jigsaw puzzle piece (see Figure 9-13). To remedy the situation, you need to install the plug-in.

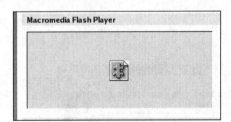

Figure 9-13: Flash content before installing the Flash plug-in

9C-1: Getting the Flash File

To start things off, go to http://plugindoc.mozdev.org/linux.html to get the plug-in tarball. Once there, click the **Macromedia Flash Player** link, which takes you down to the appropriate section on that page, after which you only need to click the link next to the word **Download**. This takes you to the Macromedia download page, where all you have to do is click the **Download** button. Once you've done that, the download commences, and 965 KB later, it finishes.

9C-2: Extracting the Tarball

To extract the **install_flash_player_7_linux.tar.gz** tarball, just double-click it, which opens the File Roller program. In the first File Roller window, click **Extract**, and in the second window click **OK**. When the process is complete, you have a new install_flash_player_7_linux folder in your Home folder. You can then quit the File Roller program.

9C-3: Installing the Flash Plug-In

To finish the job, you can choose from two alternatives, both of which are rather simple: you can run an installation script, or copy the necessary files to the correct places yourself. To go the do-it-yourself route, just copy the files **libflashplayer.so** and **flashplayer.xpt** from the **install_flash_player_7_linux** folder to your Mozilla plug-ins folder. The Mozilla plug-ins folder is in root territory, so you'll have to do this copying as root by using the command line. Here's what you have to do:

1. Open a new Terminal window and become root using the **su** command.
2. Type `cd install_flash_player_7_linux` and press ENTER.
3. Type `cp flashplayer.xpt /usr/lib/mozilla-1.4.1/plugins/` and press ENTER.
4. Type `cp libflashplayer.so /usr/lib/mozilla-1.4.1/plugins/` and press ENTER.

Now that you have copied the two files to your Mozilla plug-ins folder, you are finished. Quit Mozilla, if it's still open, and then start it up again.

If you'd rather not bother with all those **cp** commands and would prefer to let the script included in the Flash tarball do your copying for you, you can go about things this way instead:

1. Quit Mozilla, if it's still running.
2. Open a new Terminal window and become root using the **su** command.
3. Type `cd install_flash_player_7_linux` and press ENTER.
4. Type `./flashplayer-installer` and press ENTER.
5. Some introductory text appears after which you must either press ENTER to continue with the installation or press CTRL+C to cancel the process. Now is not the time to give up, so just press ENTER.
6. You are told that Macromedia Flash Player requires the installation (by the installer) of two fonts. Let it do its thing by pressing ENTER.
7. You are then told to quit any browsers you have open, so if you still haven't closed Mozilla, do so now. When you're ready, press ENTER.
8. Now you are asked for the path to your browser. Type `/usr/lib/mozilla-1.4.1` and press ENTER.
9. You are then asked to confirm the location that you've just typed in. If it looks right, type y and press ENTER. If not, type n, press ENTER, and try again.
10. You are then told that the installation is complete and asked whether you want to perform another installation. Unless you have something up your sleeve that I don't know about, you do not, so type n and press ENTER.
11. You can now close the Terminal window.

Whichever method you ended up choosing, now that you've installed Flash, give it a try. First things first, run Mozilla again; then go back to the Macromedia plug-in test page at http://www.macromedia.com/shockwave/welcome/ to see if things have changed. If all is hunky dory, the Flash section now looks like the one in Figure 9-14. Alternatively, you might want to check out some other Flash-rich site to put your new plug-in through its paces. The pages for most automobile manufacturers (VW, Volvo, Saturn, Pontiac, Ford, and so on) are usually flush with Flash content, so any of those sites would prove to be a good test.

Figure 9-14: Viewing Flash content after installing the Flash plug-in

If it appears that your installation of the Flash plug-in is successful, you can now drag the **install_flash_player_7_linux** folder to the Trash (or right-click it, and select **Move to Trash**), because its job is done. You can do the same to the **install_flash_player_7_linux.tar.gz** tarball, though I would advise you to back up the tarball to CD first, just in case you need to do this all again someday.

An Easier Way?

Now if all this Flash installation seems intimidating or a bit more than you'd prefer to bother with, there is an easier alternative. Just hang on until you complete the following chapter on installing applications via APT/Synaptic, and then use that powerful package management duo to install the file **mozilla-swfdec**. It's extremely easy to install, but nowhere near as much fun as the process I've just laid out. Ah, but then to each his own.

10

YES, YET ANOTHER WAY!

Downloading, Installing, and Updating Programs with APT and Synaptic

You've learned how to install RPM packages via the Package Manager and directly via the double-click method. However, believe it or not, there is yet a third way, called APT (Advanced Package Tool), to install new RPM-based software. In fact, anyone familiar with the Linux Debian distro or with the Fink program on Mac OS X will probably already be familiar with the APT program.

The Debian version of APT is designed to download special Debian APT packages from which it installs a program and all its dependencies. These APT packages, however, do not work on Fedora because they are not RPMs. There is, however, a special variation on the original Debian version of APT that is designed to work on RPM-based systems, such as Fedora Core. APT connects to an RPM repository on the Internet and then downloads all the programs you select, as well as the dependencies for those programs. The programs are downloaded as RPM files, which APT then installs on your system.

APT is a very easy, safe, and foolproof way of installing programs, because nothing will go missing, and it makes dependency hell pretty much a thing of the past. Of course, not every program or file is available in an APT repository, so the other methods you have learned so far are not for naught. There are also still other applications that are not available as RPMs at all, but you will learn how to deal with those in the next chapter. Nevertheless, there are plenty of files that you can download and install, or (very importantly) just update, via APT.

The one thing about APT that some people might consider a problem is that it is a command-driven application. This means that you have to run it via commands in the Linux Command Terminal. Fortunately, you can avoid this more cumbersome way of doing things by installing the program Synaptic, which is a graphical front end for APT. Synaptic allows you to use APT graphically, and thus quite easily.

Finally, there are a variety of APT repositories on the Internet, and the version of APT offered at these various repositories is usually preconfigured to download RPMs from that particular repository. In addition, the packages from one repository are not guaranteed to be compatible with those from another, meaning that conflicts could occur if you mix files from different repositories (though I must admit to having never had problems myself in this regard). To stay on the safe side and keep things convenient, user-friendly, and aesthetically pleasing, we will be using the repositories at Freshrpms for APT, and for RPMs not available from Freshrpms, we will use, whenever possible, the Freshrpms-compatible DAG repository, from which you will download several RPMs while performing some of the projects in this book.

Project 10A: Installing APT and Synaptic

In this project, you will install the APT program, which comes in the form of an easy-to-install RPM. Once you install APT, you will then use it by command line to install its graphical front end, Synaptic. All in all, both steps are very easy.

Getting the APT File

To get started, the only file you will need is the one for APT. You can get this by going to http://freshrpms.net/packages/ and clicking the link appropriate for the version of Linux you are running. After the new page appears, go to the left side of the page and click the **apt** link, which will take you to the page for that package. You will see the APT file listed at the top of the page.

To download the file, just right-click the tiny floppy-disk icon to the left of the filename, and then select **Save Link Target As** in the pop-up menu. You do not need the **apt-devel** file, so don't bother with that.

10A-1: Installing APT

As APT comes in the form of an RPM file, installation is a breeze, as you now know. Just double-click the RPM file, and then follow the usual RPM installation procedures that you learned in Chapter 8.

10A-2: Entering APT Proxy Settings

If your Internet service provider requires you to connect to the Internet via a proxy server, you will have to add your proxy settings to APT before you can do any updating or downloading. If you do not connect to the Internet via a proxy server, you can skip directly to the next step in the project (10A-3).

Inputting proxy settings in most programs is easily done in the Preferences window for that program. In the case of APT, it is a tad more complicated, but just a tad. To input your proxy settings for APT, you will need to open the **apt.conf** file. As this file is in root territory, you will have to open and alter it after becoming root.

To get started, open a Terminal window and become root. Once you've done that, type gedit /etc/apt/apt.conf and press ENTER. This will open up the apt.conf file in the Gedit text editor (in root mode). Once the file is open, scroll through it and look for an entry beginning with the word **Acquire**. When you find it, change it so that it looks similar to the entry in the following example, but use the proxy and port information supplied by your service provider or network administrator.

```
Acquire {
    Retries "0";
    Http {
        Proxy "http://proxy.yourserver.com:3128/";
```

In case your provider gives you the proxy address and port number separately (for example, http://proxy.magnumopus.se and port 6048), type a colon after the address and then add the port number after the colon. Using the previous example, that would be http://proxy.magnumopus.se:6048/. Yours will no doubt be different.

10A-3: Updating the APT Database

Now that APT is installed on your system, you are almost ready to use it. I say "almost" because you first have to tell APT to update its database so that it will know what is available for download from the online repositories and what you have already installed on your system in RPM form. To perform the update, open a Terminal window, become root using the **su** command, and then type apt-get update and press ENTER.

Checking your system and the repositories should take APT a couple of minutes the first time around, so just be patient and ponder your future (or something) until your prompt reappears. Once it does reappear, you will be ready for action.

10A-4: Using APT to Install Synaptic

Your first taste of using APT via the command line (and probably the last you'll want to have with it) is to download and install Synaptic, the graphical front end for APT.

The general format for the command to download and install a package via APT is: apt-get install package_name. In this case, you are going to be installing Synaptic, so open a Terminal window, become root, and then type apt-get install synaptic and press ENTER. APT will then begin downloading Synaptic, and, once it's done doing that, it will go on to install it. During this time, APT will show you its progress, as you can see in Figure 10-1.

After your prompt reappears, the process is complete, and you can begin using Synaptic instead.

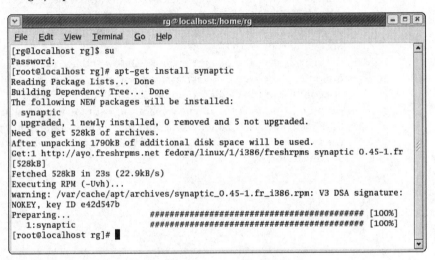

```
[rg@localhost rg]$ su
Password:
[root@localhost rg]# apt-get install synaptic
Reading Package Lists... Done
Building Dependency Tree... Done
The following NEW packages will be installed:
  synaptic
0 upgraded, 1 newly installed, 0 removed and 5 not upgraded.
Need to get 528kB of archives.
After unpacking 1790kB of additional disk space will be used.
Get:1 http://ayo.freshrpms.net fedora/linux/1/i386/freshrpms synaptic 0.45-1.fr
[528kB]
Fetched 528kB in 23s (22.9kB/s)
Executing RPM (-Uvh)...
warning: /var/cache/apt/archives/synaptic_0.45-1.fr_i386.rpm: V3 DSA signature:
NOKEY, key ID e42d547b
Preparing...                ########################################### [100%]
   1:synaptic               ########################################### [100%]
[root@localhost rg]#
```

Figure 10-1: Downloading and installing Synaptic

Project 10B: Using Synaptic to Install MPlayer

Now you are ready to get some experience using Synaptic, while at the same time rounding out your system a bit by installing a player for your MPEG and QuickTime video files. The program is called MPlayer (shown in Figure 10-2), and it is a very handy program that plays a variety of video formats, DVDs, VCDs, some video streams, and even audio files.

As you can see in Figure 10-2, MPlayer has separate control and view windows. If you prefer a single-window approach, or you want the ability to capture video frames as still images, you might want to try out gxine instead (shown in Figure 10-3), which is otherwise quite similar to MPlayer in terms of its capabilities (though it can seem a bit buggier at times).

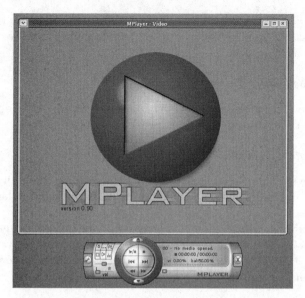

Figure 10-2: The MPlayer video player

Of course, some people may have no need for video playback at all, and thus may not wish to devote so much download time for a program that will go unused. If you are such a person, and you choose not to download MPlayer (or you choose to download gxine instead), you should download the MP3 encoder LAME, which is normally downloaded as one of the dependencies for MPlayer. LAME is used to convert WAV sound files (like those on an audio CD) into the popular space-saving MP3 sound files. You will need LAME installed on your machine by the time you reach Chapter 13, where you will be learning more about this encoding process.

Figure 10-3: The gxine video player

The instructions for installing gxine and LAME, or LAME by itself, are essentially the same as for installing MPlayer; just substitute **gxine** or **lame** for **mplayer** in the instructions that follow.

Getting the MPlayer Files

Because APT and Synaptic will automatically download everything for you, you don't need to get any files on your own for this project.

10B-1: Entering Synaptic Proxy Settings

If you are behind a firewall and had to add your proxy settings in order to use APT, you will have to do the same for Synaptic. If not, you can skip down to the next step (10B-2).

Entering the proxy settings is more easily done in Synaptic than APT. Just go to the **Preferences** menu and select **Preferences**. Once in the Preferences window, click the **Network** tab, select **Manual proxy configuration**, and then input your proxy settings.

10B-2: Installing MPlayer

Before you begin, I should mention that the download for MPlayer and all its dependencies is rather hefty (about 13MB), so make sure you give yourself some time to do this. All in all, the entire process should take about twenty minutes or more (depending on your Internet connection speed), but during most of this time, you won't have to do anything other than wait. This is all time well spent, as many of these dependencies are items that will prove useful to you later on, when you are using other programs.

Anyway, the first thing you'll want to do is run Synaptic, which you can do by going to the Main menu and selecting **System Tools > Synaptic** (some versions of Synaptic may place themselves in **System Settings > Synaptic**). Once Synaptic is running, you need to find the MPlayer program in the Synaptic package list. Just type mplayer in the **Find** box at the right side of the program window, and the package name will appear highlighted within the package pane in the middle of the program window (see Figure 10-4). Alternatively, you can click the little arrow next to **Applications/Multimedia**, and then scroll down until you see **mplayer**, and click it.

Information about the file will appear at the bottom of the Synaptic window. As you will see, there are four tabs there, each telling you something about the file you have chosen. The most important of these are **Description**, which tells you something about the file, and **Dependencies**, which tells you what other files are needed to run or to use the file you have selected. Dependencies that are not already installed on your system will appear in red, but you needn't worry about them because the Synaptic/APT combination will download and install them for you automatically.

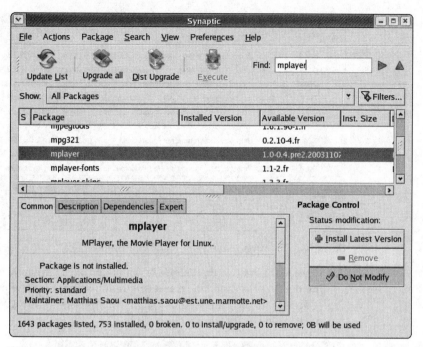

Figure 10-4: Using Synaptic to download and install MPlayer

Now you are ready to actually install MPlayer, so here are the simple steps you need to follow, many of which require no action on your part:

1. Assuming that **mplayer** is still highlighted in the package list, click the **Install Latest Version** button in the lower-right portion of the Synaptic window.

2. Depending on the packages selected and on what you already have installed on your system, you may be presented with a window asking you whether or not to "Apply additional required changes?" This will tell you what files will need to be changed (upgraded or installed). If this window appears, click **Apply**.

3. Click the **Execute** button in the main program window to start the download and installation.

4. The Operation Summary window will then open, telling you what is going to be installed, what is going to be updated, and what is going to be left alone. Click the **Proceed** button in that window.

5. Synaptic will then begin downloading all the files it needs. A window showing the progress of the downloads will appear (see Figure 10-5 on the next page). You can kick back a while and have a Dr. Pepper or something while you wait.

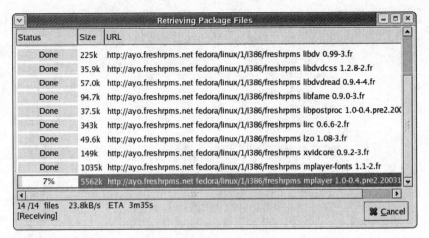

Figure 10-5: The download progress indicator in Synaptic

6. Once all the necessary files are downloaded, APT/Synaptic will begin readying the files for installation and will then install them. The progress of these processes will be indicated in a small window (see Figure 10-6). You needn't do anything except wait a short while.

Figure 10-6: The installation progress indicator in Synaptic

7. Once the installation progress window disappears, Synaptic will gray out again as it updates its package list. Once it is back to normal, the process is done.

10B-3: Running MPlayer

Now that MPlayer is installed, you can run it by going to your Main menu and selecting **Sound & Video > More Sound & Video > Movie Player**. MPlayer will then open in two parts: the controller and the actual viewing window. To test it out, try playing one of your MPEG or movie files (files with a .mpg or .mov extension). Just click the arrow at the top of the round portion of the player window (shown in Figure 10-2 on page 147), and then select the file you want to play.

If you chose to download and install gxine instead of MPlayer, you can run it by going to the Main menu and selecting **Sound & Video > More Sound & Video > gxine**. If you only downloaded LAME, you'll have to wait until Chapter 13 to learn what to do with it.

Updating the APT Package Database with Synaptic

It is a good idea to update the APT package database every so often in order to keep APT up-to-date with what is available for download. Earlier in this chapter, you used the **apt-get update** command in the Terminal to accomplish this, but it's much simpler to do via Synaptic. Just click the **Update List** button in the main Synaptic window, and Synaptic will check the online repositories and update its package list. Very simple, eh?

Finding New Packages and Upgrading Packages with Synaptic

If you just want to find out what packages are available on the APT repositories but are not installed on your machine, click the **Show** drop-down menu button at the top of the Synaptic window that, by default, says **All Packages**, and select **Not Installed**. Synaptic will then display only those packages available for download that are not yet installed on your system.

If you instead want to know which of your packages are upgradable, go to the same drop-down menu button and select **Upgradable**. Synaptic will then show you what packages on your system are upgradable, what version of a given package you have, and what more recent version is available for download. You can then choose the packages you want to upgrade, and click the **Upgrade** button. Once you are done with your selections, you need only click the **Execute** button in the main Synaptic window to start getting the files.

You can also upgrade every package that is upgradable by clicking the **Upgrade All** button at the top of the main Synaptic window (and don't mess with the **Dist Upgrade** button). Of course, this could require a lot of downloading time, so once you've clicked that button, and the **Execute** button after that, check out the Operation Summary window before committing to the process to see how much data you will have to download. A full system upgrade may require downloading over 100MB of files — a very hefty download if you are working with a dial-up Internet connection. If you think you can bear the size of the download indicated in your case, click the **Proceed** button in the Operation Summary window; if not, click **Cancel**.

Removing Packages with Synaptic

Synaptic can also be used to remove packages you have installed on your system. This is especially handy for removing RPM packages that do not appear in the Package Manager window. However, remember that APT and Synaptic deal only with RPMs. If you downloaded a program file, and then compiled and installed it yourself from source, as you will learn to do in Chapter 11, it will not appear in Synaptic.

To remove an RPM package, select **All Packages** from the **Show** drop-down menu at the top of the Synaptic window, and in the middle of the program window find the package you want to remove. Select it by clicking it, and then click the **Remove** button. Once you have clicked the **Remove** button for all the packages you wish to remove, click the **Execute** button.

Adding Repositories to Synaptic's Lookup List

If you fnd that you are frequently using a Freshrpms compatible repository, particulary DAG, to directly download files, you might find it useful to access that repository via APT/Synaptic. If you are using a dial-up modem, I wouldn't recommend this because it will slow things down a tad when you update package lists, but otherwise, it can be rather handy.

Adding repositories to Synaptic is now quite easy. After running Synaptic, go to the Preferences menu and select Repositories, which will bring up the Repositories window. To add a new repository, such as DAG, click the New button and then enter the repository information in the three text boxes at the bottom of the Repositories window (Figure 10-7). This information can be found on the homepage of the repository you wish to add. In the case of DAG, this information is located at http://dag.wieers.com/home-made/apt/.

The repository information is broken into three parts: the URL, the distribution, and the section. On the repository homepage this is usually written in one line with the different parts separated by spaces. For example, in the case of Fedora Core 1, the repository details are given as http://apt.sw.be redhat/fc1/en/i386 dag, and the placement of these three elements in the Synaptic Repository window can be seen in Figure 10-7.

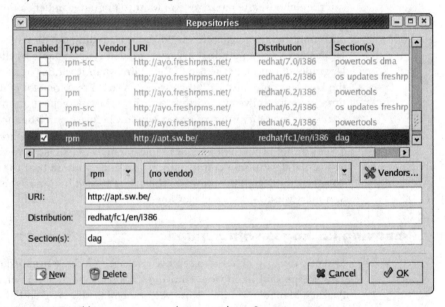

Figure 10-7: Adding repositories to the sources list in Synaptic

Hungry for More?

If you're eager to download some more stuff with APT/Synaptic, you will get further chances elsewhere in the book. If you just can't wait, however, and you just want to get hopping right now, check out my Web site for this book (http://www.edgy-penguins.org/non-geeks) for some recommendations.

11

DINING ON TARBALLS

Compiling Programs from Source (Made Kind of Easy)

For the beginner, just the mention of compiling a program from source seems off-putting enough. The words *compile* and *source* seem to instill a sense of foreboding in the heart of the new user. That certainly was the case for me, anyway.

However, this method of installing programs is a lot easier than it sounds. In fact, now that you have some experience in using the Terminal and command line, it is just plain easy — a sort of one, two, three, and you're done process.

Of course, you can live long and prosper without ever bothering to compile anything on your system. You can move along quite happily with your system as is, or you can just install programs by means of the very straightforward RPM method.

However, not every bit of software out there is available in RPM format; and, if you are filled with natural human curiosity, there will come a time when you will want to move just one step beyond. After working through this short chapter, you will be able to do just that, and I am sure you will find that your initial worries will have been for naught.

What Is Source?

In order to understand what *source* is, you should understand a bit about how a program actually gets from its primitive state on the programmer's computer to an up-and-running application on your machine. First the programmer writes a program in a programming language. You have probably heard of programming languages such as Basic or C, and there are many others. What the programmer actually writes with such a language is a set of instructions called the *source code*, or *source*. Your computer, however, cannot actually understand any of that source on its own. It is as if the computer speaks ancient Greek, and the source code is all written in French. The computer therefore needs some sort of interpreter to help it out.

The various languages that programmers use are called *high-level languages* — they are relatively easy for programmers to read. The computer, on the other hand, only understands what are called *low-level languages*, which are quite difficult for most mere mortal programmers to deal with. To convert the high-level language instructions to a low-level language, the computer needs some other program to translate.

This can be done while a program is running, in which case the translator program is called an *interpreter*. Applications that run using an interpreter are usually called *scripts*. The pyWings application in Chapter 9 is an example of such a script application.

The problem with such script applications is that they can be slower, because the computer must run an interpreter, interpret the source code, and run the actual application all at the same time. This is like having a French book translated to a Greek speaker by a live interpreter — very slow indeed.

As an alternative, many programs use a *compiler* instead of an interpreter. A compiler translates the high-level source code into low-level *machine code*, or *object code*, that the computer can understand before the application is actually run. Once this translation is done, the computer never has to bother with the high-level instructions again; it can merely read the translated version each and every time it runs the program. This is like reading a translated version of a foreign book that you can read any time you want to without assistance. Because computers can run compiled programs without simultaneously using an interpreter, compiled programs run faster. Most applications for all operating systems are, therefore, compiled.

Tarballs: The Containers of Source

Almost all source packages come in the form of tarballs (tarballs and RPM files are both referred to as *packages*, which is why the icon for such files looks like a little parcel-post box). Tarballs, like ZIP files on Windows systems or StuffIt files on the Mac, consist of a group of files, or even a single file, which have been compressed into one space-saving archive file. In Linux, the most common method of creating such archives is through the tar program, from which the tarball gets its name. Tar files, or tarballs, can be recognized by their file endings, which are .tar.gz or tar.bz2.

You may or may not realize it, but you have already used tarballs in two of the previous chapters. In Chapter 5 you dragged tarballs into your Theme Preferences window to install new window borders and control sets, and in Chapter 9 you untarred a tarball (extracted the archived files) in order to set up and use the pyWings application. The files archived in tarballs can be extracted by using the command line, but to keep things easy, you can just use the simple double-click method that you used in Chapter 9.

Project 11A: Compiling and Installing Xmahjongg

To get some hands-on experience with compiling a program from source, you will be working with a game called Xmahjongg. Now, you may think that, as you already have a GNOME mahjongg game and a KDE mahjongg game (not listed in the Main menu) installed on your system, having yet another mahjongg game is a tad redundant, to say the least. Maybe so, but in terms of gaming, the Xmahjongg game is easier on the eyes and snappier in performance. It looks prettier too, in my opinion.

More important than these gaming points, though, is the fact that the Xmahjongg package provides a perfect opportunity to learn to compile a program from source and then install it. It is not too big, it doesn't take too much time to do, and it requires no tinkering.

You can see what the final product will look like in Figure 11-1.

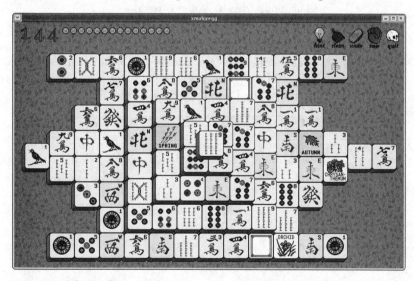

Figure 11-1: The Xmahjongg game

As you can see, it is all very simple and clearly laid out. In case you are not already familiar with this genre of mahjongg game, the idea is simple enough. Basically there are four of each tile in the pile. You must match pairs of like tiles that are open to one side. When you click the two matching open tiles, they will disappear. The object of the game is, thus, to remove all the tiles from the board. A very simple solitaire game.

To compile and install Xmahjongg, you are going to use seven commands: **cd** (to get into the xmahjongg folder), **./configure** (to configure a makefile, which provides instructions for the next command), **make** (to translate the source code into object code that the computer can understand), **su** (to become root), **make install** (to install the program), **exit** (to get out of root mode), and **make clean** (to clean up the mess). I know that sounds like a lot of commands, but as I always say, it is easier to actually do than it looks like on the page, so fear not.

Getting the Xmahjongg Files

To get started, you will first have to download the Xmahjongg file. You can get this from the Xmahjongg project page at: http://www.lcdf.org/~eddietwo/ xmahjongg/. Download the tarball **xmahjongg-3.6.1.tar.gz** or a newer version if there is one. Do not download any of the RPM files, even those that say they are for Red Hat.

Once you have the file on your hard disk, you are ready to roll.

11A-1: Untarring, Compiling, and Installing

Before you actually compile and install Xmahjongg, you have to extract the tarball's source files, or *untar* the tarball.

1. Untar the **xmahjongg-3.6.1.tar.gz** file by double-clicking the file icon. This will bring up the File Roller program.
2. In the File Roller program window, click the **Extract** button.
3. When File Roller's Extract window opens, click the **OK** button. Once File Roller is done, you can close the File Roller window. A new folder, xmah-jongg-3.6.1, will now appear in your Home folder. Figure 11-2 shows the contents of the xmahjongg-3.6.1 folder.

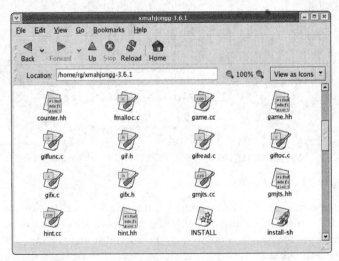

Figure 11-2: The contents of the folder created by extracting the Xmahjongg tarball

4. Scroll down through the xmahjongg-3.6.1 folder contents and look for a file called **INSTALL**. The INSTALL file is actually just a text file with a set of instructions on how to install the program. To read the INSTALL file, just double-click it, and it will open in the same Nautilus window, as shown in Figure 11-3.

In this case, you can simply close the INSTALL file, as it prescribes the same steps as I've listed below. However, in the future, when you install other programs from source, you will need to follow the instructions in the INSTALL files that come with the source files for those programs. With most INSTALL files, the instructions will match those that follow.

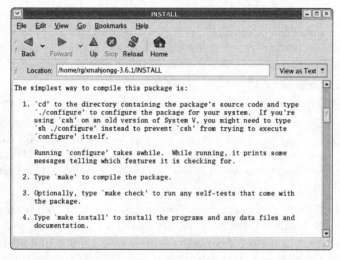

Figure 11-3: Reading a tarball's INSTALL file in a Nautilus window

5. Open a Terminal window by clicking the Terminal launcher on the GNOME Panel, and then move into the new folder by typing cd xmahjongg-3.6.1 and pressing ENTER.

The next step is sort of a setup phase that runs the configure script in the xmahjongg-3.6.1 folder. The configure script checks what files, compilers, and other things it needs, and then it searches your computer to see if those things are there, and if so, where. Based on this information, it then writes a file called **makefile**, which is a set of instructions that will tell the **make** command in the subsequent step how to set things up specifically for your system configuration.

While you are running **configure**, you will see lots of odd and mysterious things flowing down your Terminal window; this is essentially a running account of what is going on, each step of the way. Depending on the program you are dealing with, this could take a bit of time — a few seconds or a few minutes. Either way, you needn't worry. As long as the mysterious text keeps flowing and you don't get an error message at the very end of the whole process, all will be well.

6. Compile the program by typing ./configure and pressing ENTER.

   When **configure** has done its thing, you will see your prompt again, and you can go on to the next step, which is the translation step. The **make** command reads the makefile that **configure** created to see how things need to be set up on your machine. Then it proceeds to call on the compiler to translate the high-level source code into low-level, machine-readable files that can be installed in the subsequent step.

7. To perform this translation, type make and press ENTER.

   Again, you will be treated to more mysterious text flowing down the screen and a short wait, usually a tad longer than for the configure process.

   Once **make** has done its job and you see your prompt again, you are ready to install the program. However, because some of these files created by **make** must go into places guarded by root permissions, you must first become root by using the **su** command before doing anything else.

8. Become root by typing su and pressing ENTER.

9. Type your root password when prompted to do so, and then press ENTER.

   Up to this point, you have not changed your system in any way. All the changes thus far have taken place in the xmahjongg-3.6.1 folder only. Your system is still as pure as the day you started. Of course, all that is going to end now, as you are about to install into your system the files that **make** created.

10. Type make install and then press ENTER.

11. Once **make install** is done installing the program, your prompt will reappear. Now type exit and press ENTER to exit root mode.

12. Type cd and press ENTER to return to user's Home, and leave your Terminal window open for the time being.

11A-2: Running Xmahjongg

As a general rule, programs compiled from source do not automatically install a launcher in your Main menu. Although you can run a program for the first time by going to the Main menu, selecting **Run Program**, and then typing the program name in the dialog box, it is better to run the program for the first time by typing the command for the new program in your Terminal window. If anything has gone amiss during installation, the Terminal will tell you what the problem is, whereas the Run Program method would just leave you wondering what's going on.

Usually the program's command name is written in the INSTALL file or the README file within the directory that was created when you extracted the source files from the tarball (xmahjongg-3.6.1 in this case). Sometimes you won't find it there, but you can find it on the project page for that application on the Internet. Other times, however, you can't find it there either, so you'll just have to resort to guessing. Sometimes the hardest part of compiling a program from source is not, as you now know, compiling it, but rather finding out what the command to run it is. Usually, it is just the name of the tarball, minus the file endings.

It is time to make sure that all went well with the Xmahjongg program installation. In your Terminal window, type xmahjongg and press ENTER. If all is as it should be, and there is no reason it shouldn't, the Xmahjongg program will open within seconds and all will be well. You can now goof around with the game for a while, if you like, or get straight back to cleaning up, which is an easy enough process.

11A-3: Cleaning Up

Once you are all done compiling and installing your new application, you will find that you have a lot of extra files in your original source folder that you no longer need. As I mentioned before, the **make** command created translations of all the source code files, and those low-level language versions of the files were then installed in the **make install** step. Now that your installation is complete, you don't need those files anymore; they have all been copied elsewhere. The translated files in your source folder are just sitting there rudely wasting disk space.

Getting rid of these space wasters is simple enough, fortunately. The **make clean** command will remove all the extraneous translated versions of your source files. However, it sometimes happens that **make clean** will also clean out your makefile, which is bad, because the makefile often allows you to uninstall the program you've installed with it. Before running the **make clean** command, therefore, it is a good idea to copy the makefile to the desktop. Then, once you are done with **make clean**, you can check to see if the makefile is still in the project folder or not. If it is, you can trash the makefile on your desktop. If the makefile is not in the project folder, you can move the desktop makefile back into that folder.

Here are the steps:

1. Type cd xmahjongg-3.6.1 and hit ENTER to return to the xmahjongg-3.6.1 folder.

2. Type make clean and press ENTER. You needn't be root to do this.

3. After **make clean** is finished with its tidying chores, you are done, and you will have saved a bit of disk space. In the case of the xmahjongg-3.6.1 directory, you will find that it will shrink from 4.2MB to only 867KB (under one megabyte) or thereabouts.

4. Close your Terminal window by typing exit and then pressing ENTER.

5. If Xmahjongg is running as it should and you are satisfied with it to the extent that you are sure that you do not want to uninstall it, you can now haul the xmahjongg-3.6.1 folder to the Trash. If you aren't all that impressed and wouldn't mind dumping it right away, move on to 11A-4.

And that is that! You have compiled a program from source, installed it, and even cleaned up after yourself. As you can see, there's really nothing to it! It is most definitely time for a self-administered pat on the back.

11A-4: Second Thoughts — Uninstalling Xmahjongg

Let's say that you installed a program through this compiling process, and you don't like or need it — you just want to get it out of there. Usually you can uninstall the program, provided the pesky makefile is still there in the project folder (hence my warning in the previous "Cleaning Up" section), with the **make uninstall** command. You might first want to check out the INSTALL or README file to see if **make uninstall** is supported or if there is another uninstall method. Sometimes, however, the uninstall method is not specified, so you will just have to give it a go to find out if **make uninstall** works or not. There is no danger in this, because if it isn't supported, nothing will happen.

Anyway, Xmahjongg is a good example. There is no information in either the INSTALL or README files about uninstalling the program, so to find out if you can use **make uninstall**, you have to go through the more or less standard steps:

1. Open a Terminal window and become root by typing su and pressing ENTER. Then type your root password and press ENTER.

2. Use the **cd** command to move over to the xmahjongg-3.6.1 folder by typing cd xmahjongg-3.6.1 and hitting ENTER.

3. Type make uninstall and press ENTER.

    When you're done, you should see a stream of text flowing down your Terminal window for a few seconds. If you take a look at the text after it has stopped flowing and you are back at the root prompt, you will see that it actually consists of information that you now more or less understand: a series of **cd**, **rm**, and **rmdir** commands.

4. To make sure that Xmahjongg really is uninstalled, type exit and press ENTER to get yourself out of root mode, and then type xmahjongg and press ENTER to try to run the program. You should be told that the command cannot be found. If this is the case, you have successfully rid your computer of Xmahjongg.

This is basically the same way you would go about uninstalling any other package that you originally installed in this non-RPM manner. If it works, it works, and if it doesn't . . . well, then you will have to read the makefile (by double-clicking it) to see where everything was placed, and then trash all the files one by one. That's a big pain, and you might screw something up in the process, so I recommend you just ignore the program instead, at least at this stage of the game.

Project 11B: XPenguins (Optional)

Aha! Just as I expected; you are so overwhelmed by your sense of accomplishment that you've become hungry for more. To satisfy your desires, I will give you another little project that you can do on your own. It is a two-parter that will put more of your skills to work.

This do-it-yourself project is a goofy little desktop amusement called XPenguins. The program releases an absolute swarm of penguins upon your desktop, where they drop down by balloon, read books, march atop your windows and Panel, and even drill holes in things (see Figure 11-4). Admittedly, XPenguins is another one of those system resource wasters; it's absolutely useless, but, depending on your view of things, quite cute and amusing. If nothing else, having all those penguins goofing around on your screen will give your system a more Linux-ish look.

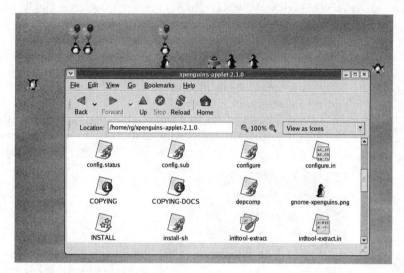

Figure 11-4: XPenguins in action

Getting the XPenguins Files

You will need two different files for this project. The first is the actual XPenguins program, which you can get from http://dag.wieers.com/packages/xpenguins. On that page, just download the newest XPenguins file appropriate for your system. If you added DAG to Synaptic's list of repositories as I explained in Chapter 10, you can also download the file by running Synaptic, typing xpenguins in Synaptic's **Find** box, and then following the standard Synaptic installation procedures.

The other file you will need is a GNOME Panel applet with which you can release the penguins to scamper about your screen when you're in the mood and then get rid of them once they begin to annoy you. To get this file, go to the XPenguins project homepage at http://www.xpenguins.seul.org. Once there, download **xpenguins-applet-2.1.0.tar.gz** (the GNOME Panel applet). If you happen to be using Red Hat Linux 8, get **xpenguins-applet-2.0.1.tar.gz** instead of 2.1.0.

11B-1: The General Steps

The first step is to install the **xpenguins RPM** as you learned to do in Chapter 8. Once you've done that, extract the **xpenguins-applet-2.1.0.tar.gz** tarball, cd to the new folder that was created when you extracted the tarball, and then follow the steps you've learned in this chapter: **./configure**, **make**, **make install**, and **make clean**, but in this case, per the instructions in the INSTALL file, instead of just typing *./configure*, type this:

```
./configure --prefix=/usr --sysconfdir=/etc
```

11B-2: Running XPenguins

You could simply run XPenguins by typing xpenguins in the Run Command window or the Command Terminal, but if you did that, getting rid of your new, pesky little friends would be more of a chore. Instead, add the XPenguins applet, which you've just compiled, to the GNOME Panel by right-clicking the Panel and selecting **Add to Panel > Amusements > XPenguins** in the pop-up menu. If XPenguins doesn't appear in the menu straightaway, try again the next time you restart your machine.

With this Panel applet (see Figure 11-5), you can bring on the penguins by clicking the top button, and then send them back where they came from by clicking the bottom button. A very convenient arrangement, to be sure.

Figure 11-5: The XPenguins Panel applet (and some more penguins in action)

11B-3: Installing Themes for XPenguins

If you like the concept of XPenguins, but not the penguins themselves, right-click the XPenguins Panel applet and select **Properties** in the pop-up menu. In the Properties window, click the **Themes** tab, and you will find a few non-penguin alternatives. If none of these satisfies you, you can go back to the XPenguins project page and download an additional package that contains several cartoon-character themes, such as the Simpsons. The theme package is available as a tarball, but for convenience's sake, just download the RPM file **xpenguins_themes-1.0-1.noarch.rpm** and install it.

12

DATA ON ICE REVISITED

Windows Partitions and USB Storage Devices

You've learned to transfer data to your computer by downloading it from the Internet (such as when you are installing applications, fonts, and other files). And you know how to transfer data to and from your computer with CDs and floppies. There are also a couple of other data sources that we have yet to discuss: portable USB storage devices and, for dual-booters, the Windows partition.

USB Storage Devices

Nowadays, tiny portable storage devices that go by names such as PenDrive, JumpDrive, ClipDrive, DiskOnKey, and so on, have become quite popular (see Figure 12-1 on the next page). Because of their small size, these "flash drives" are very handy when you have to transfer fairly large, but not gigantic, amounts of data from computer to computer (from work to home, for example). They come in a variety of sizes from 16MB to 2GB and are becoming less and less expensive (especially in the 16MB to 256MB bracket).

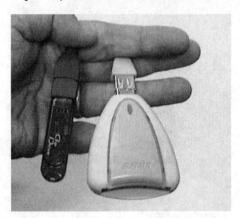

Figure 12-1: A USB flash drive and card reader

Memory cards are also popular as portable storage devices; however, to read these cards, you use a card reader (also shown in Figure 12-1). Memory cards are most commonly used in digital cameras. As these memory cards come in a variety of formats, such as CompactFlash, Memory Stick, and SmartMedia, different types of card readers are available to read the different media formats.

As you may already know, USB devices, which are recognizable by their narrow rectangular connector plugs (see Figure 12-2), have become increasing popular, largely because you can plug and unplug them while your computer is running (called *hot plugging*). While connecting universal serial bus (USB) storage devices to USB ports (which are also shown in Figure 12-2) is about as simple as things can get, accessing those devices so that you can transfer data to and from them is still one of Fedora's weaker areas, but once you go through the only slightly cumbersome one-time process of setting up your USB storage device, things will be as easy as can be. A little patience will bring great rewards, as the pyWings oracle might say.

Figure 12-2: A USB connector plug and USB ports

Device Compatibility

As with all forms of computer hardware, you have to wonder whether or not the device is compatible with your system. In the case of Windows or Macintosh compatibility, this is usually quite simply determined by reading the fine print on the side of the box that the device comes in. As you no doubt know by now, Linux compatibility is seldom specified. There also seems to be little in the way of an online guide for Linux compatibility for USB storage devices, probably because many of these devices are manufactured, or at least distributed, by rather small (sometimes no-name) companies, of which there are too many to deal with.

It is pretty safe to say that if the device claims to work on both Mac and Windows, or if it works on recent Windows versions without the need for a special driver, it will probably work on Linux. In the case of card readers, the multi-reader variety, which reads a variety of card types, is more likely to give you headaches. Better, in my opinion, to stick with those specifically designed for one type of card.

If you are the worrying kind, and you are not soothed by my words of encouragement, you can try one of the online Linux forums and ask for some recommendations, or if you have a particular model in mind, ask if anyone has experience with that particular device. And then there is the tried-and-true Google search, as I so often suggest for questions of hardware compatibility. Just type the make and model of the device in question along with the word "Linux," and see what happens.

Locating Your Device

Before you go about setting up your system to deal with your new USB storage device, it is useful to know how it is actually being handled by Linux. The mass storage driver in Linux deals with all USB storage devices as if they were SCSI (Small Computer System Interface) drives. SCSI (pronounced *scuzzy* — Ouch!) devices were once the most popular type of peripherals out there, but they have largely been supplanted by the cheaper and easier-to-deal-with USB devices. This means that such devices, whether real SCSI or USB, will be listed in your Hardware Browser as SCSI drives under the /**dev** listings: /**sda**, /**sdb**, /**sdc**, and so on, depending on how many of these devices you have. As you might have guessed, these listings (sda, sdb, sdc, and so on) stand for SCSI device a, b, c, and so on.

To see what I am talking about, plug your USB storage device into a USB port on your computer; you don't need to shut down your machine before doing this. Once you've done that, you need to find out where the device actually is, according to the computer. Now, of course, you know it is stuck into one of your USB ports, but your system has a reality all its own.

The easiest graphical way to find the USB device is to use your Hardware Browser. Just go to the Main menu and select **System Tools > Hardware Browser**. You will be asked for your root password, so type it when prompted and click **OK**. A window will then pop up telling you that it might take some time to check your hardware configuration; but before you finish reading it, the Hardware Browser window will open, and the message window will vanish. On the left side of the Hardware Browser you will see a number of headings, so click the one that says **Hard Drives** (not the one that says USB devices).

If your USB storage device is hardware compatible with Linux, it will most likely appear in the list as **/dev/sda1**, assuming it is the only device of that type you are dealing with (see Figure 12-3). If you are working with a second or third device, it might appear as **sdb1**, or **sdc1**, and so on.

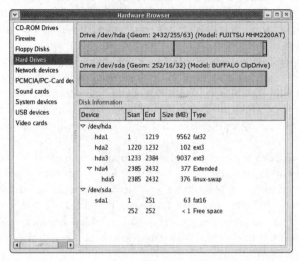

Figure 12-3: Looking at a USB storage device in the Hardware Browser

Setting Things Up — Editing the fstab File

As things are right now, your system is recognizing your USB storage device, but you still really can't use it, at least not easily. In order to set things up so that you can use your storage device anytime you want with just a couple of mouse clicks, you need to create an entry for the device in your **fstab** file.

Now I must admit that the first time I heard about this fstab file, and that I was going to alter it in some way, I sort of got the willies. Just the name of the file seemed creepy enough: f+stab. I thought the name was one of those off-the-wall Linux acronyms for something dark and dreary. Alas, I was relieved (or maybe even disappointed) to find out that fstab merely stood for *File System Table.* By modifying the fstab file, you are simply adding an item to a table. Nothing terrifying about that.

To get at your fstab file, you will use your now-beloved Terminal, so open it by clicking the Terminal launcher in your GNOME Panel. Once you've done that, become root by using the **su** command, and then type gedit /etc/fstab and press ENTER. In case you're wondering, the first part of that command opens the text editor program Gedit, while the second half tells Gedit to open the **fstab** file located in the **etc** folder. Once it all opens, your fstab file should look like the one in Figure 12-4.

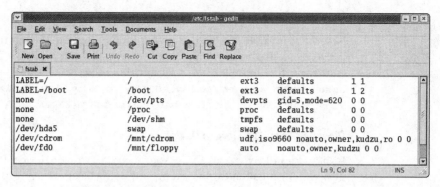

Figure 12-4: Modifying the fstab *file*

Now that the fstab file is open, you can add an entry for your new USB storage device by using the device location listed in the Hardware Browser. What you need to do is go to the bottom of the list and add something like the following:

```
/dev/sda1  /mnt/pendrive  auto  defaults,users,noauto 0 0
```

Now to explain what this all means, let's go through it bit by bit.

- The first element, **/dev/sda1** (or **/dev/sdb1**, and so on), is where the system says your device is located. This is the bit of information that you got from the Hardware Browser. The **1** in **sda1** points to the first (usually only) partition on that device.

- The second element, **/mnt/pendrive**, is the *mountpoint* for the drive. This mountpoint doesn't exist yet, but you will be creating it in the next section. The part of this element that comes after /**mnt**/ can be anything you like. If, for example, you are setting up a card reader instead of a PenDrive, you could call it /mnt/cardreader.

- The third element is the file system for the device. To keep things simple, you will be using auto, which should be self-explanatory in this case.

- The next three elements, which are strung together without spaces (only separated by commas), are the other settings for the device: defaults tells the system to handle this device in its usual way, **users** gives all users of the machine permission to use it, and **noauto** tells your system not to mount the device automatically on startup, as it is a removable device that might not be there when you start up. Make sure you don't type any spaces around the commas in this part of the entry.

- The last part, the two zeros, is a bit complicated, so just trust me on this one. Make sure that you have just one space between the two zeros.

You don't need to worry too much about lining up your new entry with the ones before it. However, if you space things out, be sure to avoid using your TAB key to make the spaces, as it causes problems in some text editors. Once you're done, click the **Save** button in Gedit and then quit the program.

Creating a Mountpoint

Now that your fstab has been edited, it is time to create the mountpoint that you listed in your fstab entry. This is quite easy, as you already know the **mkdir** command. Just go back to your Terminal window, which should still be in root mode, type in `mkdir /mnt/pendrive` (or replace `pendrive` with whatever name you gave your storage device in the fstab file) and press ENTER.

Mounting Your USB Storage Device

It should now be very easy to use your new USB storage device. Plug in the device, if it isn't already plugged in, and right-click your desktop. In the pop-up menu, select **Disks > pendrive**, and an icon for your new drive will appear on the desktop (in Red Hat Linux 9 you may have to restart your machine before your new storage device name appears in the pop-up menu). After that, you can use it like any other storage device by double-clicking it to open a Nautilus window. You can then drag files to and from the device as if it were a hard disk or floppy.

NOTE   *Fedora users should note that dragging a file from your USB storage device to your desktop will move the file, rather than copy it; therefore, once you've completed the drag-and-drop procedure, the file will be located on your hard disk but will erased from your USB device. On the other hand, dragging a file from your USB device directly to your Home folder or any other location therein will result in the file being copied rather than moved — it will be present on both the hard drive and the storage device after the drag and drop is complete. In the case of Red Hat Linux 9, all drag-and-drop procedures are treated as copies rather than moves.*

Unmounting Your USB Storage Device

Once you are done using your USB storage device, you have to unmount it before you can unplug it from the USB port. If you do not do this, then none of the files you dragged to the device will be saved there, which could be confusing. To unmount the USB device, right-click the desktop icon for the device and then select **Unmount Volume** in the pop-up menu. The icon will disappear, and then you can unplug the device if you like, though you do not have to. Make sure to close any open Nautilus windows for the drive before trying to unmount it, or the system won't allow you to do so.

Sometimes, as when unmounting floppies, your system will jump the gun a bit and tell you that it cannot unmount the drive, when in fact it is busy in the background doing just that. As I mentioned before, if you get such a no-can-do message, but the drive icon disappears anyway, you can ignore the system warning. Once the icon is gone, the drive is unmounted.

Adding Additional USB Storage Devices

Adding additional storage devices can be done in the same way that you added the first one:

1. Use the Hardware Browser to check the device location.
2. Add a new entry to the fstab file.
3. Create a new mountpoint.
4. Restart your machine.
5. Mount the drive by right-clicking the desktop, and select **Disks > **
   newdrivename from the pop-up menu.

Dual Booters: Mounting Windows Partitions or Drives

If you are a dual booter, meaning that you have both Windows and Linux installed on your hard disk, you may well want to be able to transfer files back and forth between your Windows and Linux partitions or disks. This is useful, for example, if you want to copy some of your Windows fonts to your Linux system, as you will learn to do in the following chapter. To do this, you have to mount your Windows partition or drive.

Now don't start hollering that your Windows partition is not a USB device; I know that. However, the process of setting up your system so that you can easily mount your Windows partition or drive is essentially the same as the one you learned for mounting USB drives.

Locating Your Windows Partition or Drive

Just as with USB storage devices, the first thing you have to do is locate your Windows drive or partition with the Hardware Browser. Go to your Main menu and select **System Tools > Hardware Browser**, and then type your root password when requested to do so. Once the Hardware Browser opens up, click **Hard Drives** in the left panel.

Next, look for your Windows partition, which will most likely be **hda1**. Once you've done this, check under the **Type** column to see what the file system format is for the partition. If it is **fat16** or **fat32**, you will have no problem. If, however, it is **ntfs** (which is the default file system for Windows NT, 2000, and XP) you are out of luck and will have to forgo this process, as Linux doesn't let you, as of yet, mount NTFS partitions, and not without good reason. Linux kernel support for NTFS is still buggy, thus endangering the integrity of such partitions or drives.

If you have a FAT16 or FAT32 partition, jot down the information for that partition. In the case of the example shown earlier in Figure 12-3 on page 166, the necessary info would be: /**dev/hda1 fat32**. Once you've done that, you can go on to edit the fstab file.

Adding Your Windows Partition or Drive to the fstab File

Open a Terminal window, become root, type gedit /etc/fstab, and press ENTER. When the fstab file opens in Gedit, add a new entry to the bottom of the list by typing the following:

```
/dev/hda1  /mnt/windows  vfat  defaults,users,noauto 0 0
```

Of course, if your device location is different, change the entry accordingly. You might also want to change noauto to auto. If you do this, a desktop icon for your Windows partition or drive appears in your Computer window each time you log in, thus eliminating the mount step each time you start your machine. You should note, however, that this method mounts the Windows partition as read-only, which means that you can copy files from the partition, but you can't write any files to that partition. To give yourself write permissions as well, use the following fstab entry instead, making sure to replace *username* with your own username:

```
/dev/hda1 /mnt/windows  vfat   auto,rw,uid=username,users 0 0
```

This entry gives you write permissions for the Windows partition, but it only provides read permissions to other users, which, all things considered, is a pretty safe way to go about things. No matter which route you choose, when all is as you want it, click the **Save** button, and quit Gedit.

Creating a Mountpoint

Now that your fstab has been edited, it is time to create the mountpoint that you listed in your fstab entry. Go back to your Terminal, which should still be in root mode, and type mkdir /mnt/windows and press ENTER.

Mounting Your Windows Partition or Disk

You can mount your Windows partition or drive in essentially the same manner as was described for USB storage devices. Right-click anywhere on your desktop, and then, in the pop-up menu, select **Disks > windows**. A desktop icon for your Windows partition or drive will then appear.

Double-clicking your Windows partition desktop icon will open a Nautilus window. You can then drag files to and from the Windows partition.

If you changed noauto to auto in your Windows partition fstab entry, you won't have to do anything the next time you start up your machine, as your Windows partition will be mounted automatically on startup, and the Windows partition desktop icon will appear automatically.

Unmounting Your Windows Partition or Disk

Unmounting your Windows partition or disk is done in the same manner as unmounting USB storage devices. Close any open Nautilus windows for the partition, and then right-click the desktop icon for the Windows partition or drive and select **Unmount Volume** from the pop-up menu.

13

TUX ROCKS

Music à la Linux

It's now time to move on to the audio side of things. Yes, Linux does indeed rock. You already learned about the GNOME CD Player in Chapter 7, but in this chapter you will find out even more about your system's musical talents. You will learn how to rip CDs and create MP3 and Ogg files (which have the .mp3 and .ogg filename extensions), how to change the tags of such files, and how to play those files. You'll also learn how to play a variety of audio streams.

Audio Formats

Before we go any further, it is probably best to discuss the various formats in which audio data can be stored on your computer. The de facto standards for the longest time have been WAV (created by Microsoft/IBM and using the .wav extension), AU (from Sun/Unix, and using the .au extension), and AIFF (from Apple), all of which are uncompressed formats. Files saved in these formats are, therefore, exceedingly large, with an average WAV file of CD-quality music weighing in at about 10MB per minute. To put that in perspective, my first Macintosh back in 1988 had a 40MB hard disk — more space than I would ever need, I thought at the time, but not enough to store a WAV file of Nirvana's "Come as You Are."

As computers underwent their evolution into the multimedia machines they are today, it became clear that something was going to have to be done about those disk-space devouring audio files. Audio compression formats were thus developed. These compression formats worked, to oversimplify things a bit, by cutting out the portions of a sound signal that the human ear cannot hear — sort of a dog-whistle approach. The most widely known and embraced of these audio compression formats is MP3. Audio files encoded in MP3 format can end up being as little as one-twelfth the size of the original WAV file without any noticeable loss in quality.

Another audio-compression format that was developed was Ogg Vorbis. Ogg Vorbis was a product of the open source community, and so, unlike MP3, which has always been used under the shadow of yet-to-be-exercised patent rights, was free of patent and licensing worries from the get-go. Because of that, and the fact that it was the equal of MP3 in terms of quality and performance (if not better), Ogg Vorbis became the darling of the Linux community, and its de facto audio compression format.

Grip

One of the handiest and most popular multimedia programs on your system is Grip. Grip allows you to *rip* (copy) WAV files from audio CDs and save those files as is, or *encode* them as (convert them to) compressed Ogg or MP3 files for your own personal use, on either your computer or an external device, such as Apple's iPod (though iPod cannot as of yet play Ogg files; not that many players can).

The process for ripping a CD and saving the tracks as WAV files, or of ripping the CD and then encoding its files in the Ogg file format is quite simple. Grip, as configured in Fedora, is already set up to do it quite well. To start, just place the audio CD you want to rip in your drive. The GNOME CD Player will then automatically start, but you don't need it for this ripping endeavor, so you can close it. Then, go to the Main menu and select **Sound & Video > More Sound & Video Applications > Grip**.

Grip will open, and after a couple of seconds it will display the contents of the CD in your drive. Assuming you are connected to the Internet when doing this, Grip will also list the title of the album, the artist who recorded it, and the titles of all of the songs on the CD (see Figure 13-1).

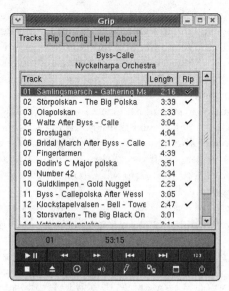

Figure 13-1: Grip displaying CD information retrieved from the Internet

Once the songs are displayed in the Grip window, you can select the songs you want to rip by clicking next to the titles under the **Rip** column. Or if you want to rip them all, you can just click the heading **Rip** at the top of that column. After you have made your selections, click the **Rip** tab to display the Rip page (see Figure 13-2).

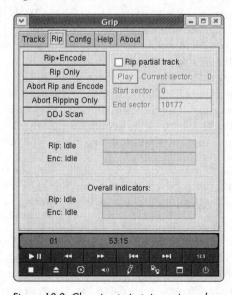

Figure 13-2: Choosing to just rip or rip and encode in Grip

If you just want to rip the tracks and save them as WAV files (which take up a lot of disk space), you can click the **Rip Only** button, and the ripping process will begin. If you want to rip the files and encode them in the much smaller Ogg format for playback on your own computer, click **Rip + Encode**, and Grip will begin to rip and then encode the files simultaneously. The encoding process will take longer than the ripping.

Once Grip has done its work and has ejected your CD, you will find your new files on your hard disk in the **ogg** folder inside your user's Home folder. If you didn't create an ogg folder when doing the projects in Chapter 5, Grip will have automatically created one for you. If you clicked the **Rip + Encode** button to encode your files in the Ogg format, Grip will also have deleted the space-wasting WAV files that it ripped from the CD.

A folder for the artist will have been created inside your **ogg** folder, there will be a folder for the album inside the newly created artist folder, and the ripped (and possibly encoded) files will be within the album folder. Thus, if you ripped a CD called *Orange Lightning Water* by Chuck Rumsfoord and the Venutians, you would find your files in ogg/chuck_rumsfoord_and_the_venutians/orange_lightning_water. Grip will also create an M3U playlist for the album outside of the artist folder (with an .m3u filename extension). Double-clicking that file will start up your default audio player, which will load the entire song list for that album and then start playing it all. Very handy.

Encoding MP3 files with Grip

Although I, as well as most Linux users, prefer the Ogg Vorbis format to that of MP3, there are many who need or want to encode files as MP3s. This is particularly true if you have an iPod-like player that cannot support Ogg files as of yet.

Fedora does not come with any native MP3 support, and the Grip application cannot encode MP3 files without such support. Without knowing it, however, you already provided Grip with the capacity to do this when you installed MPlayer in Chapter 10 using APT/Synaptic. One of the dependencies for MPlayer that APT/Synaptic downloaded and installed on your system was a program called LAME, which is an MP3 encoding program. This being the case, you are all ready to go. (I told you that those dependencies would come in handy later.)

NOTE   *If you didn't install LAME earlier for some reason, now would be the time to do so by running Synaptic, typing LAME in the **Find** box, and then following the procedures you learned in Chapter 10.*

To set up Grip so that it will encode MP3 files instead of Ogg files, click the **Config** tab in the main Grip window, and in the Config window click the **Encode** tab. This will bring up the page with encoder settings (see Figure 13-3). On this page, select **lame** from the **Encoder** drop-down list. Then, in the **Encode file format** box at the bottom of the page, change the ending in the existing string from **.ogg** to **.mp3**. That's all there is to it.

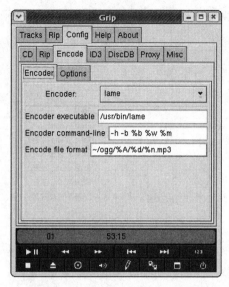

Figure 13-3: Setting up Grip to encode MP3s

If you want to go back to Ogg encoding, just change the **.mp3** ending back to **.ogg** in the bottom box, and select **oggenc** in the **Encoder** drop-down list.

Sound Juicer

Fedora Core includes an alternative CD ripper called Sound Juicer. Sound Juicer is a rather new program that is not as well known as Grip, but it is much easier to use. On the downside, it doesn't automatically create a playlist for the songs you rip and encode, and it seems (at least to me) to be a bit slower and, at times, a bit quirky.

To give it a try, go to the Main menu and select **Sound & Video > More Sound & Video Applications > Sound Juicer CD Ripper**. After you place an audio CD in the drive, the title of the album, name of the artist, and a list of the tracks on that CD will appear in the program window if, of course, you are connected to the Internet at the time (see Figure 13-4 on the next page).

Sound Juicer is set up by default to rip your CDs and encode the audio files in Ogg Vorbis format. The default location in which Sound Juicer will save these files is your Home folder. Because you have an ogg folder for this purpose already, it is probably best to make this the default location for Sound Juicer as well. To do so, go to the **Edit** menu and select **Preferences**. This will open the Preferences window where you can change the output path by clicking the **Browse** button (see Figure 13-5 on page 177). In the Select Output Location window, double-click the **ogg** folder in the Folders pane of that window and then click **OK**. You can now close the Preferences window.

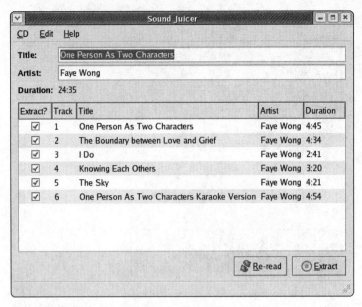

Figure 13-4: Sound Juicer displaying CD information

You may well have noticed that in the Preferences window, there are also settings for file formats other than Ogg Vorbis. Although the preference settings are there, the support files you need to use them are not included in your Fedora Core system. If you have your heart set on encoding MP3s, run Synaptic, type `gstreamer-plugins-extra-audio` in that program's **Find** box, and then follow the standard download and installation procedure outlined in Chapter 10.

To start ripping all the songs, all you need to do is click the **Extract** button at the bottom of the Sound Juicer window. If there are certain tracks you do not care to rip and encode, just uncheck the checkboxes next to the names of the songs in question before you click **Extract**. If you only want to rip and encode a few of the songs in the list, it might be better to first go to the **Edit** menu, select **Deselect All**, and then check the checkboxes next to the songs you do want to rip before clicking **Extract**.

As the songs are being ripped and encoded, Sound Juicer will show you its progress in a progress window, and when it's all done, it will also tell you in a small window that the tracks have been copied successfully. Once you get that message, click **Close** (the still-buggy Open button does the same thing). You can then eject the CD by going to the **File** menu and selecting **Eject**. If you want to rip and encode another CD, just pop it into the drive, and then, just as with the first CD, the album, artist, and titles will all appear in the program window, and you can rip away yet again.

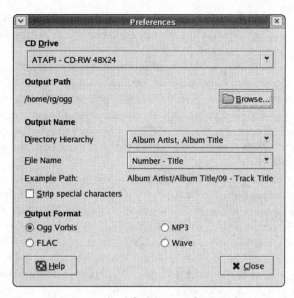

Figure 13-5: Setting the default location for Sound Juicer audio files

Rhythmbox

A new addition to Fedora Core is an audio player called Rhythmbox (see
Figure 13-6), and it is now the default audio player in Fedora Core for Ogg files.
Rhythmbox, using Sound Juicer as its ripper/encoder, is supposed to function
pretty much like the Macintosh world's iTunes application.

Figure 13-6: The Rhythmbox sound player

Unfortunately, the Rhythmbox music player seems to have been introduced into
Fedora Core before its time, as it is still sort of buggy in certain areas. I can't
really recommend it, especially when the tried and true XMMS audio player

(which I will get to shortly) is also installed on your system. I will wait for a couple more Rhythmbox upgrades (which will eventually be available via APT) before making it my default audio player.

If you still want to give Rhythmbox a look, by all means do, but just remember that if you want to play MP3 files, you have to download and install the file called **gstreamer-plugins-extra-audio** via Synaptic. Of course, if you've already done this to encode MP3 files with Sound Juicer, you're set. To run Rhythmbox, just double-click any Ogg file (or MP3 file if you've installed support), and it starts right up. Alternatively, you can go to the Main menu and select **Sound and Video > Music Player**.

The first time you run Rhythmbox, you are greeted by a three-step setup wizard. To get through the first introduction screen, just click **Forward**. In the second screen (shown in Figure 13-7), you should tell Rhythmbox where it is you keep (or plan to keep) your music files. As you have already created an Ogg folder while following along with this book, use that folder. In the **Path** input box type /home/*username*/ogg (or use the **Browse** button to locate the folder graphically), and then click **Forward**. Finally, in the third and final screen, just click **Apply**, and Rhythmbox will scan your ogg folder and add any songs it finds there to its library.

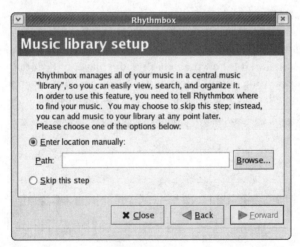

Figure 13-7: Setting up Rhythmbox

The Rhythmbox Library and Browsers

If you are familiar with Apple's iTunes, then you should pretty well understand the library in Rhythmbox too, as it is essentially the same concept. Basically, every time you tell Rhythmbox to check your ogg folder for new songs (by going to the **File** menu and selecting **Add to Library**), it scans that folder and adds any new songs it finds to its library. You can also add other single audio files, or folders containing such files, by right-clicking the target file or folder and selecting **Add to Music Player Library** in the pop-up menu. The library is thus, in essence, a database of all the songs you have in your ogg folder and any others that you point Rhythmbox to.

When you want to play songs in Rhythmbox, you just need to click **Library** in the Source pane on the left side of the program window. This will show all of the songs that you have listed in your library. You can click the play button to start playing them all, or scroll down to a song you want to start with and double-click that.

Of course, as your library grows, this can all become rather problematic — there might be a day when you are feeling a bit more Roxy Music than Britney (and thank goodness for that).

Fortunately Rhythmbox has a nice browser function that allows you to see lists of the artists and albums listed in its library. If you click a specific artist in the Artist pane, a list of albums by that artist will appear in the right pane (see Figure 13-8). You can then double-click one of the albums in that right pane to play it. If you want to play all of the albums you have by that artist, just double-click the artist's name in the left pane. All in all, a very handy feature.

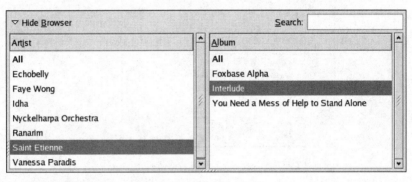

Figure 13-8: Selecting music by artist in Rhythmbox

Creating Playlists

Rhythmbox allows you to create playlists, which are your own personalized assortments of songs. To create a playlist, go to the **File** menu and select **New Playlist**. A dialog box will then open in which you can give your list a title; then click **Create**. The new list will appear in the left pane of the Rhythmbox window.

To add songs to your list, just drag the songs you wish to add from the main list to the new playlist icon. Once you are done, click your new playlist, and its contents will then appear in the main list pane. After that, just click the play button to play the songs in your new playlist.

XMMS

Now we come to XMMS, the Linux world's best known and most widely used audio player. It is pretty much a clone of the Windows world's Winamp in terms of what it can do, but it was written from scratch, and it is very cool and capable. With XMMS, you can play just about any kind of audio file and even listen to Internet broadcast streams in either MP3 or Ogg format.

XMMS actually consists of three components: the Media Player, the Equalizer, and the Playlist (see Figure 13-9 on the next page). You can run the Media Player alone or in conjunction with either or both of the other components, which you can open by clicking the tiny **EQ** button in the Media Player window for the Equalizer, or the **PL** button for the Playlist. You can also move the various components around just like a real component stereo so that they are stacked one on top of the other, side by side, or in whatever configuration you want; just drag things around until they all look the way you want them to.

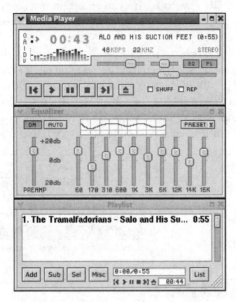

Figure 13-9: The three components of XMMS

You can run XMMS by going to the Main menu and selecting **Sound & Video > Audio Player**. You also used to be able to start it playing by double-clicking any M3U, Ogg, or MP3 file (after reinstalling the MP3 support that Red Hat, the company, removed). Now that Rhythmbox is set up as the default player in Fedora Core, though, this is no longer the case by default.

You can, however, set things up so that XMMS becomes the default audio player again, or at least appears as an option in the pop-up menu when you right-click an audio file.

To change these settings for Ogg files, follow these steps:

1. Right-click any Ogg file and then, in the pop-up menu, select **Open with > Other Application**. The Open with Other Application window will appear (see Figure 13-10).

2. Select **X Multimedia System** (XMMS) by clicking the name once, and then click **Modify**. This will open a window called Modify "X Multimedia System" (also shown in Figure 13-10).

3. In that window, choose the second item, **Use as default for "Ogg audio" items**, and then click **OK**.

Once you've done this, XMMS will be the default player for Ogg files, while Music Player (aka Rhythmbox) will still be available by right-clicking any audio file and selecting **Open with > Other Application** in the pop-up menu. Even if you later find that you like Rhythmbox more than XMMS, this way of doing things is better, all in all, as you retain Rhythmbox's functionality for playing your music, while utilizing the lightness of XMMS for quickly checking audio files when you first encounter them on the Internet or elsewhere.

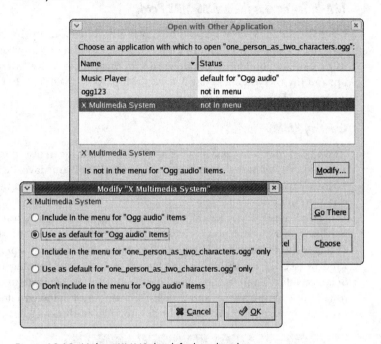

Figure 13-10: Making XMMS the default audio player

Now that you have gone through this process for Ogg files, it would be an equally good idea to do the same for MP3 files. Just right-click an MP3 file, and then follow the same procedures.

Project 13A: Installing MP3 Support for XMMS

As I mentioned, XMMS can play audio files in just about any format. However, Red Hat, the company, removed MP3 support for XMMS from its products because of those patent and licensing issues I mentioned at the beginning of the chapter. This means that if you want to play MP3s or MP3 streams with XMMS, you will need to install a patch in order to do so.

If you don't believe me, or just don't understand what I am talking about, see for yourself. Place an MP3 file on your hard disk, and then double-click it. XMMS will open, as will another small window, giving you a no-can-do-MP3s message.

13A-1: Downloading and Installing the XMMS MP3 Patch

The XMMS MP3 patch can be easily downloaded and installed via Synaptic. Just run Synaptic by going to the Main menu and selecting **System Tools > Synaptic** (or **System Settings > Synaptic**, if that is where it is on your system).

Once Synaptic is up and running, just type XMMS-mp3 in the Find box, and then follow the simple procedure for installing packages via Synaptic that you learned in Chapter 10.

13A-2: Trying Out the XMMS MP3 Patch

Once the patch is installed, you can try it out quite easily by double-clicking any MP3 file on your hard disk (and if you don't have one now, you should make one using Grip, as you learned to do earlier in this chapter). XMMS will then open up, and the file you clicked will start playing. As you will see, there won't be any no-can-do-MP3s message this time.

Creating XMMS Playlists

XMMS can play M3U playlists created by Grip, but it can also create playlists as well. Let's say that you want to create a playlist of your favorite songs by various artists, but these songs are located, quite naturally, in a variety of different folders.

To create this "My Faves" playlist, just add each song you want to the XMMS playlist window, which you can do by clicking the small **Add** button at the bottom of that window (shown in Figure 13-9 on page 180). This will open the Load Files window (see Figure 13-11), in which you can locate the first file and click **Add Selected Files**. Then in the same Load Files window, navigate to the each additional tune you wish to add to your list, clicking **Add Selected Files** for each tune. (You can ignore the **Add** button in the Load Files window.)

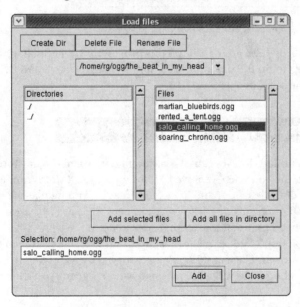

Figure 13-11: Adding songs to the XMMS playlist via the Load Files window

Once you've added all the files you want, you can see all the titles in the Playlist window (see Figure 13-12). If everything looks as you want it to, click, but don't release, the **List** button at the bottom-right corner of that window. Then select

Save from the pop-up menu, and release the mouse button. This will bring up a Save Playlist window, where you should type in /home/*username*/ogg/*playlisttitle*. m3u (substitute your own username and playlist title for *username* and *playlisttitle*). In my case, for example, I typed in /home/rg/ogg/MyFaves.m3u. Once you're done, click **OK**, and XMMS will save your new playlist. After that, all you have to do to play the list is double-click the M3U file for that list.

Figure 13-12: A new playlist shown in the XMMS playlist window

Using XMMS to Listen to Streaming Media

One of the coolest features of the Internet is streaming media, which is essentially live or taped audio or video Internet broadcasts. Such broadcasts can come in a variety of streaming formats, which are basically compression formats that allow data to move across the Net at as small a size as possible. Unfortunately, Linux cannot yet deal with the two most common of these formats, Microsoft's Windows Media Player and Apple's QuickTime, at least not in any simple way. Fortunately there are other media streaming formats out there on the Net, such as RealMedia. In addition, as streaming media formats are essentially space-saving compression formats, it is only natural that MP3 and Ogg Vorbis, both audio compression formats themselves, have also come to be used as streaming media formats for Internet audio broadcasts.

Ogg Vorbis Streams

In addition to allowing you to save music to disk in the form of Ogg files, Ogg Vorbis is also used for streaming media across the Internet. Compared to the number of MP3 streams, however, the number of Ogg Vorbis broadcast streams is still rather limited. Things seem to be changing, though, and the number of Internet broadcasters who are experimenting with Ogg Vorbis seems to be increasing, albeit very slowly.

Radio France is a good example of one of these Ogg Vorbis broadcasters. Radio France has a number of program streams for Internet listeners in Windows Media Player format. It also has now begun to "expérimente" (its word, not mine) with providing Ogg Vorbis streams for all of their broadcast programs. The stream I recommend you try out is Fip, which is an exceedingly cool eclectic collection of music of *all* genres; you will be constantly surprised by what they play. If you are worried about language, don't; there is very little talk, and roughly 80 percent of the music played is in English. I don't speak any French other than *je suis fatigué*, but I have no problems at all.

If you want to give streaming media in general, and Radio France in particular, a try, then right-click any open space in the main XMMS window, and from the pop-up menu, select **Play Location**. In the Location window that pops up, type http://ogg.tv-radio.fr:1441/encoderfip.ogg, and then click **OK**. Assuming you are already connected to the Internet, Fip should start playing after a few seconds of pre-buffering.

If you would like to be able to play Fip again in the future without having to type the somewhat lengthy URL each time, you can create a clickable launcher of sorts in your Home folder by saving the Fip location as a playlist. As in the preceding section, click, but do not release, the **List** button in the bottom-right corner of the Playlist window. In the pop-up menu, select **Save**, which will bring up a Save Playlist window. In the Selection box at the bottom of that window, type Fip.m3u, and then click **OK**.

Once you've done all that, a Fip.m3u file will appear in your Home folder. Now, whenever you want to listen to Fip, just double-click that icon, and XMMS will open and start bringing you a dose of eclectia, provided, of course, that you are connected to the Internet at the time.

If you would like to try any of the other Radio France broadcast streams, go to www.radiofrance.fr/services/aide/difflive.php#ogg, and you will find a list of addresses.

If the more traditional variety of pop and rock is your cup of tea, another broadcaster offering Ogg Vorbis streams is Virgin Radio. Virgin Radio has both standard pop/rock and classic rock broadcast streams. To listen to Virgin Radio, go to the Virgin Radio site at www.virginradio.co.uk/thestation/listen/ogg.html. Once there, click the appropriate link (modem or broadband) for the program stream you'd like to hear.

Once you do that, Mozilla will display a window (see Figure 13-13) to ask you what program you want to use to open the Ogg file type. Select **Open it with**, and in the accompanying box type /usr/bin/xmms. Then click **OK**. Mozilla will open XMMS, and the Virgin Radio stream will start playing. From now on, whenever you try to play an Ogg Vorbis stream, Mozilla will automatically start XMMS to play it.

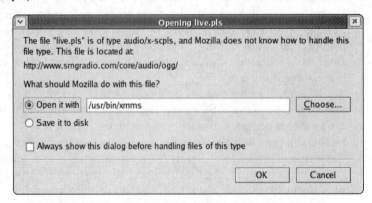

Figure 13-13: Instructing Mozilla to play Ogg streams with XMMS

SHOUTcast (MP3) Streams

As you have just learned, XMMS can play Ogg Vorbis streams, but now that you have installed MP3 support, it can also play SHOUTcast MP3 streams. To give this a try, go to www.shoutcast.com where you will see an extensive listing of SHOUTcast MP3 streams. Once you find a stream that seems of interest to you, click the **Tune In** button for that stream.

When you do this, Mozilla will pop up another one of those what-should-I-do-with-this-file windows. Just type /usr/bin/xmms in the **Open with** box and click **OK**, and XMMS will open and soon begin playing the stream. Now, any time you try to play a SHOUTcast stream in the future, Mozilla will know what to do with it.

Inputting Proxy Settings for Ogg Vorbis and SHOUTcast Streams

If your Internet provider has you behind a firewall, you will not be able to listen to broadcast streams with XMMS unless you input the proxy server settings given to you by your service provider. You can do this by right-clicking anywhere in the XMMS window and selecting **Options > Preferences** in the pop-up menu. When you do this, the Preferences window will open.

To input your proxy settings for Ogg Vorbis streams, scroll through the items in the Input Plugins pane, select **Ogg Vorbis Player**, and then click the **Configure** button, which will open the Ogg Vorbis Configuration window (see Figure 13-14). In that window, check the **Use proxy** checkbox and type your proxy information in the **Host** box. When you've finished, click **OK** to exit the Ogg Vorbis Configuration window, and then in the Preferences window, click **Apply** to apply your changes.

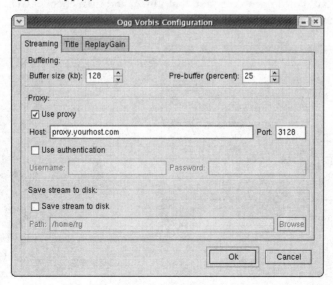

Figure 13-14: Inputting proxy settings for Ogg Vorbis streams in XMMS

To input proxy settings for SHOUTcast streams, scroll through the items in the Input Plugins pane again, but this time select **MPEG Layer 1/2/3 Player**. Once you've done that, click the **Configure** button, which will open the MPG123 Configuration window. In that window, click the **Streaming** tab, and in that page click the **Use proxy** checkbox. Now input the proxy settings you received from your Internet provider or network administrator. You should also click the **Enable SHOUT/Icecast title streaming** checkbox near the bottom of the page. Once you've done all this, click **OK** to close the window. Then, back in the Preferences window, click **Apply** once (which will make the changes take effect immediately), and then click **OK** to close the Preferences window.

Project 13B: Using XMMS Skins

In Chapter 5, you learned how to customize the look of your system by changing window border and application control themes. However, XMMS is configured to hide its window bars, and it uses controls of its own, so any cosmetic changes you make to your system will have no effect on XMMS. You can, however, directly change the look of XMMS by using its own themes, called *skins*. The default skin for XMMS in Fedora Core is called Bluecurve, and it essentially follows the default theme of the rest of the system.

Before we can move on, you are going to have to install some skins to work with. This is easily enough done by running Synaptic, typing xmms-skins in Synaptic's **Find** box, and then following the usual Synaptic download/installation steps. Once done, you will have a hefty collection of XMMS skins to work with. If you installed your Fedora Core or Red Hat Linux system from a 3-CD installation disk set, the xmms-skins package is already included on the disks, so you can install the skins by using the Package Management window instead. Just click the **Details** button next to **Sound and Video**, and then check the checkbox next to **xmms-skins** to get things rolling.

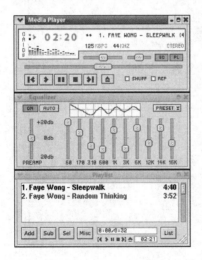 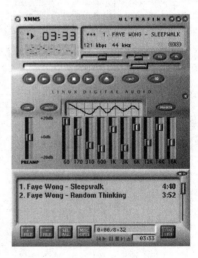

Figure 13-15: Changing XMMS skins: before and after

13B-1: Changing Skins

As you can see in Figure 13-15, what you are going to do in this part of the project is change the default Bluecurve skin (shown on the left of the figure) to the Ultrafina skin (on the right of the figure), which for my money (and I admit I don't have much) looks a lot better. You may beg to differ, but just go along with me for now. You are free to do anything you like once we part company — no feelings hurt.

To bring about this remarkable transformation, you will first need to start XMMS, if it isn't already up and running. After that, right-click anywhere on the main XMMS program window, and from the pop-up menu select **Options > Skin Browser**. This will open the Skin Selector window (see Figure 13-16), in which you will scroll down until you find **Ultrafina**. Once you see it, click it. Like magic, the transformation will be complete.

Figure 13-16: The XMMS Skin Selector window

Boy, that was simple! You can now, of course, browse through the other choices by simply clicking them, one by one, until you find one that does something for you.

As you may have noticed, there is a lot of variation in the world of skins. Some can be so wild that you can barely use them, while others may be quite dull yet very easy on the eye. There is also the configuration of your XMMS components to consider. You may agree that the Ultrafina skin looks much more handsome than the default Bluecurve skin when the components are stacked on top of one another, as in Figure 13-15 on the previous page. However, place the components side by side while using Ultrafina, and it all looks pretty weird, whereas a more traditional stereo system skin, as shown in Figure 13-17 on the next page, seems much more the ticket.

Figure 13-17: XMMS components stacked in classic stereo configuration

13B-2: Downloading Additional Skins

If you've gone through the whole lot of choices and found nothing to get your heart a-pumping, you can download still other skins from the Web. The XMMS site (www.xmms.org) has quite a few, but even more can be found on the Winamp site (http://classic.winamp.com/skins). Yes, you've guessed right; Winamp skins and XMMS skins are interchangeable. Just be sure *not* to use those skins designed for Winamp 3, which will not work. You can tell which are which by the file extensions: Winamp 3 skins end in .wal, Winamp 2 skins (the XMMS compatibles) end in .zip, and native XMMS skins end in .wsz.

Once you find some skins that you like, download them in the usual manner.

13B-3: Installing Your New Skins

Once you have downloaded some new skins, you will have to make them available to XMMS by putting them in the right place on your system. You needn't unzip them, though; you can use them as is, which saves you some minor grief. Anyway, at this stage of the game, this is most easily done by putting them in the **.xmms** folder within your Home folder.

Directories preceded by a dot are normally hidden from view, so either you can go to the Preferences menu in a Nautilus window and then check **Show hidden and backup files** in the Preferences window, or you can just open another Nautilus window, and in the **Location** box type `~/.xmms/Skins/` and press ENTER. From there on in, it's a simple drag-and-drop procedure. Just drag the downloaded skin files directly into the Skins folder, and that is that. The next time you open the XMMS Skin Selector, your new skins will be there waiting in the list. All very simple.

EasyTAG

If you are really into MP3s and Ogg files, a handy program you might want to add to your repertoire is EasyTAG, which allows you to view and change the tag information for your MP3 and Ogg files (see Figure 13-18). This is very handy when you have files that are missing or have incorrect file information (artist, title, and so on), and thus do not display that information when playing in XMMS or other audio players. It also displays the technical details of each file.

You can easily download and install EasyTAG by using APT/Synaptic, which you downloaded and installed in Chapter 10. Just open the Synaptic program, type easytag in the Synaptic search box, and then follow the procedures laid out in Chapter 10. After the installation is complete, you can run EasyTAG by going to the Main menu and selecting **Sound & Video > More Sound & Video Applications > EasyTAG**. EasyTAG will then start and scan your hard disk for all of your MP3 and Ogg files.

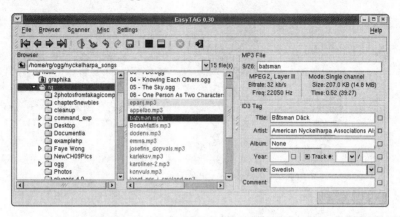

Figure 13-18: Modifying audio file tag info with EasyTAG

Audacity

If you like, or need, to really manipulate your sound files, then Audacity is a very handy program (see Figure 13-19 on the next page). Audacity is a sound editor that allows you to load files in almost any sound format (.wav, .aiff, .au, .ogg, . mp3) and edit them in a variety of ways. For example, you might want to capture just one phrase out of a speech, or your favorite guitar solo from a song, and use it as a system sound, or maybe you want to permanently boost the volume of a certain portion of a recording that didn't come out just right the first time around. Or maybe you just want to perform an old "expletive deleted" routine on a saucier portion of something you are planning to play before a class of junior high school students. You can even use Audacity to add reverberation, echo, or other effects to a sound file. And you can use it to record your own sounds via line-in or microphone.

Audacity is not included with Fedora Core, but it is easily downloaded and installed with Synaptic/APT. To get it, just run Synaptic, and then type Audacity in the **Find** window. Once it is installed, you can run it by going to the Main menu and selecting **Sound & Video > More Sound & Video Applications > Audacity Audio Editor**.

If you need more help after that, there is a pretty good quick guide, which you can access by going to the **Help** menu and selecting **Online Help**, and there is a full manual that you can use online or download from http://audacity. sourceforge.net/help.php.

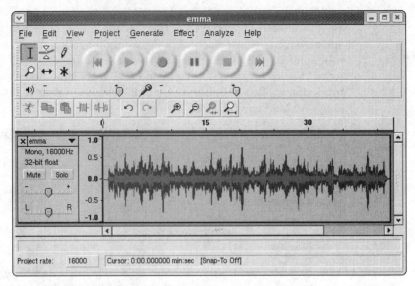

Figure 13-19: Adjusting audio files with Audacity

Project 13C: RealPlayer 10 Gold

Now that you know how to play Ogg Vorbis and SHOUTcast streams, it is time to help your system go a bit more mainstream by installing RealPlayer 10 Gold (Figure 13-20). RealMedia streams are widely available and are provided by many mainstream broadcasters, both local and international. You can play RealVideo streams, when they're available, as well.

Figure 13-20: RealPlayer 10 Gold

Linux users familiar with previous versions of RealPlayer will be happy to know that RealPlayer 10 is much improved over previous Linux offerings. One of the big advantages is that RealPlayer 10 now has a working Mozilla-compatible plug-in, which means that you can now listen to RealMedia streams that were previously unavailable to you because they could only be accessed through browser-embedded players. If you don't know what I'm talking about, take a look at the example from the Radio Sweden site in Figure 13-21.

Figure 13-21: Embedded media players in Mozilla before and after installing the RealPlayer plug-in

As you can see, the Radio Sweden site (www.sr.se), like many others, uses an embedded player for the broadcast streams it provides; however, without installing the proper plug-in, the player cannot be used, as you can see in the left half of Figure 13-21. Once the RealPlayer plug-in is installed, however, its controls automatically appear (as you can see in the right side of Figure 13-21), allowing you to use the embedded player just as you would the stand-alone version (shown in Figure 13-20).

Now, before moving on, note that RealPlayer 10 is now theme compatible. This means that if you change your system theme from Bluecurve to Crux, for example, those effects take place in RealPlayer 10 too. This means you are no longer stuck with the look that the Real folks provide you with. Yes, things are getting better.

13C-1: Getting and Installing the RealPlayer File

To download the RealPlayer 10 file, go to the download page at www.real.com/linux. Once there, all you need to do is click the **Download RealPlayer** button. When you do, a Mozilla window appears asking you what to do with the file. The default selection should be "Save it to Disk"; assuming this is the case, just click **OK**, and the download commences.

Once the download is complete, quit Mozilla, open a Terminal window, and then follow these really easy steps:

1. First, make the RealPlayer installation file executable (aka *runnable*) by typing `chmod a+x RealPlayer10GOLD.bin` and pressing ENTER.

2. Become root by using the **su** command.

3. Now type `./RealPlayer10GOLD.bin` and press ENTER.

4. When you are told to press ENTER to continue, press ENTER.

5. Accept the default installation location by pressing ENTER.

6. Let the installer begin its file-copying chores by pressing ENTER.

7. When you are asked whether to allow the installer to configure system-wide symbolic links, type `Y` and press ENTER.

After a very short while, the installer tells you that it's finished, and you can exit the Terminal window. You can now run Mozilla again.

13C-2: Setting Up Mozilla to Play RealMedia Streams Automatically

RealPlayer 10 is now installed and set up on your machine, but to use it comfortably, it is probably best to set up your Mozilla web browser so that it knows what to do when you try to play a RealMedia stream that doesn't take advantage of the RealPlayer plug-in for Mozilla. The easiest way to do this is by trying to open such a stream right away. For convenience's sake, I use the National Public Radio (www.npr.org) site for my source stream; you can, of course, choose any stream you like. If you don't know any streams offhand, just follow along with me. It doesn't really matter at this point, because our objective is merely to set up Mozilla.

First, go to the site and click the link for the program stream. In the case of NPR, you are first asked if you want to use RealPlayer or Windows Media Player. Click **RealPlayer**. After you do this, Mozilla pops up yet another what-should-I-do-with-this-file window, asking you what to do with the stream. Check the radio button next to the **Open with** box, and type `/home/username/RealPlayer/realplay` (replacing *username* with your own username, of course). Once you've done that, click **OK**, and the stream should begin playing after a few seconds of pre-buffering. The station icon for that stream, if there is one, also appears in the Real-Player window.

You probably won't have to go through this process again, because Mozilla now knows what to do with RealMedia streams. If you do happen to get asked again somewhere along the way, follow the same steps again: select **Open with**, type `/home/username/RealPlayer/realplay`, and click **OK**.

Now that you are all set up, you probably want some more streams to try out. There are plenty of sites out there with RealMedia streams, but let me steer you to some of my faves to get you started (you may already know some of these):

- **Michael Feldman's Whad'Ya Know? (comedy/game)**
  www.notmuch.com/Show
- **Sounds Eclectic (alternative/world music)**
  http://soundseclectic.com
- **Car Talk (car talk)**
  http://cartalk.cars.com/Radio/Show
- **Radio Netherlands (pop music)**
  www.rnw.nl
- **A Prairie Home Companion (Garrison Keillor, et al.)**
  www.prairiehome.org/listings
- **Radio Sweden P3 Svea (alternative/world/pop music)**
  www.sr.se/p3/svea
  (Click the **lyssna** button to listen via the embedded player.)

14

BRUSH-WIELDING PENGUINS

Linux Does Art

Now that you know that Linux rocks, it is time to don that beret of yours and move on to the artistic side of Linux. Yes, Linux does art, and as you will soon find out, there are a good number of programs on your system that allow you to create and manipulate graphic files. The most notable (and famous) of these applications is the GIMP, which you might think of as the Linux equivalent of Adobe Photoshop. To run the GIMP, just go to the Main menu, and select **Graphics > The GIMP**.

Getting Arty with the GIMP

The GIMP allows you to create bitmap graphics and, quite importantly, retouch or completely doctor image files, such as those from your digital camera. (Want to put some color in your cheeks, you say?) With the GIMP you can get rid of red-eye in your digital photos, airbrush out unwanted shadows (or even facial blemishes), give your image a canvas texture, change a photo into an oil painting, and even add a bell pepper here and there (see Figure 14-1).

Figure 14-1: Manipulating a digital image in the GIMP

The GIMP is also a very handy tool for resizing images. This can easily be done by simply right-clicking an image opened in the GIMP and then selecting **Image > Scale Image** in the pop-up menu. This will bring up the Scale Image window, where you can set the new size of the image.

The GIMP is also an excellent tool for converting images from one file format to another. You can, for example, open a bitmap (.bmp) file and save it as a PNG (.png) file, or save a JPEG (.jpg) file as a GIF (.gif) file, and so on. The GIMP supports an extremely wide variety of file formats, and it even lets you save an image file as a compressed tarball. To perform a file conversion, just right-click an image opened within the GIMP and then select **File > Save As** in the pop-up menu. This will bring up a dialog box in which you can specify the new file format by replacing the original file extension in the **Selection** box at the bottom of the window with the extension for the format you want to convert the image to.

It is lots of fun to learn to use the GIMP by just playing around with it for a while. Of course, you should make a backup copy of any file you are planning to experiment with before doing so. If you prefer working through tutorials to just finding things out by goofing around, the GIMP Documentation page (www.gimp.org/tutorials.html) has a number of links to tutorials covering various functions, features, and skill levels. In my opinion, the best of these is the GIMP Tutorials page (http://empyrean.lib.ndsu.nodak.edu/~nem/gimp/tuts).

Project 14A: Tux Paint (Optional)

If you don't really need all the power that the GIMP provides, and you are instead just looking for something simple for the kids to paint with (or even for when you just want to whip out a quick doodle or two), you can always try KPaint, which is a very lightweight equivalent of Windows Paint or MacPaint from the early Macintosh days (both lightweight programs, themselves). KPaint comes as part of your Fedora Core system, and it can be run by going to the Main menu and selecting **Graphics > More Graphics Applications > Paint Program**.

If you would like something a bit more fun and attractive, you should check out Tux Paint (see Figure 14-2). Tux Paint is a very easy-to-use, kids-oriented paint program with a highly intuitive and attractive interface that anyone of almost any age can get the hang of after a minute of use (slightly more, perhaps, for the real young'uns). If you also download and install the separate rubber stamps package, you or your kids can stamp all sorts of odd things all over the page: tropical fish, penguins, nickels, dimes, Euros, clothespins, and even bell peppers, like in the GIMP.

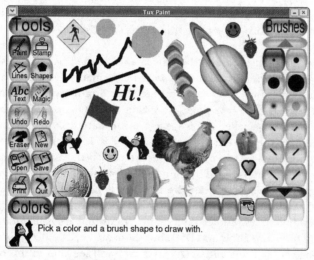

Figure 14-2: Playing with Tux Paint

Getting the Tux Paint Files

Tux Paint is not included with your Fedora Core system, so you will have to download it yourself. In addition to the main Tux Paint package, you will also need to download **SDL-ttf**, which Tux Paint needs to run, and the rubber stamps plug-in, which although optional, is really what makes Tux Paint so very cool.

To get the main Tux Paint package and rubber stamps plug-in, go to www.newbreedsoftware.com/tuxpaint/download/linux-rpm. For the main package, select the appropriate **tuxpaint** file for the version of Linux you are using. For the rubber stamps plug-in, select the link below **tuxpaint-stamps noarch-rpm**.

To get the SDL-ttf package, go to www.libsdl.org/projects/SDL_ttf and download the file **SDL_ttf-2.0.6-1.i386.rpm** from the **Binary** section right below the word **Linux**.

14A-1: Installing and Running Tux Paint

All three of the files you've downloaded are RPM packages, so there will be no problems on your end. When installing the packages, just be sure to install them in the right order to avoid dependency warnings: **SDL_ttf** first, **tuxpaint** second, and **tuxpaint-stamps** last.

Once everything is installed, you can run Tux Paint by going to the Main menu and selecting **Graphics > Tux Paint**.

Project 14B: Sodipodi (Optional)

The GIMP, like other so-called paint programs, creates bitmap (.bmp) images. These are images in which the location and color of every single pixel is recorded. The image is essentially a collection of dots, or bits. The file you create is thus a rather hefty map of these bits (hence its name), and this map tells your system where everything in your image is supposed to go when it is displayed or printed.

Drawing programs, on the other hand, create vector images, or drawings. The vector image file is a collection of mathematical formulae representing the various shapes in your image. This may sound rather unimportant to you, but such drawings have advantages in certain cases. One of these advantages is that vector image files take up less space on your hard disk than bitmaps. Another, and perhaps the most important, advantage is that shapes in vector images retain their smooth edges when the images are enlarged. A smooth circle created as a bitmap, for example, would begin to show jagged edges (the jaggies) when enlarged to any extent, while the same circle in a vector image would remain smooth and round no matter how much you increased its size.

Fedora comes with a couple of programs that are called drawing programs (OpenOffice.org Draw and Dia), but these are really more appropriate for creating simple flyers and diagrams, as you will see later in this chapter. My pick for the easiest-to-use drawing program for creating true graphics is Sodipodi — the name is Estonian for mishmash (see Figure 14-3).

14B-1: Downloading, Installing, and Running Sodipodi

Sodipodi is not included in your Fedora Core system, so you will have to download it and install it yourself. You can get the RPM file by going to http://dag.wieers.com/packages/sodipodi and then clicking the link for the newest version appropriate for your Linux version. If you added DAG to Synaptic's list of repositories as I explained in Chapter 10, you can also download the file by running Synaptic, typing sodipodi in Synaptic's **Find** box, and then following the standard Synaptic installation procedures. As the file is an RPM with no unmet dependencies, installation is very simple.

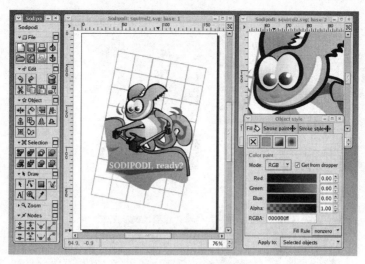

Figure 14-3: Creating real graphics with Sodipodi

Once Sodipodi is installed, you can run it by going to the Main menu and selecting **Graphics > More Graphics Applications > Sodipodi**.

If you would like to get a feel for what you can do with Sodipodi, click the **Galleries** link at the top of the Sodipodi project home page (www.sodipodi.com). You can also find a very nice tutorial on how to use Sodipodi at http://hawthorn.csse.monash.edu.au/~njh/programming/drawing-packages/sodipodi.

Viewing Your Images with gThumb

As you learned in Chapter 3, Nautilus acts as a sort of previewer for your graphics files. There are limitations to what Nautilus can do, however, so it is time for you to become acquainted with another program that comes with your Fedora Core system: gThumb (see Figure 14-4 on the next page). You can run gThumb by going to the Main menu and selecting **Graphics > gThumb Image Viewer**.

Once gThumb is up and running, you will want to direct it to the folder where you keep your images. You can do this by clicking the folder icons in the left panel of the program window, or by typing in the location in the location box above the left panel (/home/username/Photos if you created the folders I told you to in Chapter 5). Once you are there, gThumb will show you all the files in that folder in the form of slidelike thumbnail images.

So what? Well, gThumb also lets you resize an image, adjust the brightness and contrast of that image, and even rotate it by simply clicking the image you want to modify and then selecting from the various choices in the **Image** menu. You can also change the file format of a given file in gThumb (from .jpg to .png, for example), though without the various options available when doing the same in the GIMP. Finally, if you want to print out one of your images, doing so via gThumb is extremely easy. Just click the image you want to print, and then select **Print** in the **File** menu.

Figure 14-4: Viewing images in a folder with gThumb

In terms of viewing, you can also view an image using the full screen by clicking the image you want to view and then selecting **Full Screen** in the **View** menu. From the same menu, you can also view all of your images as a slide show by selecting **Slide Show**.

Project 14C: Emblems Again! Creating Your Own

One of the first things my mother asked me after she got Linux up and running was how to create her own emblems. You already learned how to deal with emblems in Chapter 5, but now that I have introduced many of the graphics tools at your disposal, it might be a good time to address my mother's question as well.

14C-1: Using an Existing Icon as an Emblem

Probably the easiest way to get started creating emblems is to use one of the icons on your system as an emblem. The only problem with that idea is that most of your system icons are 48 by 48 pixels in size, while emblems are 36 by 36 pixels. If you don't want your new emblem to look weirdly oversized and out of place, it is best to resize it.

As I mentioned in the previous section, the gThumb application is very handy for resizing images. For this project, we will use the **gnome-tigert** icon, so in the left pane of the gThumb window, navigate to **/usr/share/pixmaps**. Once there, look for the **gnome-tigert.png** file, click it once, and then go to the **Image** menu and select **Resize**. This will bring up the Scale Image window (see Figure 14-5) where you can change the width of the icon to 36 pixels (the height will change automatically, as long as the **Keep aspect ratio** box is checked). Once you are done, click **Scale**.

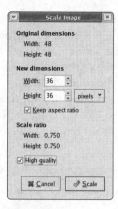

Figure 14-5: Scaling an image in gThumb

Now you need to save the newly sized icon to your Home folder, while keeping the original as it was. To do this, go to the **File** menu and select **Save As**, which will bring up the Save Image window. Save the file as gnome-tigert_emblem.png in your Home folder. You can do this either by navigating through the folders in that window or by changing the text in the Selection box at the bottom of that window from gnome-tigert.png to /home/username/gnome-tigert_emblem.png. After either method, click **Save**.

14C-2: Adding the Newly Sized Image to the Emblem Collection

Now that you have an image of the appropriate size, it is time to add it to your system's collection of emblems. To do this, open a Nautilus window, go to the **Edit** menu, and then select **Backgrounds and Emblems**. Once the Backgrounds and Emblems window opens, click the **Emblems** button on the left side of the window, and then click the **Add a New Emblem** button at the bottom of that window. This will bring up a small Create a New Emblem window (see Figure 14-6).

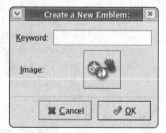

Figure 14-6: Adding a new emblem to your collection

Start out by giving your emblem a name. As the image is that of a tiger, I called mine Kitten Stuff, but you can call it something else if you like. Just type the name in the **Keyword** box.

After you have done that, it is time to work on adding your new emblem to your system's emblem collection. To do this, just click the big button next to the word **Image**. This will open the Select Image window. As your new emblem is in your Home folder, change the path at the top of the window so that it reads /home/username/gnome-tigert_emblem.png, and then press ENTER.

The Create a New Emblem window should now disappear, and your new Kitten Stuff emblem (or whatever you called it) will appear in the Emblems window (see Figure 14-7). Now you can use your new emblem as you would any other.

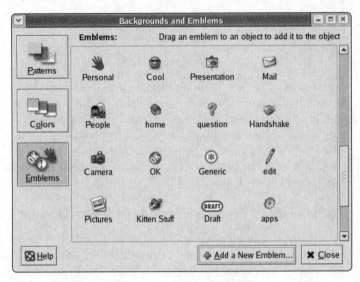

Figure 14-7: A new emblem (Kitten Stuff) in the Emblems window

Creating Your Own Icons (and Emblems)

With all the available graphics programs you've seen in this chapter, you might well be inspired to create some icons of your own. Or maybe you just want to add some sunglasses to hide Tigert's dazed and confused expression. If so, you will want to try out Icon Editor, which allows you to create new or modify existing icons, pixel by pixel (see Figure 14-8). If you've never tried this sort of thing before, it can take some getting used to, so make sure that you save whatever file you are working on under another name before getting to work (just in case you really make a mess of an otherwise handsome icon).

To run Icon Editor, just go to the Main menu and select **Graphics > More Graphics Applications > Icon Editor**.

Scanning

Scanner support in Linux is still rather spotty in terms of hardware, but this is more the fault of the manufacturers than the Linux community. Basically, to figure out whether or not your scanner will work, hook it up to your computer before starting up. Then, once you are logged in and ready, go to the Main menu and select **Graphics > Scanning**. This will bring up the Sane scanning program. If Sane can recognize your scanner as is, the main program windows will open (see Figure 14-9), and you can begin scanning.

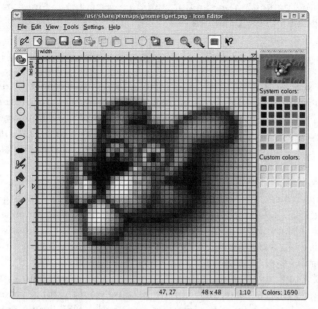

Figure 14-8: Modifying an icon in Icon Editor

If Sane cannot recognize your scanner, or if you are trying to figure out what type of scanner to buy, you will probably want to go to the Sane Web site to see what scanners are supported, or if you can get yours to work with a little tweaking. The URL for the Sane hardware support page is www.sane-project.org/sane-mfgs.html.

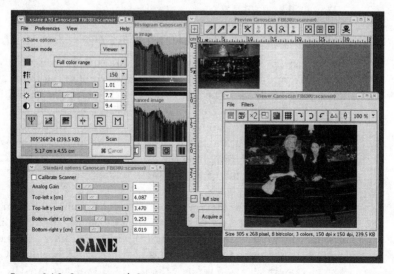

Figure 14-9: Scanning with Sane

If your scanner is part of one of Hewlett-Packard's all-in-one scanner/printer combinations (a multifunction device) you will need to install **libsane-hpoj**, which you can install via the Package Management window, which you learned to use in Chapter 8. You can find and then select **libsane-hpoj** by clicking the **Details** link next to **Graphics**.

Digital Cameras

While scanner support for Linux is still a bit spotty, support for digital cameras is significantly better. Linux supports over 400 cameras through the gPhoto2 digital camera software package, which is a part of the default installation in Fedora Core. To see if your camera is supported, go to the gPhoto2 project page (www.gphoto.org), and scroll down and click the link that says **400 cameras**. Once on that page you will find a complete list of all the cameras supported by gPhoto2. If your camera isn't on the list, it most likely means (as that page points out) that your camera is so old that there is little demand for support for it or that it is so new that there hasn't been enough time to develop support for it. Of course, gPhoto2 is constantly being updated, so if your camera isn't on the list now, it could very well be so in the future. Updating gPhoto2 with Synaptic now and again, should keep you as up to date as possible.

If your camera is not currently supported by gPhoto2 and you really want to get cracking right away, all is not lost because you can still get your images to your hard disk by setting up your system to work with a USB flash memory card reader, as I discussed in Chapter 12. After adding your card reader to your system's *fstab* file, remove the flash media card from your camera, pop it into your USB card reader, and then mount the reader by right-clicking your desktop and selecting **Disks > cardreader** (or whatever you named it). Once you've done that, it is a simple drag-and-drop process to get the images to your hard disk. Of course, you can use this method even if your camera is supported, which I think is the easiest way to deal with things.

Viewing, Copying, and Deleting Images with gtKam

If your camera is supported by gPhoto2, and you prefer to access your photos directly from your camera rather than fiddle with flash storage cards, then gtKam is the program to use. The gtKam program is essentially a graphical front end to gPhoto2 and is also installed by default in Fedora Core. Before running gtKam, however, you need to connect your camera to your computer, usually via a USB cable. Once you've done that, turn your camera on and set it to communicate with your computer. Switching the camera to **Play**, rather than **Camera**, mode usually seems to do the trick, but you should check your owner's manual just to be sure.

Once your camera is connected and set, you can run gtKam by going to the Main menu and selecting **Graphics > Digital Camera Tool**. The first time you run gtKam, you will have to set it up to recognize your camera. This is quite easily done by going to the **Camera** menu and selecting **Add Camera**. Once you do this, a small camera selection window (Figure 14-10) will appear. The easiest way to go about things is to let gtKam find your camera itself by clicking the **Detect** button.

Within a second or two, gtKam will find your camera and select the appropriate settings. Once it has done its job, just click **Apply** and then **OK**. An icon for your camera will then appear in the left pane of the gtKam window.

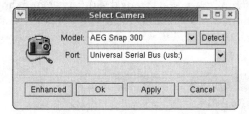

Figure 14-10: Configuring gtKam to work with your digital camera

Now that gtKam is ready, you can easily access your files by clicking the little + symbol next to the camera icon in the left pane of the gtKam window. This will reveal the folders that are present on the flash storage card in your camera. Click any folder (or folders) you wish to view, and the contents will appear as thumbnailed images in the right pane of the gtKam window (see Figure 14-11).

Figure 14-11: Accessing your images with gtKam

To copy images to your hard disk, first select the images you want to transfer by clicking them one by one. If you want to copy them all, go to the **Select** menu and choose **Select All**. Once you are done selecting your images, click the floppy disk icon at the top left of the gtKam window. This will bring up a Save As window. The default settings in this window should be fine enough, so just click **OK** to complete the job.

You can delete images from your camera just as easily by first selecting the images you want to delete. Once done, click the trash can icon (to the right of the floppy disk icon). This will bring up a handy final confirmation window (Figure 14-12). In that window, you can deal with any second thoughts you might have by unchecking the box next to any file you don't want to delete after all. Once done, click **Delete**, and the files that are still selected will be gone for good.

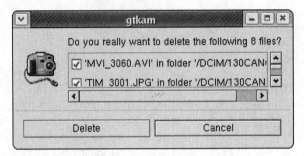

Figure 14-12: Deleting images from your camera with gtKam

15

PENGUINS BACK AT WORK

Getting Down to Business in Linux

Well, I admit it; I've been leading you on a totally hedonistic, fun-and-games, pleasure-above-all-else, wild ride through the world of Linux, with barely a mention of anything suggestive of the workplace . . . or even of work, for that matter. I am, after all, trying to get you to see that Linux is a warm and fuzzy, fun and friendly operating system.

All this focus on fun doesn't mean, however, that Linux isn't capable behind the desk. Linux can get down to business and do it as well as the next OS. I think it's safe to say that you are missing nothing and are probably gaining quite a bit in terms of home and office productivity programs in the world of Linux. In this chapter, I'll walk you through the Linux offerings in this department.

OpenOffice.org

Whether they should be or not, people are quite obsessed with office suites, even though most people seldom need more than a word processor. The de facto standard among office suites is Microsoft Office, which is available in both the Windows and Macintosh worlds. Of course, as it is a Microsoft product, you can be quite sure that there is no Linux version available.

Fortunately, Linux does have an exceedingly capable office suite in the form of OpenOffice.org, which is, incidentally, also freely available (as in "free") in Windows and Mac OS X versions. OpenOffice.org is not some lightweight sour-grapes substitute for the Microsoft Office–less Linux world; it is a full-featured contender, and in some cases, such as its onscreen font rendering, OpenOffice.org is a clear winner.

Like most other office suites, OpenOffice.org consists of a word processor, a spreadsheet program, a presentation program, and a couple of other programs. The main three applications are compatible with their Microsoft Office equivalents (Microsoft Word, Excel, and PowerPoint, respectively) in terms of both reading and writing files, and as the basic look and feel of these applications is fairly similar to Microsoft Office, switching over to the OpenOffice.org applications should be relatively easy. If you don't have any experience with Microsoft Office, you should still find it all pretty straightforward, as the basic layout is pretty intuitive. And if you are lacking in the intuition department, the built-in help files are pretty good, too.

To get OpenOffice.org up and running, launch the application you wish to use (I'd recommend the word processor for now) by going to the Main menu, selecting **Office**, and then selecting the office application of your choice. Remember that the launchers for the word processor and spreadsheet should still be on your panel too.

Turning On Tips

Once you have started one of the OpenOffice.org programs, I suggest turning on OpenOffice.org's Tips function to help you along the way as you take a further look at the applications that make up the OpenOffice.org suite. OpenOffice.org's Tips system is just like similar systems in the Windows and Mac worlds. In fact, you have a similar feature in the GNOME environment, though it doesn't carry through to OpenOffice.org.

In case you aren't sure what I'm talking about, tips are those little yellow boxes that pop up to tell you what a button or menu item does when you place your mouse over that button or menu item. Figure 15-1 shows the two types of tips available in OpenOffice.org applications: the usual short variety and the more verbose extended variety.

To activate Tips, go to the **Help** menu and select **Tips**, and if you prefer a bit more verbiage, select **Extended Tips** as well.

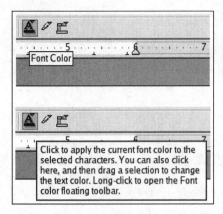

Figure 15-1: The two types of tips in OpenOffice.org: standard (top) and extended (bottom)

Getting to Know Those Other Buttons

Now that you have Tips activated, you should have no trouble figuring out what the various buttons and menu items in the OpenOffice.org applications do. There are, however, a few buttons that most likely require, or at least deserve, a bit more explanation (see Figure 15-2).

Figure 15-2: The Function toolbar in OpenOffice.org

The first odd button is situated just to the left of the printer icon. This is the **PDF** button, and you can use it to export your document as a PDF file. This button is a new feature in OpenOffice.org 1.1.0, though the actual PDF-creating function was present in previous versions of OpenOffice.org via the Print dialog box. As mentioned in Chapter 6, PDF files can still be created via the Print dialog box in OpenOffice.org version 1.1.0.

There are four other strange-looking buttons at the right end of the toolbar shown in Figure 15-2. These four buttons are all actually toggle switches, meaning that they open a certain window when clicked and then close the same window when clicked again. From left to right, these buttons toggle the Navigator window, the Stylist window, the Hyperlink window, and the Gallery.

- **Navigator window**   The Navigator window (see Figure 15-3 on the next page) is a pretty cool navigational feature that comes in handy when working with lengthy or otherwise complex documents. Navigator allows you to easily bounce back and forth between pages in a document, or even between elements therein. Let's say that you have a document with lots of illustrations in it (like this chapter), and you want to jump directly from graphic to graphic. In this case, you would click the word **Graphics** in the main pane of the Navigator window and then click the jump buttons (the odd little buttons to the left of the page number selector) to begin jumping.

Figure 15-3: The Navigator window

- **Stylist window** The Stylist window allows you to apply various styles (chapter headings, paragraph styles, numbering, and so on) to sections of text.

- **Hyperlink window** The Hyperlink window allows you to assign links to specified documents — not only to Web pages, but also to documents on an individual computer. While a hyperlink on a Web page is something we have all come to take for granted, the idea of hyperlinking between text documents sounds like a pretty radical concept. It is, in fact, a rather old one that has been around since before you or I had even heard of the Internet.

- **Gallery** The Gallery is a library of graphical elements for use in your documents or Web pages (see Figure 15-4). These elements range from various lines to buttons to colored three-dimensional doughnuts, and you can even add your own.

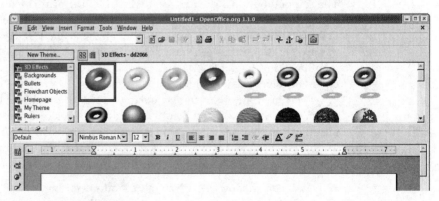

Figure 15-4: The Gallery

Inserting a graphic into your document is a simple enough task even when not using the Gallery. All you need to do is go to the **Insert** menu, select **Graphics > From File**, and then locate the image file you want to insert. It is handier to use the Gallery, however, when you intend to use certain graphics frequently. Once in the Gallery, your graphics are always only a click or two away and can be conveniently viewed in the Gallery browser window.

Adding your own graphics to the Gallery is also relatively easy to do. First you have to create a new category (called a *theme*) for each group of images you wish to add. To create a Gallery theme of your own, just click the **New Theme** button in the Gallery window. This will open the New Theme Properties window, where you should first click the **General** tab and give your theme a name. Once you've done that, click the **Files** tab, and then the **Find Files** button, which will bring up a Select path window. From there you can navigate to the folder in which you are storing your clip art, photos, or other graphics. Once you have found the folder, click the **Select** button, after which a list of all the files in that folder will appear in New Theme Properties window.

Now, you can easily add images to your new Gallery theme by clicking on the name of each image you wish to add (you might want to make sure that **Preview** is checked to make things a bit easier), and then clicking the **Add** button. Once you have done that, a copy of the image will immediately appear in the Gallery browser, where it will remain for future use. To use one of the images in the gallery, just right-click on the image you wish to insert into your document, and then select **Copy** or **Link** in the pop-up menu.

The OpenOffice.org Applications

The entire OpenOffice.org office suite consists of five applications: a word processor (Writer), a spreadsheet (Calc), a presentation creator and player (Impress), a vector drawing program (Draw), and a mathematical formula editor (Math). All of these applications can be accessed by going to the Main menu and selecting **Office**. In addition, Panel launchers for the main three applications (Writer, Impress, and Calc) are available in the default Fedora Core setup, though you probably removed the Impress launcher while following along with Chapter 3.

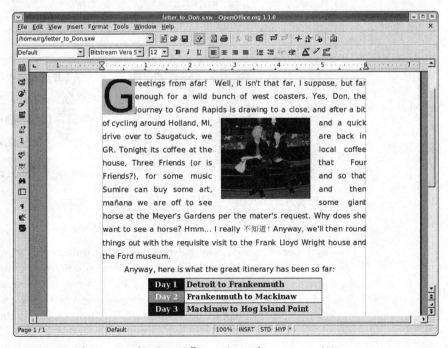

Figure 15-5: A letter created in OpenOffice.org's word processor — Writer

Let's look briefly at each of the applications, though as I'm a bit of a mathematics dunce, I don't think I will venture into the realm of what you can do with Math.

Writer

As I mentioned earlier, the word processor is the office application that the majority of users turn to most often. Fortunately, OpenOffice.org Writer is a good one (see Figure 15-5 on the previous page). It is chock-full of features and can even read and save Microsoft Word files. Like Word, it will even let you save your pages as HTML files so that you can easily change your documents into Web pages.

As I said, Writer is a very straightforward word processor, so I won't go on about it, but if you would like to see a little intro on using Writer, check out the first steps tutorial at the OpenOffice.org Web site (www.openoffice.org/writer-firststeps/writerfirststeps.html).

Calc

Calc is the OpenOffice.org spreadsheet application, and it is similar to Excel in terms of capabilities and general layout (see Figure 15-6). It can also, quite importantly, read and save Microsoft Excel files.

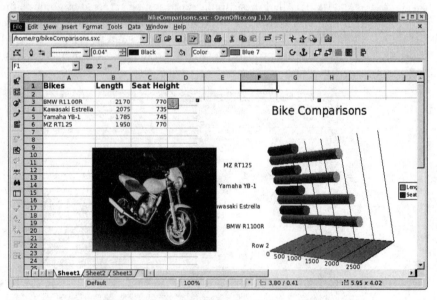

Figure 15-6: A spreadsheet created in OpenOffice.org Calc

As most people who use spreadsheets generally understand what they are all about and, after a bit of poking around, can figure out how to use them, I won't go into any sort of primer about using Calc. However, as there are many others who don't see any need to even try using spreadsheets, I will mention a few of the simpler things that can be done with Calc, in the hope of enticing some of you into trying it.

Most people who don't use spreadsheets think of them as a sort of giant calculator used for computing uncomfortably large sets of numbers, like payrolls (which was the original purpose of such applications). That's right, of course, but spreadsheets can be used for everyday tasks too, such as projecting household budgets, calculating grade point averages (for teacher or student), figuring out how long it will take you to save up for your trip to Hungary, or even for something as weird as comparing the seat heights for the four or five motorcycles you are trying to choose among. And when doing any of these minor mathematical tasks, you can easily create graphs in order to make all the abstract numbers speak to you visibly.

If numbers are just not your thing, you can still use Calc for creating lists of information, such as birthday lists, class rosters, shopping lists, address lists . . . whatever. You can even have Calc put the lists into alphabetical order, or sort them by date of birth, and so on.

Impress

Impress (Figure 15-7) is OpenOffice.org's answer to Microsoft's PowerPoint, with which it is compatible. It allows you to create graphically attractive slides for use in presentations and also allows you to create notes or handouts to accompany them. While these features make Impress quite handy in business and education settings, you may not find it of as of much value as a home user.

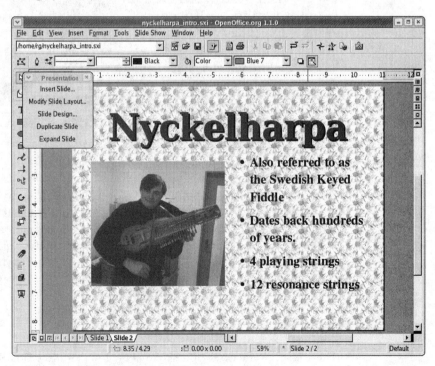

Figure 15-7: Preparing a presentation in OpenOffice.org Impress

Draw

More useful to the home user is OpenOffice.org Draw. Although Draw isn't all that great a program for creating true graphics in the art sense, it is very useful for creating flowcharts, organizational diagrams (like seating arrangements for wedding receptions or conferences), or any other document in which you want a bit more control over the placement of text and graphics (especially when the two are combined), such as for fliers, awards, diagrams, and newsletters. In this sense, OpenOffice.org Draw can be used quite effectively as a simple page layout program, as you can see in Figure 15-8.

Figure 15-8: A newsletter created (and displayed) in OpenOffice.org Draw

Math

Finally, we come to OpenOffice.org's Math. As I am a bit out of it in terms of math, I can't really tell you much more about Math other than it is a mathematics formula editor that allows you to produce complex mathematical formulae and then paste them as embedded objects into other OpenOffice.org programs. It is strictly an editor and does not calculate. I think I am safe in saying that most common folk have no need for it in their everyday lives, unless, of course, you write Math textbooks for a living.

Another Office Suite

There is yet another free office suite in the Linux world called KOffice, which is the KDE office suite that is also included in Fedora Core. I've never found much use for KOffice, as it is not as intuitive to use as one would expect, and it comes with a lot of rather useless extras that just waste space, at least in my mind.

If you are interested in KOffice, however, you can find out more by going to http://koffice.kde.org. If you think you'd like to install it after giving that site a look, you can do so quite easily via the Package Management window. Just go to the Main menu and select **System Settings > Add/Remove Applications**. When the Package Management window opens, scroll down to the **Office and Productivity** section and click the **Details** link. Once you've done that, the Package Details window will open — just check the checkbox next to **koffice**. Click **Close** to close the Details window, and then click **Update** in the Package Management window.

AbiWord

AbiWord used to have the distinction of being the only true cross-platform word processor because it came in Linux, Mac, and Windows versions. This, along with the fact that it was free, meant that many people used it. However, now that OpenOffice.org is also available on all three platforms (and is equally free), AbiWord has lost its claim to fame in that regard.

Nevertheless, AbiWord still has its place in the total scheme of things. Most importantly, AbiWord is fairly quick. After all, there may be some of you who don't really need all the power of Writer (at least not all of the time) and would prefer something that pops up as soon as you click the launcher, and that doesn't take more than a minute or so to figure out how to use (see Figure 15-9).

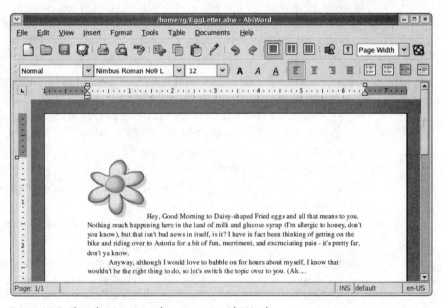

Figure 15-9: The other Linux word processor — AbiWord

AbiWord has a very straightforward and easy-to-use interface, which you should be able to figure out without much, if any, help. It also has a couple of rather interesting features, such as its auto-resize function, which magnifies the onscreen document size (fonts, images, and everything) or shrinks it as you increase or decrease the size of the program window. Another is AbiWord's ability to read and save files in an amazing number of formats, including Microsoft Word (.doc), OpenOffice.org Writer (.sxw), and many other familiar (and some unfamiliar) formats.

If you have used AbiWord in the Linux environment in the past, then you may have come away from AbiWord less than pleased with its absolutely dreadful onscreen font rendering. I personally found the look so annoying that I couldn't stand using it. Fortunately, things have changed. Fonts now look quite good (though not as good as the absolutely beautiful onscreen font rendering in OpenOffice.org), as does the whole interface, which has been, shall we say, totally GNOME-ized. All around, AbiWord is just plain better.

You can easily install AbiWord with APT/Synaptic. Just run Synaptic, type abiword in the **Find** box, and then . . . well, you know the drill by now. If you installed your Fedora Core or Red Hat Linux system from a 3-CD installation disk set, AbiWord will be on those disks, so you can install it via the Package Management window if you prefer. Just click the **Details** button next to **Office/Productivity**, and then check the checkbox next to **abiword**. Once you have AbiWord installed, you can run it by going to the Main menu and selecting **Office > More Office Applications > Word Processor**.

Some Other Cool Productivity Apps

In addition to the traditional office suite applications, there are a number of other applications included with your system that can be grouped together under the "productivity" label. You've already heard mention of (and perhaps even installed) the Linux home finance program, GnuCash, but there are many other applications that are installed and available to you, such as the following:

- Gcalctool, a calculator with both basic and scientific modes (from the Main menu select **Accessories > Calculator**)

- Gpdf, the GNOME PDF file viewer (from the Main menu select **Graphics > More Graphics Applications > PDF file viewer**)

- Kdeprintfax, a fax sending and receiving utility (from the Main menu select **Accessories > kdeprintfax**)

- Dia, the diagram creator (from the Main menu select **Office > Dia Diagrams**)

- Mr. Project, the work-project manager (from the Main menu select **Office > Project Management**)

In addition to these more or less standard utilities, there are also some other rather interesting applications installed on your system. One of these is KTimer, which allows you to run a command at the end of a given time period (see Figure 15-10). For example, let's say that you want to make sure that you take a break from your work every hour so as to keep yourself sane. You can set up KTimer so that it will bring up your favorite game, Xmahjongg, in one hour by selecting the number of seconds in the **Delay** box (3,600 seconds is an hour), checking the **Loop** checkbox (if you want this to happen again and again, every hour), and entering the command you desire to be executed (xmahjongg in this example). You can run KTimer by going to the Main menu and selecting **Accessories > More Accessories > KTimer**.

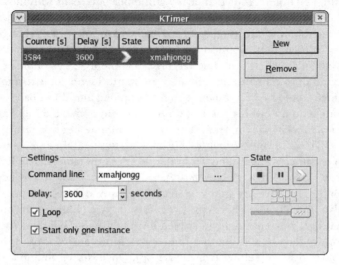

Figure 15-10: Setting up an hourly command with KTimer

Another fun and handy application is KJots (see Figure 15-11). KJots is a notepad of sorts, and it is organized into books and pages. Books are general topic areas that you create, and they are filled with pages, where you write, or jot down, your notes. There is also a Hotlist section at the bottom of the window, where you can place buttons that take you directly to those books you need most often. All in all, it's a very simple piece of software, but once you start using it, you'll find that it is quite useful. To run KJots, just go to the Main menu and select **Accessories > More Accessories > Kjots**.

Figure 15-11: Making notes with KJots

Making Your Own Tarballs (and ZIP Files) with File Roller

One of the most useful non–office applications is one you are already familiar with: File Roller. You've untarred a number of tarballs with the assistance of File Roller while doing the projects in this book. However, until now you haven't learned how to use it to create a tarball of your own. Let's change that right now.

You might be wondering why on earth you would want to create a tarball. Well, let's say that you want to send a document and a couple of images to a friend of yours via email. The files you want to send come to a total of 669KB, which would make a somewhat lengthy upload and download via a modem connection. To bring this size down a bit, and to make things easier to manage on the receiving end, you can pack these all together in a tarball.

To make your tarball (or ZIP file), go to the Main menu and select **Accessories > File Roller**. This will open the now-familiar File Roller window. In that window, click the **New** button. A New Archive window will open. With this window, you are first going to create an empty archive, into which you can later place the files you wish to pack together. Type a name for the archive, and type .zip as the extension if you are sending the file to a Windows user, or .tar.gz if you are sending it to another Linux user (Linux and Mac users should actually be able to deal with either type of archive). Once you've done that, click **OK**, and the still-empty archive will be created.

The easiest way to fill your archive with files is to just drag the files you want to the File Roller window of your new archive. You can add the files one by one, or you can add them by dragging and dropping an entire folder. Once you do this, File Roller will archive the files, and the new additions will appear in the File Roller window (see Figure 15-12). Oh, and don't worry, your original files will still be where they were — safe and untouched.

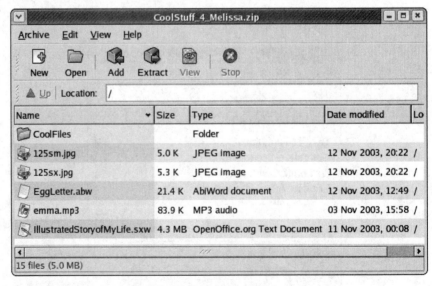

Figure 15-12: Creating a tarball or ZIP file with File Roller

Once the files appear in that window, you are done, and you can close File Roller and send your archived file to your friend. Note, however, that sometimes when the first item you drag to the archive is a folder, it will not appear in the archive window until you add yet another file, even though it is in fact there. This is a quirk in File Roller, but it is just superficial, so if the only item you are going to archive is a folder, worry not. You cannot save an empty archive, so if your archive appears in your folder or subfolders, you know you were successful.

Project 15A: Checking Your System for Viruses (Optional)

While we are still dealing with the serious side of things, we might as well make brief mention of viruses. It is true that most of the viruses that make the news are aimed at Windows systems and make use of Windows versions of Outlook and Outlook Express email clients to spread themselves far and wide. This does not mean, however, that Linux is immune to viruses. Because many Linux users think that viruses only happen to Windows, Linux systems are often unprotected and are an attractive potential target, especially as the number of Linux users continues to grow. There is also always the possibility that your system may be used as a way station of sorts, passing a virus from someone else to one of your associates (and guess who'll get the blame). So, while you really don't have too much to worry about yet, it is always better to be safe than sorry.

As Windows is the number one target of viruses, the number of virus-scanning applications for Windows is far greater than the number for Linux. Of these Linux applications, many are somewhat cumbersome for the beginner to use, and most require you to pay for the right to use them. One program, called F-Prot Antivirus, by an Icelandic company called Frisk Software International (www.f-prot.com), however, is available for free for "personal users on personal workstations." If you are part of the readership I had in mind, then this means that F-Prot Antivirus is free for you. F-Prot Antivirus comes as an RPM file and is thus very easy to install. It is also very easy to use, even though it is run from the Linux Command Terminal and, thus, has no graphical interface.

Getting and Installing F-Prot Antivirus

To get F-Prot Antivirus, click the **RPM Package** link on the F-Prot download page at www.f-prot.com/download/download_fplinux_personal.html. You will then be presented with a form in which you will have to supply your name, email address, location, and country. When you are finished filling in the form, click the **Submit and start download** button at the bottom of the page. When the download process is done, the **fp-linux-ws.rpm** file will appear in your Home folder. Just double-click the file to install it.

15A-1: Using F-Prot Antivirus

Before using F-Prot Antivirus, it is probably best that you update its virus database so that you can catch the newest of the viral meanies. To do this, you use an update script that is installed along with F-Prot Antivirus. Open a Terminal window, become root with the **su** command, type `/usr/local/f-prot/tools/check-`

updates.pl, and press ENTER. The script will then contact the F-Prot server, check for updated virus information, download whatever there is available, and then install it — while, of course, telling you everything it is doing along the way.

Once you have updated the virus database, you are ready to use F-Prot Antivirus. As I already mentioned, F-Prot Antivirus is command driven, but the commands themselves are quite simple. The basic command structure consists of the main command, **f-prot**, plus the directory or files you want to scan. For example, if you want to scan your entire hard disk to see if you have any viruses there, you first become root, and then type f-prot / and press ENTER. F-Prot then scans your entire hard disk to check for known viruses. This will probably take, depending on the speed of your system and the number of files on it, around 30 minutes, so you had better do it while having lunch. When the scanning is complete, F-Prot Antivirus will show you its results, as in Figure 15-13.

As you can see, F-Prot Antivirus tells you how many files it scanned, how long it took to do so, how many of those files were suspicious (meaning files that seemed odd to F-Prot, but did not match up with any known virus in the database), and how many were actually infected.

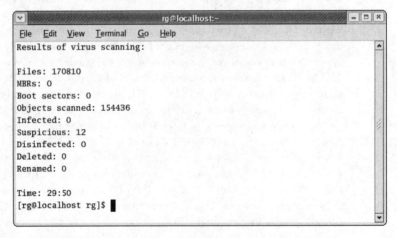

Figure 15-13: The results of an F-Prot Antivirus scan

One of the problems with the simple command string used in the previous example is that F-Prot Antivirus will give you no feedback while it is doing its business — you will see nothing in the Terminal until F-Prot is finished, it displays its results, and your user prompt reappears. I find this a bit disconcerting, so I prefer to add the **-list** flag to the **f-prot** command, which makes F-Prot show you every file it is scanning while it is doing so. This reassures you that F-Prot is doing what it is supposed to be doing (and gives you some indication of its progress).

If this sounds better to you, open a Terminal window, become root, type this command, and press ENTER:

```
f-prot -list /
```

If you only want to scan your Home folder, then type this version of the command and press ENTER:

```
f-prot -list /home/username/
```

You can also scan just a single file, if you like, by using this version of the command:

```
f-prot /home/username/mysuspiciousfile.xxx
```

Of course, in this last version I left the **-list** flag out, as there is only one file being scanned. No need to show a list of F-Prot's progress when you already know the file it is scanning.

That is all easy enough. However, all you have done is scan your disk to look for viruses. If you want F-Prot Antivirus to disinfect any infected files it finds, you need to add yet another flag to the command string, **-disinf**. To use the **-disinf** flag along with your command, you just need to type the following and press ENTER:

```
f-prot -disinf -list /
```

When F-Prot finds a file in need of disinfection, it will first seek your okay before doing so.

You now know just about all that you need to know to use F-Prot Antivirus, but if you would like to read the documentation itself and find out about a few more options available to you, you can do so at www.f-prot.com/support/helpfiles/unix/linux_ws/index.html.

16

FONT FEATHERED FRENZY

Adding New Fonts to Your System

There are basically two kinds of fonts: bitmap and outline. The difference between these two is essentially the same as that between bitmap and vector graphics, which I discussed in Chapter 14.

Bitmap characters are stored as a map of dots — the bitmap. The main limitation of bitmaps is that they only look good at the size and resolution they were designed for. Just like bitmap images, the more you enlarge a bitmap character, the worse it looks. This is particulary noticeable in rounded characters, such as O and P, where "the jaggies" becomes an issue.

Outline fonts, on the other hand, are similar in concept and design to vector graphics. Each character is stored as a mathematical formula, and just like vector graphics, outline characters keep their clean shape no matter how much you enlarge them. The main outline font formats are Type 1, or PostScript, which was developed by Adobe, and TrueType, which was developed by Apple. As free TrueType fonts are so easy to deal with, so readily available on the Net, and so easily handled in Fedora Core, I will focus on TrueType fonts in this chapter.

Your Fedora system comes with a wide variety of very usable and, at least to my eyes, rather handsome TrueType fonts. However, these tend to be a bit on the conservative side of the aesthetic spectrum, and many users tend to want to add a few somewhat more distinctive, usually wilder, fonts to the system repertoire. In my own case, I had this really cool idea of writing messages to my friend in old Scandinavian runes. Of course, my friend wet-blanketed the whole idea, so it all came to naught.

You probably won't be interested in sending cryptic runic messages to your friends, but you may want to print out an award for some event using some sort of Gothic font, or you might be preparing a newsletter for your local chapter of the snail breeders' society and want to use a font that is round, bubbly, and slimy. Whatever your penchant, purpose, or desire, you will probably come to the point when you want to install some other TrueType fonts on your system.

Before you install anything, of course, you have to find some fonts. The Internet is a good source, of course, and there are many sites that have a variety of freeware, shareware, and for-sale TrueType fonts available for download. When choosing and downloading fonts, it is best to select those designed for Windows rather than those for Mac. Fonts designed for the Windows world will most likely be in the form of ZIP files, and this will pose no problem for you, because once they are on your machine you can extract them with File Roller. Simply double-click them, just as you have with the other tarballs you have used thus far, and go through the File Roller steps you learned in Chapter 9. Once you've done this, the font file will appear as an icon showing an upper- and lowercase sample of the first letter in that font (see Figure 16-1).

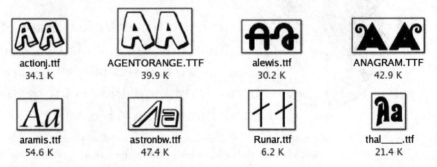

Figure 16-1: Font icons display the first letter in the font

In addition to getting a glimpse of what the fonts look like through these icons, you can also see all, or at least almost all, of the characters in a given font by double-clicking the font icon. A window, as shown in Figure 16-2, will open, showing you most of the characters in A-to-Z format and then in the traditional "The quick brown fox jumped over the lazy dog" format that you may well remember from your junior or senior high school typing classes.

Figure 16-2: Previewing a font by double-clicking the font icon

Installing Fonts

At the present time, there are two ways in which Fedora deals with fonts, which means there are two ways to install fonts, depending on what applications you want to make the fonts available to. Rather than twist your mind by explaining the technical aspects of these differences, I will instead just tell you how to install fonts by each method and which applications each installation method will make the fonts available to. Fortunately, the easier of these two installation methods will probably be the only one in the future, but for now you'll need to know about both.

Project 16A: Installing TrueType Fonts Using the Easy Method

This first font installation method is the easier, and newer, of the two, and it requires almost no effort on your part. For the sake of convenience, I will refer to the installation process for such fonts as "the easy method."

Fonts installed using the easy method can be used by the *fontconfig* font subsystem, which handles the fonts for the vast majority of applications installed on your system. Such fonts will be available to GNOME and KDE applications, to

Mozilla, and, with a tad more tinkering, to OpenOffice.org. These fonts are also available to your system for customizing GNOME and KDE. Basically, if you're not trying to install fonts for use with the GIMP, this easy method is the method to use.

Slightly different installation steps are required depending on whether you install the fonts locally (for use only by the user who installs them) or globally (for use by all users on the computer). To keep things easy, I will begin with the local installation process, as that is by far the easiest of all.

Getting the Font Files

The Internet is awash in free fonts. For this project, I will point you to the www.fontfreak.com site, which has a very nice collection of fonts. Once you get to the FontFreak splash page, click **ENTER**, which will lead you to the main page. Once there, click the button on the left that says **PC Fonts**, which will bring you to the first page of PC fonts. You can browse through the various pages until you find some fonts to your liking. Which fonts you download is completely up to you.

As you will also need fonts for Project 16B, you might as well download them now too. All in all, for the two projects, you will need eight fonts, which you should download to your Home folder (not to one of the subfolders). Be sure to unzip your font files before going on to the installation steps.

16A-1: Installing Fonts Locally Using the Easy Method

For the first step of this project, let's use one of the fonts that you downloaded. After you've decided which font to use, follow these steps:

1. Open two new Nautilus windows by clicking the Home folder launcher on your GNOME Panel twice.

2. In the **Location** box of one of the Nautilus windows, type fonts:/// and press ENTER. Once you've done this, the window will be filled with the font icons you have installed on your system.

3. From the other open Nautilus window (your Home folder window), select the unzipped font you want to install, and drag it to the **fonts:///** folder window. The first time you do this, a hidden **.fonts** subfolder will automatically be created in your Home folder.

NOTE   *You will have noticed that when you dragged your new font from your Home folder window to the **fonts:///** window, the icon for that new font file did not immediately appear. If you don't like this lack of immediate feedback, you can check your **.fonts** folder by typing ~/.fonts in the **Location** box of one of the Nautilus windows. This will show you what fonts you have installed locally — at this point there should be only one.*

4. Open a Terminal window (do *not* become root), and type the following:
   fc-cache ~/.fonts/

   Make sure there is a space between fc-cache and the tilde (~), and that there is no space between ~/ and .fonts. Then press ENTER. This updates your font cache so that your system will know that the new fonts are there and completes the installation process. The fonts are then available for use, though you will have to quit and restart any programs you have open before you can access the fonts in those programs.

16A-2: Alternative Approach to Installing Fonts Locally Using the Easy Method

If you prefer truly immediate feedback on your installation progress, you can try the following variation of the installation process, which yields the same results as in 16A-1. However, because this installation method uses the **.fonts** folder that is created in step 3 of 16A-1, you must go through the process in 16A-1 with at least one font file prior to trying this installation method. Let's use two more of the fonts you downloaded.

1. Assuming that you have already closed the two windows from 16A-1, open two new Nautilus windows by clicking the Home folder launcher on your GNOME Panel twice.

2. In one of the open Nautilus folders, type ~/.fonts/ and press ENTER.

3. In the other open Nautilus window, your Home folder window, highlight both of the fonts you want to install by holding down the CTRL key and then clicking the icon for each font. Then release the CTRL key, right-click either of the highlighted fonts, and select **Copy Files** in the pop-up menu.

4. In the **.fonts** window, right-click any open space in the window, and select **Paste Files** from the pop-up menu. The fonts will then appear in the Nautilus window.

5. Open a Terminal window (do *not* become root), and type the following:
   fc-cache ~/.fonts/
   Make sure there is a space between fc-cache and the tilde (~), and that there is no space between ~/ and .fonts. Then press ENTER.

As I mentioned before, this alternative procedure yields exactly the same results as the procedure in 16A-1. The only difference is that you will immediately see that your fonts have been copied to the **.fonts** folder. Which method you choose in the future is, therefore, strictly a matter of personal preference.

16A-3: Uninstalling Fonts Installed Locally Using the Easy Method (Optional)

Regardless of whether you used the installation method outlined in 16A-1 or 16A-2, you can uninstall any fonts installed locally via the easy method by doing the following:

1. Open the **.fonts** folder in your Home folder by typing ~/.fonts/ in the **Location** box of a Nautilus window, and drag the fonts you want to remove to the Trash.

2. Open a Terminal window (do *not* become root), and then type fc-cache ~/.fonts/ and press ENTER.

16A-4: Installing Individual Fonts Globally Using the Easy Method

The fonts you have installed thus far can only be used by you when you log in under your usual username. If, however, you want to install fonts that can be used by you and everyone else who uses your computer, the process is slightly different. We'll use only one of the fonts you downloaded for this part of the project.

The font folder for globally installed fonts is in root territory, so you will need to become root to install fonts in this way. Follow these steps:

1. Open a Terminal window and become root by using the **su** command.
2. Copy the file you want to install globally to the global font folder by typing the following command and pressing ENTER:
   `cp /home/`*username*`/`*fontname*`.ttf /usr/share/fonts/`
   Be sure to include spaces between `cp` and `/home`, and between `.ttf` and `/usr`. Also, be sure to use your username instead of *username*, and the name of your font in place of *fontname*. For example, if your username is **thucuc**, and your font is called **arachnid**, the first command would be
   `cp /home/thucuc/arachnid.ttf /usr/share/fonts/`
3. Go back to the Terminal, and type in `fc-cache /usr/share/fonts/` and press ENTER to update the fonts cache and thereby complete the installation process. You still need to be root to do this.

16A-5: Installing Several Fonts Globally Using the Easy Method

If you want to install several fonts globally at the same time, you can do so quite easily. The process is essentially the same as in 16A-4, with a slight variation.

1. Create a new subfolder in your Home folder window called `ezglofonts`.
2. Place all of the fonts you want to install via this method into the new **ezglofonts** folder. Let's use two of your new fonts for now.
3. Open a Terminal window and become root by using the **su** command.
4. Copy all of the fonts in your **ezglofonts** folder to the main global font location by typing the following command and pressing ENTER:
   `cp /home/`*username*`/ezglofonts/*.ttf /usr/share/fonts/`
   Note that you do not need to type in the names of the fonts, as the wildcard character (*) is essentially telling your system to copy all files ending in .ttf within the **ezglofonts** folder. You should replace *username* with your own username, of course.
5. Go back to the Terminal, and type `fc-cache /usr/share/fonts` and press ENTER to update the fonts cache. You still need to be root to do this.

Now that you are done, you can back up the font files in the **ezglofonts** folder to CD or floppy and then trash the files. Keep the folder, however, so that you can use it again in the future.

16A-6: Uninstalling Fonts Installed Globally Using the Easy Method (Optional)

If want to remove any fonts that you installed using the global installation method in 16A-5, you can do so rather easily in the following manner:

1. Open a Terminal window and become root.

2. Type `rm /usr/share/fonts/`*fontname*`.ttf` and press ENTER. Be sure to substitute the name of the font you want to remove for the word *fontname*.

3. Update your font cache by typing `fc-cache /usr/share/fonts/` and pressing ENTER.

16A-7: Making Fonts Available to OpenOffice.org Applications

If you want to make the fonts installed either locally or globally using the easy method available to OpenOffice.org applications, you will have to go through a few extra steps. Fortunately, these steps are not very difficult.

1. Go to the Main menu and select **Office > OpenOffice.org Printer Setup**.

2. When the Printer Administration window opens, click the **Fonts** button at the bottom of the window.

3. The Fonts window will then open. Click the **Add** button at the bottom right of the window.

4. The Add Fonts window will then open. In the **Source directory** input box, type either `/home/username/.fonts/` (with no space between the backslash and the period!) to make locally installed fonts available, or type `/usr/share/fonts/` to make globally installed fonts available. A list of the fonts in the specified folder will then appear, though it might take a few seconds. If they do not appear after that, then just click in the input box again and they will.

5. If you want to make all of the fonts available, just click **Select All** and then click the **OK** button. If you only want to make some of the fonts available, hold down the CTRL key and select the fonts you want to install by clicking them. (If you only want to install one of the fonts, of course, you needn't hold down the CTRL key.) Once you are done selecting the fonts, click the **OK** button.

6. An installation progress window will open for the briefest of moments, after which you will see a tiny window saying that *x* number of fonts have been installed. Click **OK**.

You can also remove fonts for use by OpenOffice.org while in the Fonts window by selecting the fonts you want to remove and then clicking **Remove**.

Project 16B: Installing TrueType Fonts for Use with Core X

Now that you've learned the easy font installation method, let's try the second method, which is a bit more cumbersome, at least initially. This method, which I'll call the "X method," installs fonts globally for use with the much older *core X* font subsystem. In general, you don't really need to worry too much about this method unless you need to install fonts for use with the GIMP, which is not handled by fontconfig.

16B-1: Installing Fonts Using the X Method

To install fonts with the X method, follow these steps:

1. Create a new folder in your user's Home folder window and call it myxfonts.
2. Drag the fonts you want to install into the new **myxfonts** folder. Let's use the remaining two fonts you downloaded earlier.
3. Open a Terminal window and become root.
4. Create a new system folder for your new X fonts called xsysfonts by typing the following command and pressing ENTER:
   mkdir /usr/share/fonts/xsysfonts/
5. Copy the fonts from your **myxfonts** folder to the system **xsysfonts** folder by typing the following command and pressing ENTER:
   cp myxfonts/*.ttf /usr/share/fonts/xsysfonts
   This will copy all of the fonts in your **myxfonts** folder, so make sure that only the fonts you want to install are there.
6. Type cd /usr/share/fonts/xsysfonts and press ENTER to move over to the **xsysfonts** folder.
7. Type ttmkfdir > fonts.scale and press ENTER. Don't forget to put a space on either side of the > character. This, to put it simply, translates the names of the fonts in the directory into the lengthy font-naming format that the core X font subsystem understands. The font **grudge.ttf**, for example, becomes **-misc-Grudge-medium-r-normal — 0-0-0-0-p-0-iso10646-1** in core X lingo.
8. Type in mkfontdir and press ENTER. This creates an index of the fonts in the directory so that the core X font subsystem knows what's in there.
9. Finally, teach your system where to find the new **xsysfonts** folder by typing in the following command and pressing ENTER:
   /usr/sbin/chkfontpath -a /usr/share/fonts/xsysfonts

NOTE *You don't need to perform step 9 again when adding additional fonts in the future using the X method.*

You're done, so restart your machine and take a well-deserved break with the beverage of your choice. Once you're done drinking, and your computer has booted back up, you will find that your fonts appear in the font menus of most of the programs on your machine, including OpenOffice.org.

To make things easier on yourself in the future, I recommend backing up all the files in the **myxfonts** folder in your Home folder to CD or floppy. After doing that, you can trash the original fonts still in the **myxfonts** folder so as to avoid installing them again by accident and to save disk space. You might as well keep the folder itself, however, as you might want to use it again when you install new fonts in the future.

16B-2: Uninstalling Fonts Installed with the X Method (Optional)

To uninstall any of the fonts you install using the method introduced in 16B-1, follow these steps:

1. Open a new Terminal window and become root.

2. Type cd /usr/share/fonts/xsysfonts and press ENTER.

3. Type rm *fontname*.ttf (replacing *fontname* with the name of the font you want to remove) and press ENTER. Repeat this step for each of the fonts you want to remove.

4. After you have finished removing all the fonts you want to remove, type ttmkfdir > fonts.scale and press ENTER. Remember to put a space on either side of the > character.

5. Type mkfontdir and press ENTER.

6. Exit out of the Terminal. The fonts will be gone once you restart your system, though you needn't do that immediately.

Project 16C: Dual Booters: Installing Fonts from Your Windows Partition (Optional)

Now that you've learned how to mount your Windows partition (Chapter 12), there's no reason for you not to take advantage of the many fonts you have there just gathering dust. Transferring font files from your Windows system to your Linux partition for use in Fedora is fairly similar to the methods you just used in Projects 16A and 16B.

16C-1: Locating Your Windows Fonts

Regardless of which font installation method you will use to install your Windows fonts on Fedora, the first three steps in this process are the same:

1. Mount your Windows partition as explained in Chapter 12.

2. Open a new Terminal window.

3. Check the location of your Windows Fonts folder, and then in the Terminal window type cd followed by a space, followed by the Fonts folder path, and then press ENTER. Very likely, your Fonts folder path will be /mnt/windows/ WINDOWS/Fonts, but it might be slightly different (/mnt/windows/windows/Fonts, for example) depending on the version of Windows you are using.

Depending on which font installation method you will be using, the next steps differ.

16C-2: Installing Windows Fonts Locally Using the Easy Method

To install your Windows fonts locally for use with the *fontconfig* font subsystem (and most of the applications on your system), follow these steps:

1. Copy the font that you want to install to your **.fonts** folder by typing the following command and pressing ENTER:

   `cp fontname.ttf ~/.fonts/`

   You should *not* be root when doing this. Be sure to replace *fontname* with the name of the font you want to install, and replace *username* with your username. If you want to go wild and copy all of the fonts in your Windows font directory (that's a lot of fonts, mind you!), you can type *.ttf instead of *fontname*.ttf. Be sure that you have a space between cp and *fontname*.ttf and between *fontname*.ttf and ~/.fonts/.

2. Type `fc-cache ~/.fonts/` and then press ENTER. The installation will then be complete. If you want to make these fonts available for use in OpenOffice.org applications, you will also need to follow the procedure outlined in 16A-7.

16C-3: Installing Windows Fonts Globally Using the Easy Method

To easily install your Windows fonts so that all users on your machine can use them, follow these steps:

1. In your Terminal become root, and then copy the font you want to the system font folder by typing the following command and pressing ENTER:

   `cp fontname.ttf /usr/share/fonts/`

   Type `cp *.ttf /usr/share/fonts/` instead and press ENTER if you want to install all of the fonts in your Windows font directory.

2. Type `fc-cache /usr/share/fonts/` and then press ENTER, which will complete the installation process. Again, to make these fonts available for use in OpenOffice.org applications, you will now need to follow the procedure outlined in 16A-7.

16C-4: Installing Windows Fonts Using the X Method

If you would like to install your Windows fonts using the X method (for use with applications not handled by the *fontconfig* font subsystem, such as the GIMP) follow these steps:

1. In your Terminal become root, and then copy the font you want to the **xsysfonts** folder by typing the following command and pressing ENTER:

   `cp fontname.ttf /usr/share/fonts/xsysfonts/`

   Type `cp *.ttf /usr/share/fonts/xsysfonts/` instead and press ENTER if you want to install all of the fonts in your Windows font directory.

2. Type `cd /usr/share/fonts/xsysfonts` and press ENTER.

3. Type `ttmkfdir > fonts.scale` and press ENTER.

4. Type `mkfontdir` and press ENTER.

The fonts will be ready for use when you restart your system.

Windows Fonts for Non–Dual Booters

So what happens if you have a Linux-only setup, and consequently no Windows fonts, but you still have to deal with documents you receive that are written with Windows fonts? Well, fortunately you are in luck, because you can download and install the group of fonts known as Microsoft TrueType Core Fonts, which includes Arial, Times New Roman, Courier New, Comic Sans, and a few others. These fonts are actually packaged as Windows executable files (.exe), so you will also need to install a utility called **cabextract** in order to extract the fonts (the .ttf files) from the .exe files.

The cabextract utility can be downloaded and installed with Synaptic. Just type cabextract in the **Find** search box, and then follow the usual procedures that you learned in Chapter 10. To get the fonts, go to http://sourceforge.net/projects/corefonts. On that page, scroll down until you get to the **Latest File Releases** section. There you should find three items: **cabextract**, **corefonts**, and **the fonts**. To proceed, click the **Download** link next to **the fonts**, which will take you to the download page, from which you can select the fonts you want. I would recommend installing at least Arial, Courier, and Times, because they are not only pretty standard fare out there in the computing world, but they also provide you with significant foreign language support, which could come in handy even if you don't consciously care about such things.

Once the files are downloaded, use the newly installed cabextract to get to the fonts in those .exe files. To make it easy, it is probably best to first create a new folder inside your Home folder, call the new folder mscorefonts, and then drag all the .exe files you downloaded into that folder. Once you've done that, open a new Command Terminal window and do the following (you don't have to be root to do any of this):

1. Type cd mscorefonts and press ENTER. This will take you into the mscorefonts folder.

2. Type cabextract *.exe and press ENTER. This will tell the newly installed cabextract program to extract the contents of all files ending in .exe within the mscorefonts folder.

If you look inside the mscorefonts folder, you should see the original .exe files, your new fonts (the .ttf files), and maybe even a file called **fontinst.inf**, which you can ignore. To install the fonts, just install the .ttf files by following the instructions earlier in this chapter for installing fonts using the easy method.

Customizing Your System Fonts

Now that you know how to get and install fonts, you might be itching to use some of them to further customize your system. To get started doing this, just select **Preferences > Font** in your Main menu, which will bring up the Font Preferences window (see Figure 16-3 on the next page).

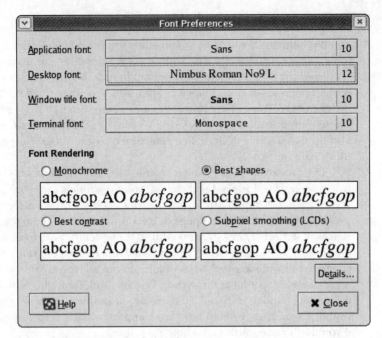

Figure 16-3: Setting system font preferences

As you will see, you can change four groups of fonts on your machine: those for your desktop; those for the titles of your windows; those for menus, applications, and the contents of Nautilus windows; and those you use when typing commands in the Terminal.

The choices you make will take effect immediately, so you will soon know whether or not you can live with them. Unlike the other aspects of customization, the font choices you make could drive you stark raving mad. Sure, it is easy and fun to live with the gaudiest desktop imaginable, the wildest and most mismatched color scheme on the planet, and the goofiest icon scheme ever to be seen by post-Neanderthal man, but if your font selections get too out of hand, watch out! Of course, you are free to do what you want, but don't blame me if you start baying at the moon.

Project 16D: Creating Your Own Fonts with PfaEdit (Optional)

After all this font talk, it seems only appropriate that we end this chapter by giving you the means to create your own fonts (or at least modify someone else's). PfaEdit allows you to create or modify TrueType, PostScript, and bitmap fonts (see Figure 16-4). The interface itself seems a bit dated, but don't let that fool you; PfaEdit is quite capable and easy to use.

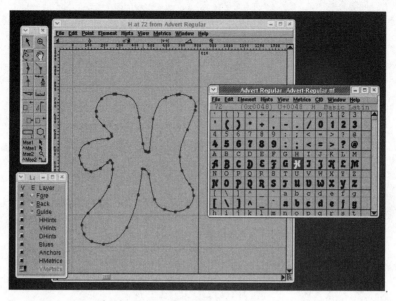

Figure 16-4: Using PfaEdit to create fonts

16D-1: Downloading, Installing, and Running PfaEdit

You can download PfaEdit from http://dag.wieers.com/packages/pfaedit. On that page, download the package appropriate for your system. If you added DAG to Synaptic's list of repositories, you can also download the PfaEdit via Synaptic. To do so just type pfaedit in Synaptic's **Find** box and then follow the procedures you learned in Chapter 10. As the package is an RPM file with no unmet dependencies, installation will go quite smoothly.

PfaEdit does not place a launcher in your Main menu once installed, so to run it you will have to either open a Terminal window, type pfaedit and press ENTER, or go to the Main menu, select **Run Application**, and then type the command pfaedit and click **Run**. Rather than do this every time, you will no doubt want to create a launcher on your own, so check out Appendix A for the launcher specs.

If you would like an overview of PfaEdit and font creation in general, go to the PfaEdit **Help** menu and select **Help**. Be sure to also check out the really great tutorial on font creation with PfaEdit by clicking the **Example** link on that overview page, or you can go to the tutorial directly, at http://pfaedit. sourceforge.net/editexample.html.

17

TUX SPEAKS YOUR LANGUAGE
Linux for Multilingual Users and Language Learners

These days, almost all operating systems are, at least to some degree, multilingual or capable of becoming so. This is true of Linux as well. Just open your Web browser and you can read, without performing any special installations, pages in any European language, including those with Cyrillic alphabets, such as Russian. You can even view pages in Chinese, Japanese, Thai, Arabic, and Hebrew, to name but a few, with only a tad more effort.

But the multilingual capabilities of Linux are much greater than this, and the way that Fedora Core has things set up makes it quite easy to take advantage of these capabilities. As you will soon see, you can even set up your system to give you a totally foreign language environment, allowing you to function completely in the language of your choice. Add to this the ever-expanding number of free programs available for language study, and you have a truly meaningful language-learning tool.

Read-Only Language Support

If all you want is to be able to read Web pages or documents written in a foreign language, you don't need to install any additional language support. In fact, it is possible that you won't have to do anything at all, depending, of course, on the language in question.

Documents or Web pages written in the Roman alphabet, such as Swedish, Italian, Malaysian, or Tagalog require no additional moves on your part. If in Chapter 16 you installed one of the Microsoft TrueType Core Fonts (specifically Arial, Courier New, or Times New Roman), you will also be able to read pages and documents written in many other languages that use the Roman alphabet but that require special diacritics, such as Vietnamese, as well as languages with alphabetic writing systems that are not Roman, such as Arabic, Hebrew, Thai, or the Cyrillic-based languages (Russian, Ukrainian, Serbian, and Bulgarian).

For other languages, however, you will probably have to install fonts for that language. When you come upon a page written in a language for which you have no font support, the text will be displayed as odd symbols, like the Hindi page shown in Figure 17-1.

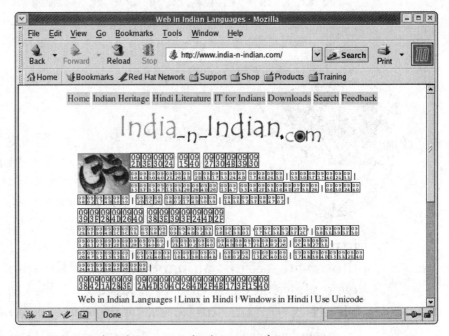

Figure 17-1: A Hindi Web page viewed without proper font support

Once you've installed the appropriate font set for the language of the page you want to view, the odd symbols will be replaced by the appropriate characters in that font. (In this case, I installed the indic.ttf font, which I downloaded from www.india-n-indian.com/download by right-clicking the **Free Indic TTF Font** link.) The result is the page being displayed as it should be (see Figure 17-2).

Figure 17-2: The Hindi Web page after the indic.ttf font is installed

Other than Hindi, the languages that will most likely require you to install specific font packages are Chinese, Japanese, and Korean. These fonts are all included on Install Disk 2. You can find the fonts by double-clicking the **Fedora** folder on that disk (the **RedHat** folder, if you are using Red Hat Linux 9 instead of the disks included with this book), and then the **RPMS** folder within that. Once you have found the fonts, copy the font package you want to the Tarballs_and_RPMs folder on your hard disk. The filenames for these fonts begin with **ttfonts**:

- **ttfonts-ko** for Korean
- **ttfonts-zh_CN** for the simplified Chinese characters used in the People's Republic of China
- **ttfonts-zh_TW** for the traditional Chinese characters used in Taiwan
- **ttfonts-ja** for Japanese

Once you've copied the files, you can install the fonts via the usual double-click method for RPMs.

If you prefer (or need) to, you can download and install any or all of these fonts with Synaptic/APT. To do this, just type ttfonts in the **Find** box in the main Synaptic window. Once you've done that, click the search arrow next to that box. You can then select the fonts you wish to install from the list that Synaptic produces as the result of your search.

Changing the Character Encoding in Mozilla

If you install your new fonts but still cannot view the pages in the language for which you installed the fonts, try changing the character coding in Mozilla. You can do this by going to the Mozilla **View** menu and selecting **Change Coding**. From the submenu there, you can select the appropriate coding for the language of that page. Mozilla will usually do this automatically, but sometimes the author of the page may neglect to include the character coding for that page in the HTML, in which case Mozilla, not knowing that the page is prepared in another language, will open in the default language of your system.

Typing Nonstandard Characters

Typing characters that are not standard in English, such as é, ç, ß, ø, æ, and å, can be done quite easily in Linux without any modifications. In most situations, you can do this by using the Unicode Character Map utility included in your system, which can be found in the Main menu under **Accessories > Unicode Character Map**. A window, like the one shown in Figure 17-3, will then appear.

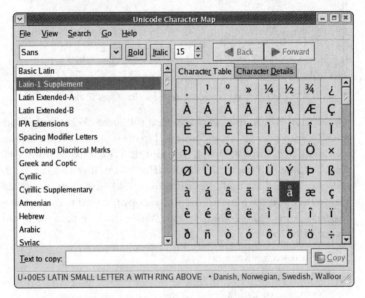

Figure 17-3: Inputting characters with the Unicode Character Map

To input the character you want, just select the language or character set in the left pane of the window, and then, in the right pane, click the character you want to input. The character will then appear in the little input box at the bottom of the window in the **Text to copy** box. Just click the **Copy** button and then paste the character wherever you want to place it.

In certain applications, such as OpenOffice.org, this method will not work. In these cases, the program most often offers a method of its own. In OpenOffice.org, for example, you can click **Insert** in the menu bar and then select **Special Character**. A selection window will open, and you can select the character you want there. Once you've done that, click the **OK** button, and the character will appear in your document, after which the selection window will close by itself.

Keyboard Layout Switcher

If you often type in a particular foreign language, it might be more convenient for you to use the **Keyboard Layout Switcher** GNOME Panel utility. This utility lets you switch quickly among various keyboard layouts. For example, if you often type in Swedish, and thus use the characters å, ä, and ö quite often, using the appropriate keyboard layout would be easier than repeatedly using the Unicode Character Map. Of course, you will have to familiarize yourself with the keyboard layout, or *keymap*, for each language you choose, but this is a relatively easy task.

The Keyboard Layout Switcher is already included in your system, so there is no need to install it. To access it, simply right-click somewhere on the GNOME Panel where you would like to place a launcher for it. Then, from the pop-up menu select **Add to Panel > Utility > Keyboard Layout Switcher**. A small icon that looks like a keycap with an American flag on it will appear in the panel.

Now, this alone will give you nothing except your default keymap, so you must configure Keyboard Layout Switcher if you want to be able to use other keymaps. To do so, just right-click the icon, and from the pop-up menu select **Preferences**, which will open the Preferences window.

To add a keymap, click on the **Add** button on the right side of the window. After you do this, another window with a list of keymaps will open up. Scroll down to the keymap for the language you want to add, and then click it. The keymaps available for that language will then appear; simply select the keymap you want, as shown in Figure 17-4. When one is available, it is usually best to choose the **xkb** layout, as it is usually coded with the most options (right-to-left text input in Arabic or Hebrew, for example).

Figure 17-4: Adding keymaps to the Keyboard Layout Switcher

Once you have selected the keymap you want, click the **Add** button and then click **Close**. This will leave you with the main Preferences window, which will then show your new keymap installed. After closing the Preferences window, the keyboard layouts can be changed by clicking the icon in the Panel. You can also change between keyboard layouts by going to the **Options** tab of the Preferences window and assigning a keyboard shortcut.

If you just want to choose a single keyboard layout to replace your present one (such as British English instead of American English or German instead of Spanish), you can do so by going to the Main menu and selecting **System Settings > Keyboard**. You will first be asked for your root password and then you will see a list of keyboard layouts that you can choose from.

Viewing Your System in Another Language

One of the many things that originally attracted me to the Linux world was being able to install language support for languages other than English. On one of my machines, I have installed support for Chinese, Japanese, Swedish, and my default, English. With just a simple logout and a few more clicks, I can log back in with an interface in a totally different language. I can have a Chinese system or a Japanese system or a Swedish system whenever I want.

This is very useful if you are going to be doing a lot of work in a foreign language, or even if you are studying a foreign language and want to give yourself as much exposure as possible to that language. It is also very handy when you have users with different native languages using the same machine. At my university, for example, where my Japanese and Chinese students sometimes use my computer, the additional language support allows them to log in using their own language. All in all, it is a very useful feature.

Taking advantage of this feature in the GNOME environment is very easy and, depending on the language you wish to use, it may require little to no special installation measures. The rule of thumb is essentially the same as for the read-only language support I mentioned earlier — if you want to view your entire system in languages with Roman-based writing systems (French, Spanish, Danish, German, Malaysian, and so on), then you don't have to do anything. And once you have installed one of the Microsoft TrueType Core Fonts, you are ready for all those languages with non-Roman writing systems I mentioned earlier as well.

Support for Chinese, Japanese, and Korean is another matter. The writing systems of these three languages are sufficiently complex as to require not only the installation of the appropriate fonts, but also the installation of a fair number of other applications to handle the input and conversion processes. Whenever possible, it is best to install additional language support for these languages during the initial system installation process described in Chapter 2. If you have already installed your system without support for these languages, but would like to add it without having to reinstall your whole system again, check out the Web page for this book (www.edgy-penguins.org/non-geeks) for information on what packages you will need to install.

Note that if you are going to be using KDE as your desktop environment in the future (or if you are already doing so on the sly), you will also need to install special KDE language files for each language you want login support for. You can find the appropriate RPM files in the RPMS folder of Install Disk X. The files will all have names like kde-i18n-Czech, kde-i18n-Arabic, and so on. If you prefer, you can use Synaptic/APT instead to add such support. To do this, just type kde-i in the **Find** box of the main Synaptic window, and then choose from the list of results for the language you want to install.

Multilingual Login

Logging in to your computer in another language is really easy. The first thing you'll have to do is get to your login screen. You can do this by starting up your computer as always and waiting for the login screen to appear, or, if you are already up and running, by selecting **Log Out** in your Main panel menu.

Once you are at your login screen, click the word **Language** at the bottom left corner of the screen.

A window with a list of all the languages available, even the ones you didn't install, will then pop up. From that list, click the language that you want to use (provided you have already installed it, of course), and then click **OK**. The language-list window will then close automatically, and you can proceed as usual by typing in your login name and password (each followed by pressing the ENTER key, of course).

A little window will then pop up asking you if you want to use the language you've chosen as your default language forever and ever. You can either click **Just for This Session** or **Make Default** depending on your personal preferences. Whatever you do end up choosing, fear not; it's no big deal to change back at a later point in time by logging out of your system, logging back in to your system under your previous default language, and clicking **Make Default**.

Your startup process will then continue, and everything will progress as it usually does. Depending on what language you've chosen, once your desktop appears you will be in another linguistic world. Your menus, desktop icon captions, and even the little Tips windows that pop up when you run your mouse over a Panel icon, will all be in the selected language. (Figure 17-5 shows the Trash and Start Here icons in a variety of languages.) Most applications you open will also appear with menus and buttons in that language.

Figure 17-5: Desktop icons in English, Hebrew, Japanese, Icelandic, and Turkish

Chinese, Japanese, and Korean Input

This section only applies to those of you who have installed Chinese, Japanese, or Korean as additional languages, or those who are planning or thinking about doing so. Of course, you can also read on if you're just curious about such things. I include this special section on these languages because they are a bit more complex to use than others.

Unlike most European languages and many other alphabet-based non-European languages, such as Thai, Arabic, and Hindi, where pressing a letter on the keyboard prints that letter to the screen, Chinese, Japanese, and Korean require a kind of conversion process, which is handled by a special application (actually a set of applications) called an Input Method Editor (IME). Of course, this is a Windows-world term, but I will use it for convenience's sake. In any case, each language has its own IME, and Fedora automatically installs the appropriate IME for each of the languages you choose to install.

Although Chinese, Japanese, and Korean all require the use of an IME to get words onto the screen, the way each operates is unique due to the different writing systems of each language.

Chinese

While most people (at least those in the linguistic know) would think that Chinese would be the most complicated system, due to the fact that the writing system consists of thousands of characters, it is in fact the simplest. The Chinese IME simply takes the Romanized keyboard input, known as *pinyin*, and converts it into Chinese characters, or *Hanzi*. For the IME, it is essentially a simple dictionary lookup task — big dictionaries, simple IME.

Here are some tips for using the Chinese IME:

- CTRL + SPACE toggles the IME.
- Select *Hanzi* by pressing the number next to the appropriate choice in the selection palette; pressing the SPACE bar selects the first choice in the list.
- The following are the Chinese TrueType fonts: AR PL KaitiM GB, AR PL SongtiL GB, ZYSong 18030.

Japanese

The Japanese IME has a considerably more complicated task to perform, as it has three writing systems to deal with: *Kanji* (ideographic characters borrowed long ago from China), the phono-alphabetic *hiragana* (used mainly for tense and case endings), and *katakana* (used mainly for words borrowed from other languages). Still, the standard input method for Japanese is primarily via the standard Roman keyboard layout, plus a few extra special-function keys. Thus, typing in Japanese is a two-step process whereby the IME first converts the Romanized text into *hiragana* as it is typed , and then converts it to appropriate *Kanji, katakana,* or *hiragana* elements after the SPACE bar is pressed.

You can see an example of these steps in Figure 17-6.

In the first line, the IME has already converted the input *rinakkusdenihongonyuuryokumodekimasu* (which means *You can also input Japanese in Linux*) to *hiragana* on the fly. In the second line, the user has pressed the SPACE bar, which caused the IME to convert the *hiragana* string into the appropriate *Kanji, hiragana,* and *katakana* elements. The first word, "Linux," has been converted to *katakana* text, as it is a borrowed word, while "Japanese input" and "can" have been converted to *Kanji*; the rest stays in *hiragana*.

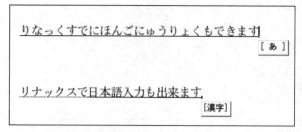

Figure 17-6: Using the Japanese IME

Here are some tips for using the Japanese IME:

- SHIFT + SPACE toggles the IME.
- Press SPACE to convert *hiragana* strings into appropriate *Kanji, katakana,* and *hiragana* elements.
- Press ENTER to accept conversions, BACKSPACE to reject.
- The Japanese TrueType fonts are Kochi Gothic and Kochi Mincho.

Korean

The job of the Korean IME is again quite different from that of the Chinese and Japanese IMEs, as the language itself is written in a very different way. Korean is written either entirely in alphabetic letters, called *Hangul,* or in a combination of *Hangul* and ideographic characters borrowed from Chinese called *Hanja.* While the *Hanja* are essentially the same as their Chinese and Japanese counterparts, *Hanzi* and *Kanji,* the Korean phonetic alphabet, *Hangul,* has it own unique appearance, as you can see in the Korean word for Korea, *Hangug(k),* in Figure 17-7.

Figure 17-7: Korea (Hangug) written horizontally in Hangul

This seems quite simple; however, the representation is not quite correct, as Korean is quite unique in the way that its alphabetic characters are put to the page. Unlike the usual side-by-side positioning of *hiragana, katakana,* and most other languages written with an alphabet, *Hangul* letters are grouped in pairs, triplets, or even quadruplets, which are written, as a general rule, clockwise. The IME, therefore, must take the input (usually based on a Korean alphabetical keyboard layout) while it is being typed and it must adjust the size, spacing, and positioning of each letter as it puts them into appropriate clusters (see Figure 17-8 on the next page).

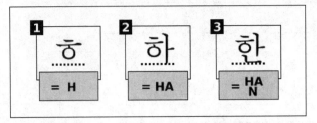

Figure 17-8: An example of the clustering process in the Korean IME

Here are some tips for using the Korean IME:

- SHIFT + SPACE toggles the IME.
- Press SPACE to accept *Hangul* clusterings.
- To convert *Hangul* to *Hanja*, press F9 before accepting *Hangul* clustering to bring up the *Hanja* selection palette. Click the appropriate choice in the palette, and then press ENTER.
- The Korean TrueType fonts are Baekmuk Batang, Baekmuk Dotum, Baekmuk Gulim, and Baekmuk Headline.

Kdeedu Language-Learning Programs

If you are learning a foreign language, you will be interested to know that there is a very useful set of programs available to you in the Kdeedu (KDE Edutainment) package, which includes a Spanish verb trainer (KVerbos), a French alphabet pronunciation program for kids (KLettres), and two flash card programs (KVocTrain and FlashKard). It also has some educational applications that have nothing to do with language learning (such as a cool star atlas).

To install any of the individual Kdeedu programs, you must install the entire kdeedu package. You can do this quite easily by using Synaptic. After starting up Synaptic, type kdeedu in the **Find** box and then follow the standard procedures you learned in Chapter 10. If you installed your system from a 3-CD Fedora or Red Hat Linux 9 installation set, you can just copy the kdeedu RPM file to your hard disk from the RPMS folder on Install Disk 3. After that, just double-click on the file to install it.

Flash Cards

As I mentioned, there are two flash card programs included in the Kdeedu package. The more complex of these is KVocTrain, which you can run by going to the Main menu and selecting **Run Program** (none of the Kdeedu apps appear in the GNOME menu). In the Run Program window, type in kvoctrain and then click **Run**.

KVocTrain is, in my opinion, needlessly complex in terms of creating your own word lists for study; however, it is quite good when studying or appending the various study lists available for it online. These files, which end in **kvtml**, include vocabulary lists, verb conjugations, and even non-language items, such as world capitals and musical key signatures. To get some of these lists, go to the Kdeedu Contributed Learning Files page at http://edu.kde.org/contrib/kvtml.php and download whatever you want to your hard drive. I would recommend creating a special folder inside your Home folder in which to keep these files. You might call the new folder kdeedu_data.

Once you've opened the files in KVocTrain, you can view the entries in them in list form or as a flash card or multiple-choice quiz (see Figure 17-9).

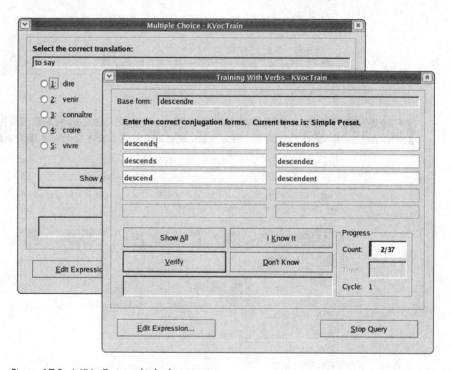

Figure 17-9: A KVocTrain multiple-choice quiz

If you are interested in a more straightforward way of creating your own flash cards, FlashKard is a more appropriate choice (though it can also use the same .kvtml files that KVocTrain uses). To run FlashKard, just go to the Main menu and select **Run Program**, and in the Run Program window, type flashkard and then click **Run**. FlashKard will then appear, and you can start inputting words that you want to study (see Figure 17-10 on the next page). After you have created a vocabulary list, you can quiz yourself, in typical flash card fashion, by going to the **Function** menu and selecting **Quiz**.

Figure 17-10: FlashKard in input and quiz modes

Project 17A: Installing the StarDict Dictionary (Optional)

One of the handiest programs available for language learners, or anyone else who needs to function in a multilingual world, is the GNOME dictionary program called StarDict (see Figure 17-11). It is a straightforward dictionary that can provide definitions in a wide variety of languages all at once.

Figure 17-11: Looking up words in StarDict

Once the program is up and running, it will display definitions from all the language dictionaries that you installed when you installed StarDict. This works in any direction, so definitions will appear for any word you type, regardless of the language. For example, I have the Eng-Swe, Swe-Eng, Ger-Swe, Swe-Jpn,

Jpn-Eng, Eng-Jpn, Chi-Eng, and Eng-Chi dictionaries all installed. If I type an English word, I will get definitions in Swedish, Chinese, and Japanese. If I type a Swedish word, I will get definitions in English and Japanese, and so on.

StarDict is also a great utility for reading text in files or Web pages because as long as the StarDict program is running, it will display definitions for words you select with your mouse in other programs. Figure 17-12 shows this inline function in action in a Web page. This inline function is called *Scan Selection*, and it also works when you are typing text into a document, or even in dialog boxes within the system itself. If you select a word, StarDict will scan it and tell you what it means.

Figure 17-12: StarDict provides inline definitions for selected text

Getting the StarDict Files

To get the latest version of StarDict, go to http://stardict.sourceforge.net and download **stardict-2.4.2-1.i386.rpm** (or a newer version) to your Tarballs_and_RPMs folder. If you happen to notice a StarDict RPM file on your installation disks, do not use it. It is not the same.

In order to use the dictionary, you will also need to download some dictionary files, usually a pair of dictionaries for each language pair (for example, English-German and German-English). You can get these by clicking on the **Dictionaries** link near the top of the Web page. Once you get to the Dictionaries page, you will see some additional links: **dictd-www.dict.org**, **dictd-www.freedict.de**, **dictd-www.mova.org**, ***Quick**, **zh_CN**, **zh_TW**, and **ja**. The FreeDict link (dictd-www.freedict.de) should have most of what you want, though you can try them all to see what they have. When you do start downloading, download the RPM files, not the tarballs — to keep things simple, of course.

17A-1: Installing StarDict and Dictionaries

The StarDict program and all the dictionaries for it are in the form of RPM files (or at least they should be if you did what I told you to do), so you will have no problems installing them. Just start off with the StarDict RPM package and double-click it. The rest of the procedure is the same as you learned in Chapter 8, so you should have no headaches.

Once done with the main program, go on to the dictionaries, which you can install in the same manner. All very easy.

17A-2: Running StarDict

Running StarDict is easy. Just go to your Main menu and select **Accessories >
More Accessories > StarDict**. StarDict will then start up and place a small applet
in the GNOME Panel. When you click this applet, it allows you to hide and show
the main dictionary window. If you right-click it, you can turn the Scan Selection
function on and off. This is very handy, because as soon as StarDict is up and
running, it will start popping up definitions any time you highlight any item of
text anywhere, which could, it seems to me, bring on the early onset of some
form of dementia.

Hungry for More?

There are, of course, other language-learning programs out there, many of
which are language specific. If you are interested in finding more, have a look at
my site for this book (www.edgy-penguins.org/non-geeks/multilingual.html),
where I list some other language-learning applications I have found and tested
on Fedora Core. There are already a couple entries for Japanese language-
learning apps (Gjiten and Kanjipad) as I am writing this, and I am always on the
lookout for more.

18

TUX UNTETHERED

Going Wireless with Linux

When notebook computers first came out, the greatest thing about them was that they freed people from their desks. People could do whatever they needed or wanted to do on their computer, wherever they wanted. As a cross-legged-on-the-floor kind of guy, a laptop was really great for me, as I could plop it down on the floor in front of the TV, and then sit there writing and gaming while playing my copy of *Wall Street* for the umpteenth time on the VCR. Yes, everything was great, but then came the Internet. Laptops suddenly became tethered to telephone lines and Ethernet cables.

Fortunately, laptops have been unleashed again as the computer world goes wireless. With the right wireless hardware, you can now use your computer just about anywhere you can catch a wave, so to speak. Whether you happen to be at your breakfast table, on your backyard deck, in the library of your university, or at your local Starbucks, you can now go online without having to physically hook your computer up to anything.

Should I Go Wireless?

Whether or not you should join the fray and go wireless is still primarily a question of personal choice and need. For example, if you don't have a laptop, there is little reason to bother, as you can't really move a desktop computer around easily; and the fact that Linux support for desktop wireless hardware is not really ready for prime time doesn't help matters. If, on the other hand, you have a laptop that you would like to use while sitting in the Santa Fe Depot in San Diego waiting for your train to L.A., or while sitting in your hotel room looking for things to do during your vacation in Seattle, or while sitting on your front porch taking in a bit of sun, then why not go for it? Whether you are ready to commit, still considering, or just plain curious, read on. . . .

Wireless Protocols

To get up to speed in the wireless world, you should first be aware of the three wireless protocols commonly in use today: 802.11a, 802.11b, and 802.11g, which are collectively referred to as *Wi-Fi* (short for wireless fidelity). In case you are wondering, a *protocol* is basically a data transmission format that has been generally agreed upon, in this case by the Institute of Electrical and Electronics Engineers (IEEE). Of these three 802.11 protocols, average home users need only concern themselves with 802.11b and 802.11g, as the hardware for these protocols is considerably less expensive than that for 802.11a, which is primarily used in large office environments.

The faster of the two protocols is 802.11g, which has a transmission speed of 54 Mbps compared to the 11 Mbps speed of 802.11b. Linux support for 802.11g wireless cards, however, is still developmental at best, which means that for now you had better stick to the 11 Mbps 802.11b protocol when selecting a wireless card. Although this may sound like an undesirable limitation, it is pretty much irrelevant in the real-world scheme of things. The somewhat lower speed of the 802.11b devices will most likely matter very little to you unless you are forking out an awful lot of money to your Internet provider each month for some extreme bandwidth. After all, the average transmission speed of most home cable Internet connections is still less than the 11 Mbps speed of 802.11b, so don't fret too much. Just remember that a traditional dial-up telephone modem has a transmission speed of 56 Kbps, or 56 *thousand* bits per second; 11 Mbps is 11 *million* bits per second. That is plenty fast for the average mortal.

Another reason you shouldn't feel so hampered by having to use an 802.11b wireless card is that the 802.11b protocol is still more commonly used than the newer 802.11g. Most public wireless access areas *(hot spots)*, such as airports, university campuses, and hotels still use the 802.11b protocol. Even if the 802.11g protocol is used in such places, or even if someone in your family has an 802.11g-based system up and running in your house, you can still connect to the Net over that system with your 802.11b network card, because the two protocols are compatible (though your 802.11b card won't be able to use the extra speed of the 802.11g network).

NOTE   *An 802.11a card isn't compatible with an 802.11b or 802.11g network.*

Wi-Fi Hardware

To create your own home Wi-Fi setup, you need at least two pieces of hardware: a wireless access point (WAP) and a wireless network interface card (NIC), both of which you can see in Figure 18-1. These two devices act like a pair of transceivers, communicating with each other via radio signals rather than over a wired connection. The WAP transmits data it receives from the Internet source device (such as your cable or ADSL modem) and receives data transmitted by your computer's NIC. The NIC, for its part, receives transmitted data from the WAP and transmits data from the computer back to the WAP.

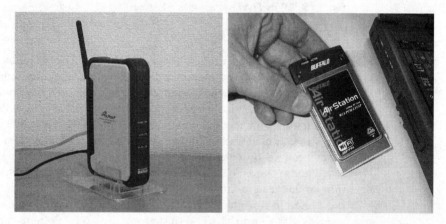

Figure 18-1: All you need for a Wi-Fi setup: an access point and a network interface card

The basic differences between a wired and wireless Internet connection setup can be seen in Figure 18-2 on the next page. In the typical wired setup, a cable from your high-speed Internet source device is directly connected to your computer by an Ethernet cable. If you are using a cable modem, for example, you would have an Ethernet cable going from your cable modem directly into the Ethernet port of your computer.

In a Wi-Fi setup, the Ethernet cable connects your Internet source device directly to the wireless access point, rather than to your computer. The wireless NIC is connected to your computer. This is frequently a PC Card, which you plug into one of the PCMCIA ports on your laptop (or into a special adapter on desktops). The NIC and access point then communicate with each other via radio waves rather than a hard wire connection — a sort of virtual wire, if you like.

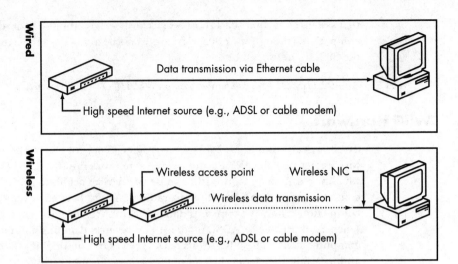

Figure 18-2: Wired and wireless Internet connections compared

Wireless Access Points

If you want to set up a wireless system in your home or office, the first thing you will need to get is a wireless access point. Fortunately, Linux compatibility is not really much of an issue in this department because the access point doesn't physically interface with your computer. In addition, as your 802.11b wireless NIC will work with access points using either the 802.11b or 802.11g protocols, it doesn't really matter what kind of wireless access point you choose. This is not to say that you needn't pay attention to what you are getting, though.

While whatever Wi-Fi access point you use should work right out of the box without the need for any special settings, there are a number of settings that you might want to consider specifying, especially for security reasons. For example, you may wish to restrict access to your wireless access point to certain hardware devices so that someone parked out on the street can't access your network. Each piece of hardware *(node)* on a network has its own unique ID, referred to as a *MAC* (Media Access Control) *address.* If you want to make sure that only your wireless NIC can access your WAP, you can do so in your WAP settings by specifying your wireless card's MAC address.

You can usually change the WAP settings by opening a Web browser and then punching up the IP address of the wireless access point, which is generally printed somewhere in the user's manual. This will present you with a Web page in which you can change or input the various settings. As Web browsers are not native to any one system, changing your settings with a Linux machine is no different from changing the settings with a machine running another operating system.

Of course, a few WAPs require you to use Internet Explorer to handle such browser-based settings, and because a Linux version of Internet Explorer does not exist, you will find yourself stuck unless you have a Mac or Windows machine to complete the job. Worse yet is the fact that some WAPs do not support browser-based settings at all. Instead, they require you to install special Windows software to do the job. When selecting hardware for your wireless setup, it is obviously best to stay clear of this sort of WAP.

Wireless Network Interface Cards

Whether you set up a home or office wireless access point, or you only need to access public WAPs (like at Starbucks), your machine will need a wireless NIC. Because these cards plug directly into your system, you must find and use a card that is Linux-compatible. Fedora Core comes with several wireless drivers built in, so if you use a card that is compatible with one of those drivers, all will be smooth sailing for you. Most wireless NICs are PC Cards that pop into the PCMCIA slot on the side of your laptop computer (see Figure 18-3).

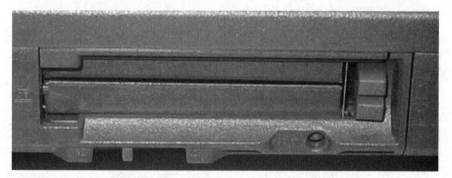

Figure 18-3: A pair of PCMCIA slots

Unfortunately, built-in Linux support is still pretty much limited to wireless NICs of the PC Card variety. Although there are also NICs that plug into one of your machine's USB ports or PCI slots, the drivers available for such devices do not come with your Linux system. Therefore, I don't really recommend using a non-PC-Card NIC, because adding a driver to Linux is not the simple slip-in-the-CD-and-double-click procedure that it can be on other systems. In fact, adding a driver to Linux involves mucking around with the Linux kernel itself, which is a cumbersome and even daunting process, especially for a beginner. Most drivers eventually make their way into future releases of the Linux kernel, so I strongly recommend sticking to hardware that is supported by the drivers included with your system.

If you would like to find out a bit more about the state of Linux wireless support, there is an excellent site that you will be pointed to by almost everyone you ask about such things: www.hpl.hp.com/personal/Jean_Tourrilhes/Linux/Wireless.html. As you will soon find out, the only problem with the site is that there is so much information that you may end up being more confused than when you started out.

Rather than baffling yourself needlessly, it is probably better to just look at what wireless NICs are supported by the drivers included in Fedora Core. The following list is taken directly from the configuration files in Fedora Core, so choosing a card from any of the following lists should ensure compatibility.

Devices supported by the orinoco_cs driver:

> Cabletron RoamAbout 802.11 DS
>
> Compaq WL100 11 Mbps Wireless Adapter
>
> 11 Mbps Wireless PC Card
>
> 3Com 3CRWE737A AirConnect Wireless LAN PC Card
>
> ELSA AirLancer MC-11
>
> Intersil PRISM2 11 Mbps Wireless Adapter
>
> Lucent Technologies WaveLAN/IEEE Adapter
>
> MELCO WLI-PCM-L11
>
> MELCO WLI-PCM-L11G
>
> Netgear MA401RA Wireless Adapter
>
> NCR WaveLAN/IEEE Adapter
>
> PLANEX GeoWave/GW-CF110
>
> ZCOMAX AirRunner/XI-300

Devices supported by the airo_cs driver:

> Aironet ARLAN 4500 and 4800
>
> Cisco 340 and Cisco 350 series
>
> Xircom Wireless Network Adapter CWE1100

Devices supported by the wavelan_cs driver:

> AT&T WaveLAN Adapter
>
> Digital RoamAbout/DS
>
> Lucent Technologies WaveLAN Adapter
>
> NCR WaveLAN Adapter

Devices supported by the ray_cs driver:

> RayLink PC Card WLAN Adapter

Devices supported by the netwave_cs driver:

> Xircom CreditCard Netwave

Despite the large number of cards listed, you should be aware that many of these are no longer manufactured, while several others are now sold under different names, either through Original Equipment Manufacturer (OEM) arrangements or because of corporate mergers or acquisitions. If you already have one of the listed cards, you can try it out easily enough by simply plugging it in and seeing how things go by following the setup steps in the following "Setting Up Your Wireless Card" section.

If you already have a card but it is not listed above, you might want to check it too, because it might be one of those supported cards under a different brand or model label. You can find out your card's make and model by using **cardctl** (a PCMCIA card control utility). To do this, insert your wireless NIC into the

PCMCIA slot of your computer, open a Terminal window, become root by using the **su** command, and then type /sbin/cardctl ident and press ENTER. The actual hardware make and model of the card will then appear in the Terminal window. If it matches one of those listed, you can be pretty sure that it is going to work. If not, you can still go through the setup steps in the following section to see what happens.

If you are going to go out and buy a card and do not want to waste your hard-earned cash experimenting, you will want to check things out more thoroughly. As always, a direct call for advice on one of the many Linux lists would be a good way to get such advice. I took a look at the archives of the Fedora_List mailing list and came up with a few reports of cards that were said to work "out of the box," without the need for any special drivers. I then punched up those devices on froogle.google.com to see what was still available (and in what price range). These included the Dell Truemobile 1150 ($39 to $49), the Compaq WL 110 ($110 to $200), and the Netgear MA401 ($42 to $65). The Cisco 350 was also mentioned as working without a hitch for some, but it was also a source of grief for others.

Not mentioned anywhere on the list (at least not where I could find it) was the Buffalo AirStation WLI-PCM-L11GP ($43 to $61), which is the card I've been using for some time now without a hitch. Although the card, as labeled, does not appear on the previous compatibility lists, performing a check with cardctl revealed that the card is telling my machine it is a Melco WLI-PCM-L11, which is on the list, so looks can be deceiving — even in the computer world.

Setting Up Your Wireless Card

Setting up a Linux-compatible wireless PC Card is relatively simple. It is probably best, though not essential, to go through the setup process in the vicinity of a wireless access point so that you know that you've succeeded. Therefore, if you have your own WAP at home or in the office, connect your WAP to your Internet source, and then turn the WAP on. If you are only going to be using public WAPs, perform the setup process on your next visit to Starbucks or another wireless hot spot.

Once you're within reach of a WAP that is up and running, plug your wireless NIC into the PCMCIA slot on your computer. Almost immediately after doing that, you should hear two beeps, which tells you that all is going to be well. Any LEDs on the card may light up at this time. If not, they will do so after you finish configuring the card. If you hear only one beep after inserting the card, then it is most likely not compatible with any of the preinstalled drivers.

If your machine does not allow you to hear system beeps or other sounds for some reason, or if you're just the double-checking kind, you can visually check to see whether or not the drivers for your card have been loaded by using the **lsmod** (list loaded modules) command. To do this, open a new Terminal window, type in /sbin/lsmod, and then press ENTER. The results should look something like those in Figure 18-4 on the next page. The driver for your card (**orinoco_cs** in the example) should appear near the top of the list and also next to **pcmcia_core**. Of course, your card may use one of the other drivers listed earlier, so your results may be considerably different.

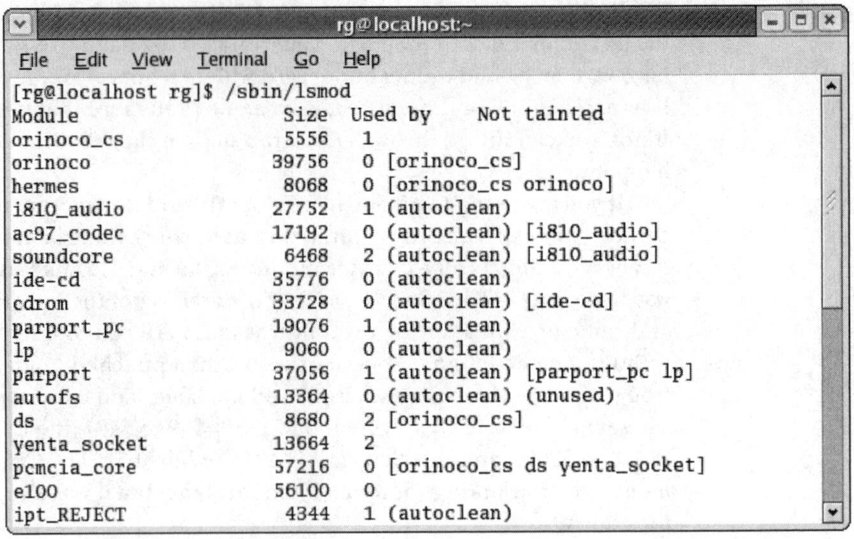

```
┌─────────────────────────────────────────────────────────────────────┐
│ ⌄                            rg@localhost:~                    _ □ ✕  │
├─────────────────────────────────────────────────────────────────────┤
│ File   Edit   View   Terminal   Go   Help                            │
│ [rg@localhost rg]$ /sbin/lsmod                                    ▲   │
│ Module               Size  Used by     Not tainted                   │
│ orinoco_cs           5556  1                                         │
│ orinoco             39756  0 [orinoco_cs]                            │
│ hermes               8068  0 [orinoco_cs orinoco]                    │
│ i810_audio          27752  1 (autoclean)                            │
│ ac97_codec          17192  0 (autoclean) [i810_audio]               │
│ soundcore            6468  2 (autoclean) [i810_audio]               │
│ ide-cd              35776  0 (autoclean)                            │
│ cdrom               33728  0 (autoclean) [ide-cd]                   │
│ parport_pc          19076  1 (autoclean)                            │
│ lp                   9060  0 (autoclean)                            │
│ parport             37056  1 (autoclean) [parport_pc lp]            │
│ autofs              13364  0 (autoclean) (unused)                   │
│ ds                   8680  2 [orinoco_cs]                            │
│ yenta_socket        13664  2                                        │
│ pcmcia_core         57216  0 [orinoco_cs ds yenta_socket]           │
│ e100                56100  0                                        │
│ ipt_REJECT           4344  1 (autoclean)                       ▼    │
└─────────────────────────────────────────────────────────────────────┘
```

Figure 18-4: Results of the lsmod command showing the loaded drivers for a wireless NIC

Once your card is inserted into the PCMCIA slot and the appropriate drivers are loaded, it is time to configure the system to deal with the card, which is all very easy. Follow these steps:

1. Open the Network Configuration window by going to the Main menu and selecting **System Settings > Network**. As most computers these days have Ethernet support built onto the motherboard, an Ethernet device will very likely be listed in the window, as is the case in Figure 18-5. If you are not connected to the Internet or another network via that device, its status will be appropriately listed as **Inactive**, so you can safely ignore it.

2. Next, you need to add your wireless device to the device list, which you can do by clicking the **New** button. This will bring up a wizard for adding network devices, shown in Figure 18-6.

3. On the Select Device Type page, select **Wireless connection** and then click **Forward** to move on to the next page of the wizard.

4. On the Select Wireless Device page, two listings should appear: one showing your card by name, and one that says Other Wireless Cards. Select the listing with your card's name and then click **Forward** to move on. Note that the name in the listing for your card might be different from what is written on the card's label, though that is not a problem.

5. On the Configure Wireless Connection page, accept the default settings unless instructed otherwise by your Internet provider. Click **Forward** when you are done. (You can always go back and change these settings later if your connection doesn't work.)

Figure 18-5: Network Configuration window

6.   On the Configure Network Settings page, if your Internet provider automatically provides IP addresses via DHCP (as discussed in Chapter 4), simply accept the default settings by clicking **Forward**. If, however, your provider does not utilize DHCP, you will have to get the necessary settings from the network administrator or service provider, enter them yourself on this page, and then click **Forward**.

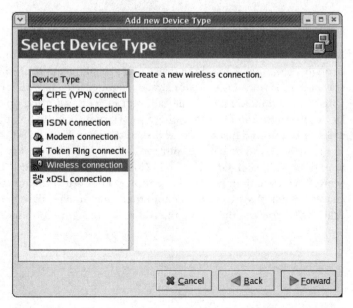

Figure 18-6: Adding your wireless device with the Add Device wizard

7. On the Create Wireless Device page, you will see a summary of all the choices you have made thus far. Click **Apply**.

8. Once you've completed the wizard steps, a small window will open asking whether you want to save your settings. You do, so click **Yes**.

9. You will then be presented with yet another, albeit smaller, window telling you that the changes have been saved and that you might have to restart your computer for the changes to take effect. Click **OK**.

This will leave you with the Network Configuration window, where you will now see your wireless card in the device list (see Figure 18-7).

Figure 18-7: A new wireless card added to the list of network devices

Before you close the Network Configuration window, there is one more thing I strongly recommend you do in order to make activating your wireless card more convenient. If your device is not already highlighted, click on it once to select it. Once you've done that, click the **Edit** button. This will bring up the Wireless Device Configuration window, where you should click the box next to **Allow all users to enable and disable the device**, as shown in Figure 18-8. This will allow you to activate and deactivate your card without first becoming root. Once you have done that, click **OK**, which will close the Wireless Device Configuration window. You will then be asked in another window if you want to save your changes (click **Yes**), and then be told that your changes have been saved (click **OK**). You can then close the Network Configuration window.

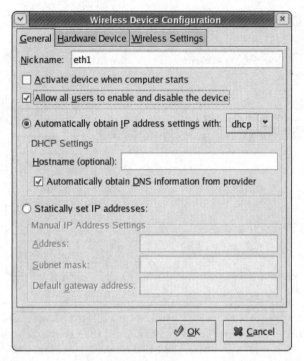

Figure 18-8: Configuring your wireless NIC to allow for easy user activation

Activating Your Wireless Network Interface Card

Now that you have configured your wireless NIC, you need to activate it in order to use it, and there are two ways to do this. As you were warned when setting up the card, though, you may have to restart your computer before you can use your new device, so if your card doesn't work immediately when you activate it, restart your computer and try again.

The more traditional way of activating a wireless card is essentially a point-and-click approach, utilizing the Network Device Control window. To open the window, go to the Main menu and select **System Tools > Network Device Control**. Once the Network Device Control window opens (see Figure 18-9 on the next page), you can conveniently activate and deactivate your configured network devices without having to enter root mode. To activate your device, select it in the device list by clicking on it once and then clicking the **Activate** button. After a moment or two of probing (the progress of which will be shown in a small window), your device will be activated and that will be indicated in the Status column. This point-and-click approach can be used not only to activate and deactivate wireless devices, but wired devices as well, making it convenient if you use both connection methods.

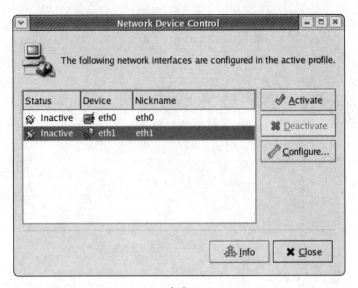

Figure 18-9: Activating your network devices

The other way to activate your wireless card is rather simple: Pull your card out until you hear your machine beep once, and then reinsert the card, after which your machine will beep twice, the LEDs on the NIC will start blinking, and all will be well with the world. I like to call this the *tactile approach*. It is quick, effective, and exceedingly straightforward. That said, it is only fair to point out that hardware is hardware, and as such it can wear out or become damaged over time, so keep that in mind if you take a shine to this manner of doing things. After all, some PCMCIA slots can seem a bit flimsy. Just use your best judgment.

A Quick Fix for the "Wi-Fi Quirkies"

While using certain wireless NICs under Linux, you may experience what seems like a system freeze. It doesn't happen very often, but it usually occurs while some sort of Internet operation is going on, either in the background or foreground. I like to call this the *Wi-Fi quirkies*, though you can just call it a pain in the posterior if you like. You will know when the quirkies strike because you won't be able to do anything, not even move your mouse.

Fortunately, the solution to this is quick and easy — the tactile approach, which I explained in the previous section. Just pull your wireless card out of the computer for a second and — *beep*— everything will go back to normal. Stick the card back in to reactivate and use it, and — *beep beep* — you can go right back to whatever it was you were doing on the Internet. It's a simple and sure-fire way of solving the problem (and it sure beats kicking the machine).

19

LEAVING THE NEST

Getting Ready to Move Out on Your Own

We've just about come to the end of our Linux adventure together. However, before I cast you off on your own, there are a few areas left that I should cover so as to round out your total Linux knowledge base up to this point. This chapter really consists of four parts: The first deals with system settings, the second with KDE, the third with keeping your system up to date, and the fourth with a collection of odds and ends that just didn't fit nicely anywhere else but are important nevertheless.

Some Useful System Settings

Although we've already gone over most of what you need in terms of system settings (thematic and printing preferences and the like), there are a couple of other areas that warrant at least a little mention.

Direct Login (Bypassing the Login Screen)

If you are the only person using your machine, you may be wondering why you need to bother logging in every time you start up your machine. Well, actually you don't have to; it is possible to set things up so that the system will automatically log you in, thus bypassing the login screen.

To set things up this way, go to the Main menu and select **System Settings > Login Screen**. You will then be prompted for your root password, so type it and click **OK**. The Login Screen Setup window will appear (see Figure 19-1).

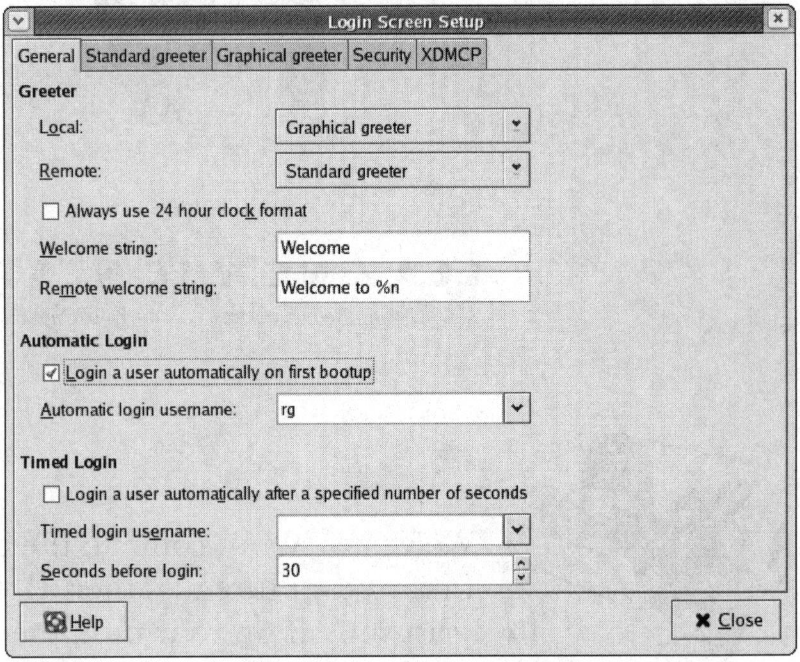

Figure 19-1: Changing the auto-login settings in Fedora Core

In the Login Screen Setup window, go down to the **Automatic login** section, and check the **Login a user automatically on first bootup** checkbox. Then, in the **Automatic login username** drop-down menu, select your username. Once you've done that, click the **Close** button.

Now, the next time you boot up your machine, you will bypass the login screen and go directly to your desktop. Of course, if you need to get back to the login screen for some reason or other (such as when switching into KDE, which I'll discuss shortly, or switching into another language mode), you can still do so by simply going to the Main menu and selecting **Log Out**.

Changing Your Screen Resolution

Screen resolution, to give you a very non-technical explanation, refers to the size of everything that appears on your monitor. A high resolution (such as 1024 by 768) gives you more desktop area to work with, but it makes everything appear a bit smaller. A low resolution (such as 640 by 480) makes everything bigger and easier to see, but it also gives you much less desktop space to work in. You may also find that certain monitors just look better at certain resolutions than at others. An LCD monitor that I just hooked up to one my machines looked really flat and blurry at 800 by 600, but when I changed it to 1024 by 768, it was beautiful. You might want to experiment a bit with your screen resolution settings if your screen doesn't look as good as you think it should.

The numbers, in case you were wondering, refer to the number of pixels (or dots) displayed in the screen's width and height, respectively.

Changing your screen resolution is quite easy in Fedora. All you have to do is go to your Main menu and select **Preferences > Screen Resolution**. The Screen Resolution Preferences window will open, and you can select the resolution you want in the **Resolution** drop-down menu. It is also a good idea to check the specs for your monitor to see if the resolution choice you make requires any change in the refresh rate for your monitor.

Once you have selected your preferred resolution, click **Apply**, and the resolution will immediately change. A small window will open, asking whether you want to return to the default resolution or keep the changes you've just made (see Figure 19-2). You can click whichever button meets your desires at the moment.

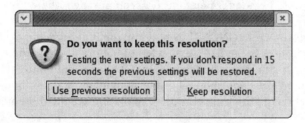

Figure 19-2: Changing screen resolution

Changing Your Color Depth

Color depth refers to the number of colors displayed on your screen. The basic color level is 256 colors; this is sometimes called 8-bit color, as the computer must send eight bits of data to create one pixel on the screen. However, if you want to view graphics, especially photos, a color depth of 256 colors will cause those images to look muddy and blotchy. In this case, it is better to increase your color depth to thousands of colors (called 16-bit color), which should be more than enough.

You may be wondering why you shouldn't just go wild and pick millions of colors (32-bit color), which would be a logical enough way of looking at things — a sort of why-take-the-Bug-when-the-Cadillac-is-in-the-driveway view of things. Well, to stick with the metaphor, the reason is gas mileage, so to speak. Basically, the more information you have to send to your screen, the more computing power and memory you use, and that slows things down. Consequently, a computer running a text-only, black-and-white system (a 1-bit system) would be considerably faster than the same computer running an 8-bit color system, which would be faster than 16-bit color, which would be faster than 32-bit color.

If you want to change your color depth, then you have to go to the Main menu and select **System Settings > Display**. After providing the requested root password, you will see the Display Settings window, in which you can change your color depth (you can also change the screen resolution here too). Once you are done, click **OK**. The changes will take effect after you log out and then back in again, or after you restart your machine.

KDE

I've kept you in the GNOME world for as long as I can, but it is human nature to want to see what is on the other side of the fence. However, I'd like to say a few words before you journey off to KDE land.

Up until now, I have not dealt with KDE in this book other than in regard to a few KDE applications. As I mentioned earlier, this is because I feel that GNOME is much easier for beginners to deal with. GNOME is also the default environment in Fedora and it is thus a bit more developed (at least in Fedora). And finally, I just like it better in terms of look, feel, and convenience (after all, it has the ever-useful Nautilus emblems and CD Burner). If you really want to hear more about the reasons for my GNOME orientation, then take a trip to the Edgy Penguins site (www.edgy-penguins.org/compurants) where I spell it all out.

Once you do get over to the "other side," you will find that KDE looks amazingly similar to GNOME, as both use the Bluecurve theme, though the window borders in the KDE version are of the pre-Fedora variety. There are other subtle differences here and there, of course, but armed with your new-found Linux skills, you should be able to handle yourself without difficulty. I am a firm believer in the learn-through-exploration school of thought.

Booting into KDE

To boot into KDE, get to your login screen either by starting up your machine or by logging out of your current GNOME session. Click the word **Session** at the bottom of the login screen. This will open a small window in which you should select **KDE** and then click **OK**. Type your username and user password and press ENTER, and a small message window will open, telling you that you have selected to use the KDE desktop for the following session and that you will need to use the Switchdesk utility if you want to make KDE your default environment. The only choice you have in this window is to click **OK**, so click it, which just tells the system, "Yeah, yeah, I understand, let's get on with it."

Now if you are a Red Hat Linux 9 user, you too will be presented with a small message window; however, yours will ask you on the spot if you want to make KDE your default environment for future logins. I would recommend clicking **No** your first time out, until you know whether you really prefer KDE or not. Either way, it doesn't really matter, as you can always make GNOME your default desktop again by going through the same process.

Differences Between KDE and GNOME

There are a few things you should know about the KDE environment to make your stay over there a good one: how to kill misbehaving windows, how to take care of general environmental issues (such as customizations and the like), and how to take screenshots. All of these are quite different in KDE.

To get rid of misbehaving windows in KDE, just use the CTRL + ALT + ESC key combo. After pressing these three keys at the same time, your cursor will turn into a rather ominous skull and crossbones, which you can then use to zap away any window that refuses to budge. Of course, if your misbehaving window suddenly starts behaving, or if you suddenly change your mind, you can cancel the scull and crossbones cursor by right-clicking your mouse anywhere — no damage done.

To take care of general KDE environmental matters, use the KDE Control Center, which you can access by going to the Main menu and selecting **Control Center** (see Figure 19-3). After it opens, you can click the + sign next to **Appearance & Themes**, where you can perform most of the thematic customizations that you did in GNOME, though many of the KDE themes will be different from those in GNOME, and adding new ones is a bit more cumbersome. Note that you cannot use the themes you installed in GNOME in KDE — they just ain't the same.

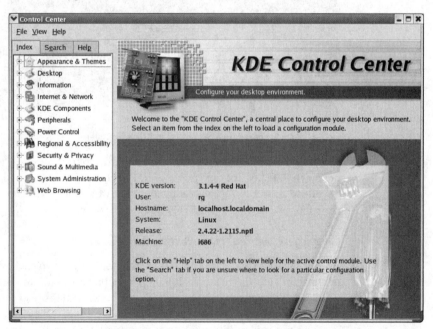

Figure 19-3: Customizing KDE with the KDE Control Center

To take screenshots in KDE, you must use the KDE screen capture program, which you can access by going to the Main menu and selecting **Graphics > Screen Capture Program**. The program allows you to take shots of either the whole screen or a single window (through use of a timer), and it is pretty straightforward and easy to understand.

Finally, before leaving you to your own resources in KDE land, I will mention one feature of KDE that I do find rather handy. This is the ability of Konqueror (KDE's answer to Nautilus) to create thumbnails of all the images in a designated folder and then set them up as a Web page, an example of which you can see in Figure 19-4. To take advantage of this cool feature, navigate to the folder that has the images you want to thumbnail, and then in the **Tools** menu of the Konqueror window, select **Create Image Gallery**. The rest should be clear to you after that.

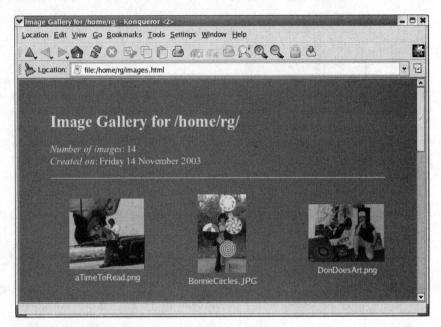

Figure 19-4: An image gallery created in KDE's Konqueror

If you find that you like this thumbnail feature but don't really want to have to deal with KDE to take advantage of it, I have a set of instructions you can download for a simple program called Jigl, which does the same thing (www.edgy-penguins.org/LFYM/newprojects.html).

Changing Default Desktop Environments

So let's say that you've taken a liking to KDE and want to stick with it for a while, or that you've been giving KDE a try for a while and want to come back home to GNOME. To change your default desktop environment, you will have to use the Switchdesk utility.

You can run Switchdesk by going to the Main menu and selecting **System Settings > More System Settings > Desktop Switching Tool**. This will bring up a very simple window (shown in Figure 19-5) from which you can choose KDE (or GNOME, if you want to switch back after making KDE your default environment). After making your choice, click **OK**, and you will get another message window telling you that your default desktop system setting has been updated, and the change you made will take effect after restarting. Just click **OK** to close that window. Don't go messing with the TWM selection at the bottom, as it will take you to a creepy place you won't want to be. I won't say more than that, but if you do ignore my warning and end up not knowing how to get out of TWM land, just left-click the completely empty TWM desktop, and select **Exit** from the pop-up menu.

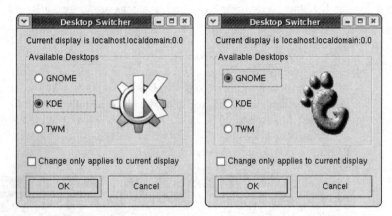

Figure 19-5: Changing the default desktop environment with Desktop Switcher

Keeping Your System Up to Date

As you no doubt already know, things move quickly in the computer world, and as such changes will already have been made to your operating system before you even get it installed on your machine. This is true not only of Linux but also of Windows, Macintosh OS, and every other operating system. These changes are available to users in two forms: updates and upgrades.

Updating

Almost all operating systems have some mechanism by which you can update your system. Updates are minor changes to your system or any application within it. These are usually released on a need-be basis in order to fix some bug (such as the Package Manager bug in Fedora 1), take care of some recently discovered security vulnerability, add some feature, or add additional hardware support (such as support for more recent digital camera models). Depending on what your needs, concerns, and download speed happen to be, you may want to download every available update, pick and choose among updates, or just not bother at all.

If you are interested in updating your system, you may recall that you've already learned one way to do so in Chapter 10. As pointed out in that chapter, using Synaptic is a very easy way to keep your system up to date. It also has the additional advantage of allowing you to update not only the standard Fedora RPM packages, but also those non-Fedora add-on RPMs, such as Frozen-Bubble, which you downloaded from FreshRPMs (and DAG, if you also added that to the Synaptic repositories list).

You can also update your system using the Up2date utility, which allows you to download updates directly from the Red Hat Network. This only works, however, with those RPM packages that come as part of the Fedora system, not those you add later from other sources. As the Fedora packages on FreshRPMs are the same as those on the Red Hat Network, I don't much see the advantage in going the Up2date route myself, but then you may see things differently, so I'll leave that up to you.

To use Up2date, right-click on the Red Hat Network Alert Notification Tool (next to the clock in the GNOME panel) and select **Launch up2date**. You will then be prompted for your user password, so enter that and click **OK**. The first time around, you will be told that you need to install a key to use the Red Hat update agent, so click **Yes**, and the key will be installed very quickly. The update agent will then appear. The agent is a handy wizard which leads you through the update process. Just click **Forward** in each screen until to you reach the Available Package Updates screen (Figure 19-6).

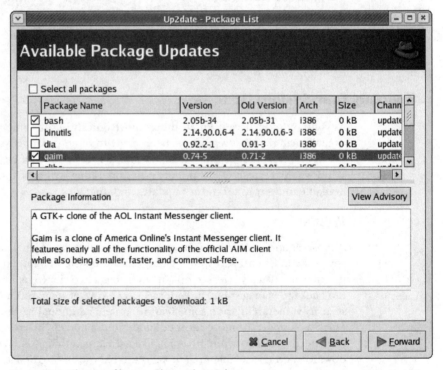

Figure 19-6: Choosing files to update with Up2date

The Available Package Updates list shows you all the updates that are available for your system. You can individually check the items you wish to update (or check **Select all packages** if you want them all), and then click **Forward**. Up2date will then download and install the selected updates and then tell you when it's done. Once you get to that All Finished screen, click **Finish**.

Upgrading

While most Linux distributions have an 8-month to 16-month life cycle between major version releases, the Fedora Project plans to significantly shorten this cycle so that new versions of Fedora Core will be released two to three times a year. While this might seem a bit too much to deal with, you really needn't worry because you don't need to upgrade your system with every new release of Fedora Core.

As I mentioned in Chapter 1, the Fedora Project folks themselves state that changes in Fedora Core will be "evolutionary, not revolutionary," and many changes, after all, will be of the under-the-hood variety and thus quite likely of little concern to you. If you still haven't been soothed by my words, just remember that there are still a good many people out there in the Linux world who are still quite content using Red Hat Linux 7.2, which was first released in 2001 (and let's not forget all the Windows 2000 users who still haven't switched to Windows XP, or Mac OS 9 users who haven't switched to OS X).

Whether you choose to upgrade depends on you. If you are satisfied with your system the way it is, then why bother? However, if one of the future Fedora releases contains some feature that you think you'd like to have, go ahead and upgrade.

The safest road to upgrading is by downloading and burning ISOs of the operating system, as I discussed in Chapter 7. This isn't such a good idea, however, if you don't have a broadband Internet connection, as each ISO could take you a couple of days to download. It also makes no sense at all if you don't have a CD burner. In such cases, it is probably worth your time and peace of mind to just order the installation CDs from one of the services listed at the very end of Appendix B. The CDs from such services are priced very reasonably, delivered quickly, and will save you a lot of time.

Once you have a set of installation CDs in your hands, then you can go about upgrading by roughly following the installation process you learned in Chapter 2. Of course, before you perform any upgrade, it is always a very good idea to back up the data on your machine. Once you've done that, just go through the installation process as normal until you get to the Upgrade Examine screen of Step 6 (see Figure 19-7 on the next page).

At this point you need to decide whether you want to perform a true upgrade or a fresh install. An upgrade allows you to keep your settings, add-on applications, and even data (back up first anyway, just in case). However, with an upgrade you might also end up keeping any problems you had before. Opting for a fresh install, on the other hand, wipes your Linux partitions clean before installing an entirely new system in its place. I prefer the latter method, but which you choose is up to you. You can always try the upgrade route first, and then if you have any problems you can just do a fresh install later.

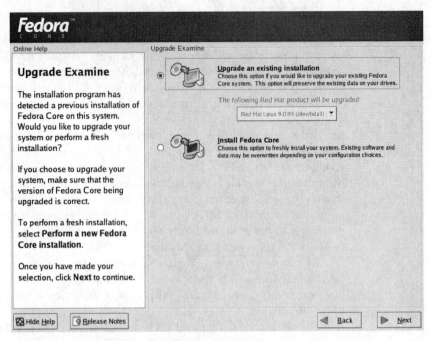

Figure 19-7: Choosing to upgrade a previous version of Fedora

To perform an upgrade, choose **Upgrade an existing installation**. The rest should be quite automatic after that, and when you are all done, you should have a newly upgraded system with all your previous settings in tact. To perform a fresh installation, choose **Install Fedora Core** and then follow the rest of the steps just as they are written in Chapter 2. If you have a dual-boot setup and are performing a fresh install, you do not need to go through the dual-boot procedures given in Chapter 2 again; just follow the standard installation procedures but be sure to select **Remove all Linux partitions on this machine** when you get to Step 9.

One last thing worth mentioning: If you are using APT and Synaptic, as you learned to do in Chapter 10, you will probably have to reinstall those two files when you upgrade your system. So just go to www.freshrpms.net and download a new version of APT that matches the version of your newly upgraded system. If you've performed an upgrade rather than a fresh install, you may find that if you try to install the APT file by double-clicking on it, you will get a message telling you that APT is already installed. You want to upgrade that version of APT, so install it via the command Terminal instead. This is quite easily done by first becoming root using the *su* command, and then typing rpm -Uvh apt* (be sure that you don't have any other file called apt in your home folder when you do this), and then tapping ENTER. Once you've done that, follow the procedures for updating the APT database and then installing Synaptic that you learned in Chapter 10.

Odds and Ends

Now we come to a short collection of essentially unrelated items that did not make it into the book elsewhere, either because I hadn't yet introduced the necessary skills when the relevant topic came up, or because this was the most appropriate place for it. In any case, all of the topics here, though unrelated to one another, are worth a mention.

Running Java Applets

While the Mozilla browser is capable of dealing with Java commands, it is not capable of running Java applications, or *applets*, as is. Such applets come in many forms. Most browser-based online games, for example, are Java applets. If you've ever looked for a house online and took a virtual tour of one the listings so as to have a look around the place, you also were most likely using a Java applet.

In order to use Java applets in Fedora Core, you need to install two components: the Java Runtime Environment (JRE), and a plugin so that Mozilla knows where and how to access the JRE. In the past, gettting the JRE successfully up and running in Linux was quite the pain, and the many "how do I..." questions on the various online Linux forums is testimony to that fact. Fortunately, the DAG respository now has both the JRE and Mozilla JRE plugins available as RPMs, thus making everything clean and easy.

To get both files, go to http://dag.wieers.com/packages/j2re and download the most recent JRE file. The JRE file is quite big at 18.8MB, so be prepared for a somewhat lengthy download. The Mozilla plugin will prove a much quicker download, as it is only a 198KB file. It is available on the same page as the JRE, but closer to the bottom.

Once you have downloaded both files, it is easy enough to install them via the double-click method you learned in Chapter 8. As the Mozilla-j2re RPM is dependent upon the j2re RPM, you will have to install the j2re RPM first. After you are done, you will probably want to test things out to make sure that all went according to plan. For a quick, easy, and totally off-the-wall example of a simple Java appet at work, go to http://java.sun.com/applets/other/BouncingHeads. Once you get there, be a bit patient because, depending on the speed of your Internet connection, it will take the applet a bit of time to load and then start running.

Checking ISOs with md5sum

Now that you are a Linux user, you will no doubt download future versions of Fedora Core in the form of ISOs from the Internet. Most download sites also provide what is called a *checksum*, or *md5sum*, file that you can use to check the integrity of the downloaded ISOs. The question most newbies have, however, is how to check the integrity of their newly downloaded ISOs with that file.

Here's how to do it.

Place the ISOs and the md5sum file in the same folder. It doesn't matter if there are other files, or even different ISOs, in that folder or not — just make sure there are no other md5sum files in that folder. Next, open a Terminal window and type this command:

```
md5sum -c MD5SUM
```

If your md5sum filename uses lowercase letters replace MD5SUM with md5sum. Then press ENTER. The output in your Terminal window should look something like that in Figure 19-8.

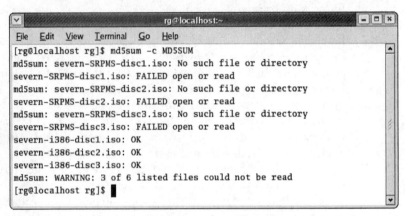

Figure 19-8: md5sum results in the Terminal window

As you can see in the example, the md5sum of the Fedora Core beta (code-named Severn) checks not only for the main installation ISOs, but also for the source ISOs. As I did not download the source ISOs, md5sum could not find them. It did, however, find the three installation ISOs I had downloaded, checked them, and found them to be okay.

Man Pages

As you make your way through the Linux world, you are eventually going to hear mention of *man* pages. Man (manual) pages are basically the original Linux online documentation system, and you will discover that there is a man page for almost every application and command on your system.

Despite the fact that man pages are loaded with just about all the pertinent information you would ever need to have, there is a rather problematic aspect to the whole thing: Man pages are nearly impossible for newbies to understand. Fortunately, you can pretty much get by without using man pages in the beginning, as there are usually other forms of help available (README files in tarballs or GNOME and KDE documents, for example).

However, as you get more and more used to your system and you have a bit more of an understanding of the world of Linux, you might actually come to understand the contents of the man pages, little by little. Man pages are opened and viewed through your Command Terminal. To view a man page, you just type the word man followed by the name of the command, application, or utility you want to find out about. For example, to see the man page for the **cp** (copy) command, you would type man cp and then press ENTER.

As you can see in Figure 19-9, the man page will open up in your Terminal window. To scroll up or down through a man page, just use the up and down cursor keys; to move up or down a page at a time, use the PAGE UP and PAGE DOWN keys. Finally, when you get to the end of a man page and you want to get back to the normal Terminal window and your now-familiar user prompt, just press the Q key.

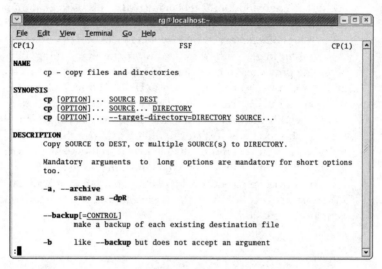

Figure 19-9: The man page for the **cp** *command*

If you would like to see a complete collection of the standard Linux man pages set in HTML format (with a clickable index), have a look at http://linux.ctyme.com.

Checking the Ink Levels on an Epson Printer

Finally, we come to one last utility that may be of value to many readers, as Epson inkjet printers are pretty common. If you are using an Epson inkjet printer and would like to know how to check your printer's ink levels, you can download and install the **gimp-print-utils** package with Synaptic/APT by typing gimp-print-utils in the **Find** box. This package includes the **escputil** program.

To use the program, first check the device location of your printer in the Hardware Browser. Start the Hardware browser by going to the Main menu and selecting **System Tools > Hardware Browser**, and once the browser is open, click **Printers** in the left pane. Your printer will probably be **/dev/lp0**.

Once you know your printer's location, open a Terminal window, become root, and then type escputil -r /dev/lp0 -i (changing the device location if yours is different) and press ENTER. Once you've done that, your present ink levels will appear in your Terminal.

Project 19A: Programming for Linux? (Absolutely Optional, but Kind of Fun)

I should first say that I am not very keen on programming. I guess my mind is just too jumbled and illogical to deal with it, and I probably had my fill of code after keying in all those Atari games in my early computing days. Nevertheless, many people want to know what it takes to program and what they need to do it.

Most of what you need is included in your Fedora Core system, and there are, in fact, many options. The language that seems to be most popular and that is supposedly easiest for newbies to deal with is called *Python*. As you may recall, the pyWings oracle, which you installed in Chapter 9, was written in Python.

In order to get a little taste of this programming thing, I'll give you a couple of sample programs you can play with. The first program in almost any programming book is a silly little thing called "Hello, World." All the program does is print out the words "Hello, World" to your screen. This always seemed weird to me, as the only person looking at the output of the program is the person who keyed in the code, not "the world." So let's change that standard intro program just a bit, and make it more valuable to your self-esteem. Let's do a "Hey, good looking" program instead. It really is the same thing anyway.

To write the program, open Gedit by going to your Main menu and selecting **Accessories > Text Editor**. In the Gedit window, type the following two lines — quotation marks too:

```
print "Hey, good looking!"
print "You are looking fine today."
```

Once you've done that, click the **Save** button, and save the program to your Home folder as goodlooking.py.

You've now written a program, be it ever so humble. Now, open up a Terminal window, and run the program by typing python goodlooking.py and pressing ENTER. The output will appear in the Terminal window (see Figure 19-10).

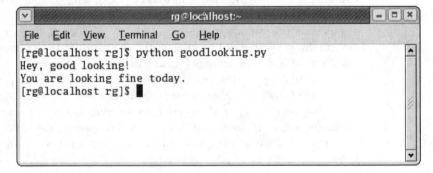

Figure 19-10: Running the "Hey, good looking" Python program

Makes you feel kind of good, doesn't it? Now, if you want to get a tad more carried away, you can create a simple window for this ego-affirming program of yours by using tkinter. As you may recall, you installed tkinter in Chapter 9 for use by the pyWings oracle, which used tkinter for the same purpose.

To write the program so that it will open in a window of its own, open Gedit again, and this time type the following:

```
from Tkinter import Label, mainloop
Label (text='Hey, good looking!\n'
'You are looking fine today.').pack()
mainloop()
```

Note that there are no spaces anywhere after the word **today** in the third line and no spaces between **mainloop** and () in the last line.

Save this new program to your Home folder as goodlooking2.py. Once you've done that, go back to your Terminal window and type python goodlooking2.py and press ENTER. Your new program will then appear in its own window (see Figure 19-11).

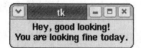

Figure 19-11: The "Hey, good looking" program in its own window

Well, that was all pretty harmless. If you find this programming thing interesting and want to find out more about Python, go to the Python site at www.python.org, which has links to several online tutorials.

Project 19B: Running Windows Programs Under Linux with Wine (Optional)

Despite the fact that there is a Linux equivalent to most of the Windows programs that people use or need, there may be one or two programs that you will come to miss. For me it's a freeware version of the Austrian card game Schnapsen. Fortunately, it is possible to run some Windows applications from within Linux with the help of a program called Wine.

The folks at Wine seem keen on pointing out that Wine is not a Windows emulator, preferring to call it a Windows compatibility layer. Whatever way you choose to look at it, its function is to allow you to run Windows apps without having Windows installed on your machine. That said, it is only fair to point out that Wine is still a work in progress. It works fairly well with some programs and not at all with others. There are some commercial versions of Wine that might work better in some cases (check out the links on the Wine homepage — www.winehq.org), but there's no harm in giving the free official version a try first, especially now that you are about ready to move beyond non-geek status.

19B-1: Downloading and Installing Wine and WineSetuptk

Wine is not included in your Fedora Core system, but you can get it quite easily by going to www.winehq.org/site/download and clicking the Sourceforge icon under the **Official Wine Versions** heading. Once on the Sourceforge page, scroll down to the **RedHat Packages** section and then download the version appropriate for the system and processor you are using. For example, if you are running Fedora Core I on a Pentium II (or newer) machine, you would download wine-20040121-1fc1winehq.i686.rpm.

Another file that you will want to download is WineSetuptk, which is a graphical setup utility for Wine. To get the file, go back to the page where you started and scroll even further down to the **Support Files** section. Once there, download the **winesetuptk** RPM file (not the tarball). Once both files are on your hard disk, install Wine first and then WineSetuptk by simply double-clicking each file and then following the usual procedure you learned in Chapter 8.

19B-2: Setting Things Up

There isn't really much you need to do to get Wine set up — WinSetuptk does most of the work for you. Run WinSetuptk by typing winesetuptk in either a terminal window or the Run Application dialog (**Main menu > Run Application**), after which the Wine Configuration Wizard will appear (Figure 19-12).

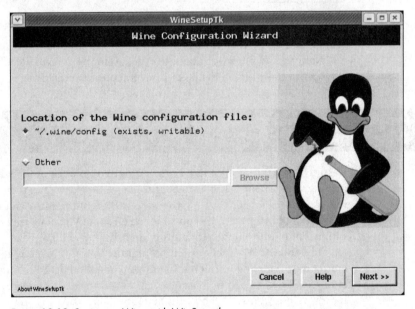

Figure 19-12: Setting up Wine with WinSetuptk

The wizard is basically a simple three-click write-nothing process. Just click **Next** in the first screen, **Next** in the second screen, **Finish** in the third screen, and Wine will then create a sub-folder within your Home folder that acts as a pseudo Windows partition (/home/username/.wine/fake_windows), complete with all the folders you would normally find on a real Windows C: drive. If you are a dual booter, you can choose to use your real Windows partition instead of creating a fake one in the second screen of the wizard, but I would be reluctant to recommend doing that, at least not until you know what you're doing.

19B-3: Installing and Running a Windows Program Under Linux

Once Wine is installed and set up, it really can't do anything unless you try to run a Windows program. That being the case, in this part of the project you are going to download, install, and run a Boggle-like game from the Windows world called BookWorm Deluxe (Figure 19-13). BookWorm Deluxe is one of the Windows games available from PopCap Games (www.popcap.com), many of which seem to work fairly well under Linux with Wine.

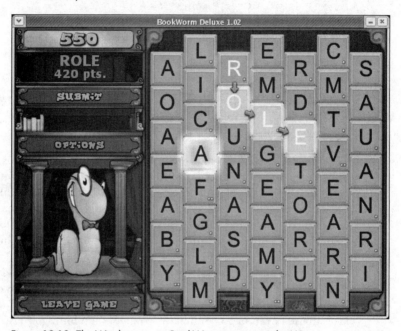

Figure 19-13: The Windows game BookWorm running under Wine

You should be aware that the games that you download from PopCap Games are all trial versions, not freebies, which means that you will eventually have to pay for any game you should want to keep using beyond the number of free games allowed. We have one foot in the Windows world right now, after all. For the purpose of this project, however, this fact should not be of great concern to you — you are just learning how to do things, and using some pretty cool games as your learning tools. And after all, who knows? You might find the games cool enough that you actually want to pay for them. Even if you don't begin to feel that way, you can still play the free online Java versions of the games (available at the same site) if you installed the Java Runtime Environment and the Mozilla Java plugin earlier in this chapter.

To download BookWorm Deluxe, go to the PopCap Games site (www.popcap.com), and click the **Deluxe Games** button on the left side of the window. Once on the Deluxe Games page, simply click the **Download Free** button next to BookWorm. Once the download is complete, you will have a file called Bookworm_setup.exe in your Home folder. Double-click that file and Wine will spring to action for the first time as it runs the Windows installer (Figure 19-14) for BookWorm Deluxe.

Figure 19-14: A Windows installer running under Wine.

All you really need do to start the installation process is click **Next.** The installer will create a BookWorm folder within a PopCap Games folder within the Program Files folder of your fake_windows partition. As the installer nears the end of the process, you will get a warning message telling you that the installer couldn't create some link, after which you will be told that the installation has been aborted and that you probably cannot run BookWorm Deluxe. Just ignore all that, as all will be fine (in this case, at least).

Now you can run BookWorm Deluxe. The most straightforward way of doing this is to head over to your new fake_windows partition. You can do this by opening a Nautilus window and typing /home/username/.wine/fake_windows/Program Files in the **Location** box of that window and then hitting ENTER. Once there, double click the **PopCap Games** folder, and then the **BookWorm Deluxe** folder within that. Finally, just double-click **BookWorm.exe** and you will soon be impressing all those around you with the great depth and breadth of your vocabulary.

If you're interested in what other applications are supposed to run under Wine, have a look at the Wine application database at http://appdb.winehq.org, which also tells what version of Wine a given application is known to work under, and what limitations, if any, a program has when running under Wine.

20

WHAT TO DO IF TUX STARTS ACTING UP

Problem Solving

It happens to everyone, no matter what operating system you are using — something goes wrong, and you are stuck with nowhere to go. Don't feel bad, and most importantly, *don't panic*. I repeat: *DON'T PANIC!* Nothing but trouble comes when you do. Going into a panicked frenzy usually turns a simple problem into a big one. Nothing is ever as bad as it seems . . . usually.

When something weird does come up and you don't quite know what to do, take your hands off the mouse and keyboard immediately. I mean that literally — *hands off!* Resist the urge to act.

Once you've done that, sit back, take a deep breath, and think. What is actually happening? What did you do that got you to this point? Hopefully, after this brief period of reflection, the problem will have solved itself, as it so often does. If not, take a break. Go downstairs and have a bowl of granola, or clam chowder, or (better yet) change that flat tire on your bicycle that's been keeping you from riding for three weeks. Then, once you're done, come back to this book and look through this section to see if your problem matches anything I've mentioned here.

To be honest, I really haven't had much trouble with my Red Hat or Fedora systems up to now. In fact, I've had fewer problems than I mention in this section. Nevertheless, computers are computers, and operating systems, whether Windows, Mac, or Linux, are sufficiently complex to freak themselves out on occasion, as my friend put it. As it is impossible to anticipate every possible mishap that might occur to everyone, I've limited this section to the mostly minor problems that I or those around me have had. If you come up with problems of a different nature, try one of the online forums or mailing lists mentioned in the Appendices and ask your question there. Be sure to say that you are a Linux newbie, so that the responders will dumb-down their comments a tad. If you can't grasp what they tell you to do, don't be afraid to seek clarification.

I will only deal with operating system failures here; hardware failures are a different story entirely, and there is nothing much you can do in such situations other than replace the offending unit (most commonly a hard disk that conks out). Hardware failures are system independent, so they would happen even if you were using Windows on your machine. Don't blame Linux if such problems happen on its watch, because it isn't the cause.

Problems and Solutions

One of my windows seems to be hanging, and it isn't even a surfer. It won't do anything, not even close.

I know the problem well. No matter what you do to the window, it won't respond; it won't even go away. Yes, this happens, but fortunately this is a minor problem that can be dealt with in a number of ways. One of the following should do the trick:

- Just wait a few seconds. It could be that your system will recognize the problem and pop up a window telling you what you already know: The application isn't responding. If such a window does appear, just click the **Kill** button, and you'll be ready to go. If you try to run the application again, it should start up; if it's a Nautilus window giving you trouble, it should automatically restart itself once you kill it. If after killing your application you can't open it again, restart your system. All will be well then.

- If all is still not well after that little exercise in patience, try using the Force Quit button you added to your panel in Chapter 3. Just click the button, and the cursor will turn into a crosshair. Place the crosshair over the window that is causing you grief, and then click again. Press ESC if you decide that you don't want to use the killer crosshair after all.

- If that approach also fails for some reason (or if you are a Red Hat Linux 9 user who doesn't have the Force Quit button), go to the Main menu and select **Run Application**. In the dialog box type xkill. Your cursor will then turn into a funny-looking square within a square. Place that square over the misbehaving window, and click the left mouse button. The program, or window, will then shut down. If you decide that you don't want to click on anything with your square-within-a-square cursor, just right-click, and your cursor will return to normal.

- Yet another alternative is to go to your Main menu and select **System Tools > System Monitor**. The System Monitor window will then open, showing all the running processes (and you'll be surprised how many there are). Find the culprit in the list, and select it by clicking once. Then click the **End Process** button at the bottom of the window, and the misbehaving program will close. Most likely, you will never have to go through this procedure, unless you want to, of course. Still it isn't a bad thing to know about.

I sometimes get a message saying that this or that GNOME application has unexpectedly quit. After that the program starts back up by itself. Is this normal?

No, it's not "normal" as normal goes, but it does sometimes happen in GNOME. No need to worry, as it seems to be taking care of things itself.

My GNOME Panel is gone or not responding.

Hmmm. Seems to me that the easiest thing to do is just press CTRL + ALT + BACKSPACE together. Your GNOME session will end, and you will be back at your graphical login screen so that you can start anew. This should work in KDE (or any other GUI) as well, if something of a similar nature happens to you.

Holy molasses! Everything seems to have gooped up and I can't get anything done.

Yes, yes, ghosts all over your screen, repeated window frames, menus seem to bleed into windows, and it all just seems like an unsightly pudding on your monitor, eh? My first suggestion is to just sit there for a minute or two. Your machine might just be too slow to handle things fast enough, and thus just needs some time to catch up. If things stay that way, however, just as with the previous problem, try the CTRL + ALT + BACKSPACE keys together, and you'll be back at your graphical login screen without the goop.

My windows all leave trails behind them when I move them. Looks cool, but I'd prefer it didn't happen.

Your video color depth is probably more than your hardware setup can handle. Try downing it from **millions of colors** to **thousands of colors**. As explained in Chapter 19, you can do this via the Display Settings window, which you can open by going to the Main menu and selecting **System Settings > Display**.

If that doesn't do the trick, try reducing your screen resolution too (in the Main menu select **Preferences > Screen Resolution**). If that doesn't cut the hay either, try adding more system memory (or getting a new video card with lots of memory built in).

Blackout! My GUI has disappeared, and I'm suddenly stuck in all-text mode. I want to get out, but I don't even know how I got here. Take me back to Kansas, Great Wizard!

Yes, this is a fright the first time around, though it fortunately has only happened to me once. Your screen is black, and it just reads **[username@localhost username] $**. It looks like a dreadful throwback to the scary days of DOS, even though it is Linux. Ouch! But don't despair, Dorothy. There is a simple way around this.

Your whole screen has become one giant Terminal window. So first become root in the usual way, and then type in the following command and press ENTER:

```
/sbin/shutdown -r now
```

The **-r** flag tells the **shutdown** command to restart after shutting down, so, naturally enough, if you don't want to restart the machine, you can omit this flag. The **now** part at the end tells the **shutdown** command to do its stuff now, not later, which, given the circumstances, is no doubt what you want it to do.

After doing all that, things will go as they should: The usual shutdown output will display on the screen, and the machine will stop, restart, and return you to your friendly graphical login screen. You're back in Kansas again, Dorothy . . . and Toto too.

Ghostly problem. My login screen is all white. All I can see is the cursor blinking in the center of the screen. What should I do?

Yes, this happens sometimes. Fortunately it is all quite temporary. Just go through the usual login steps, entering your account name and password as if you could see the login window. Despite the sudden case of whiteout, everything still functions as it should, and the login screen should be back to normal the next time you come to it.

When I leave my computer running and step out of the room for a while, I often come back to find that my machine's logged me out and I'm back at my login screen. What gives?

Assuming that the cause is not one of your children or a mischievous coworker, then the culprit is probably one of your screensaver modules. There are a couple of ways to find out which module is causing the problem.

The first way is the trial-and-error method, by which you turn off all the modules and then enable them one by one, letting each one do its thing for a while to see if it is the problem. If your problem doesn't recur, you can enable the next one and check it. And so on. The other way is to simply enable only one module and use it for a while. If your problem doesn't recur, then you know that that module is safe. When you get sick of it, change to another module and use that one for a while. Eventually, you'll discover the broken module.

My printouts look lousy. The text is all jagged, and paragraphs get blurry here and there. What can I do?

First, make sure that your problem isn't just a dirty inkjet printer. Try cleaning it first. If that doesn't work, try trashing your present print queue and creating a new one. Be sure to use the default driver for your printer. If the printouts still look lousy, try a different driver and see if that does the trick.

I can't seem to eject my CD!

Good, an easy one. First, make sure that there are no open Nautilus windows that show the contents of your CD. If there are open windows, close them and try to eject the disk again. If that doesn't work, open a Terminal window, type `umount /mnt/cdrom` and press ENTER. If that doesn't do the trick, try doing the same thing after becoming root. And if all that fails, just restart your machine with the CD stuck in your drive, and right after the machine restarts (and before you get to any of the Fedora screens) push the eject button on the CD drive — not the usual Linux way of doing things, but it works.

What happened? I suddenly can't burn CDs anymore.

If you can read CDs without a hitch, but you just can't burn them all of a sudden, the problem could be due to a USB storage device. The Linux kernel treats both CD drives and USB storage devices as SCSI devices (even if they are not). If you start up your machine with a USB storage device plugged in, the system might set up the SCSI devices so that the USB storage device is listed as `scsibus0`, and the CD drive as `scsibus1`. When you try to burn a CD, the CD burner looks for the drive at `scsibus0`. If it's not there, the burner doesn't know what to do.

You can check to see if this is your problem by opening a Terminal window, becoming root, and then typing in `cdrecord -scanbus` and pressing ENTER. If your CD drive is listed as `scsibus1` rather than `scsibus0`, you'll know that you've identified the problem. To solve this problem, just unmount your USB storage device, unplug the device from your machine, and then restart the machine. Everything should be back to normal once your system is up and running again. At that point, you can also plug your USB storage device back in, if you like.

Why can I hear sound when I play audio streams or audio files on my hard disk, but I can't hear anything when I try to play an audio CD?

Sounds to me as if you installed a new sound card and forgot to connect the CD to it. Your CD drive should have three sets of wires coming out the back: a multicolor set with a translucent white connector at the end, a very wide and flat set of gray wires that are molded together so that they look like the biggest and ugliest tapeworm in the history of tapeworms, and a pair of normal-sized black wires ending in a rather small flat connector. This last connector (see Figure 20-1 on the next page) is probably still connected to your motherboard. You should connect it instead to the appropriate slot (usually labeled **CD**) on the new sound card. If you need a bit more help, I have a set of instructions on how to install a sound card that you can download from my Web site for this book (www.edgy-penguins.org/non-geeks).

Figure 20-1: Connecting your CD drive to your new sound card

I followed your directions for installing new icon themes, but nothing happened. You told me to check here if this happens, so . . .

The problem you are experiencing is just one of those system quirks that happens sometimes. Fortunately, it is easily remedied. First, untar the icon file **ICON-Tux-n-Tosh-0.1.tar.bz2** (or whatever other file you are trying to install) by double-clicking it and then going through the usual File Roller procedures. This will create a new folder named **TuxnTosh** (or named for whatever icon set you are installing).

Now open a new Nautilus window, and in the **Location** text box of that new window type /home/username/.icons and press ENTER. This will bring you to the "hidden" icons folder (as mentioned, your folder name may vary). Finally just drag the **TuxnTosh** folder from the first window to the .icons window. Once you've done that, you should be able to go to the Theme Details window and find the icon set in the list of installed icon themes.

Whoa! I'm seeing all sorts of oily colors pulsating before my eyes, and I feel like there are frogs jumping up and down my spine. I've painted half my face blue and I look like the bad seed from an episode of Dragnet. I also have a mad urge to run naked through my local Wal-Mart screaming "Neewollah!"

You're obviously turning to the wrong place for help, as your problem seems a bit off topic and definitely out of my line of expertise, but I'm relatively sure it all has to do with something you did in high school, unless you're trying to make a sociopolitical statement of some sort. It also seems that you are well acquainted with the 1956 film classic *Picnic,* starring Kim Novak and William Holden — a cult film waiting to happen if there ever was one. My advice is to go back and ask the pyWings oracle and see what it has to say. I will merely end now by offering you a heartfelt

Neewollah!

(For those of you who don't know what this means, see the film.)

A

LAUNCHER SPECIFICATIONS

While working your way through this book, you will have installed a number of applications for which launchers are not automatically created. This is especially true of applications you compiled yourself from source. For your convenience, I have included the commands and icon locations for such launcher-less applications so that you can create launchers yourself if you want to (as you learned to do in Chapter 3).

Project 9A: pyWings

Command: pywings.py

Icon: /home/username/LocalApps/pywings/icon.xbm

Project 9B: pyChing

Command: pyching.py

Icon: /home/username/LocalApps/pyching/pyching.png

Project 11A: Xmahjongg

Command: xmahjongg

Icon: none

NOTE *There is no specific application icon for Xmahjongg, so you can create your own or just use* /usr/share/icons/Bluecurve/48x48/apps/gnome-mahjongg.png, *which is the icon for the GNOME mahjongg game.*

Project 13C: RealOne Player

Command: /home/username/RealPlayer9/realplay

Icon: /home/rg/RealPlayer9/realplay.xpm

Project 16D: PfaEdit

Command: pfaedit

Icon: none

NOTE *There is no specific application icon for PfaEdit, so you can create your own or just use* /usr/share/icons/Bluecurve/48x48/apps/fonts.png.

Command and Launcher Specs for Programs Hidden in GNOME

This section of the appendix lists of many of the programs that you have on your system but that are not listed in the Main menu within the GNOME environment. You can run any of these applications by simply typing the command in a Terminal window or by going to the Main menu, selecting **Run Program**, and then typing your command in the window that opens.

If you find that you take a real shine to any of these programs, you will probably want to create your own launcher for that program (as you learned to do in Chapter 3) to make things convenient for you in the future.

Games

Kolor Lines

A KDE version of the Lines game, with squishy balls.

Command: klines

Icon: /usr/share/icons/Bluecurve/32x32/apps/klines.png

Patience

A KDE version of the Klondike solitaire card game.

Command: kpat

Icon: /usr/share/icons/Bluecurve/48x48/apps/kpat.png

Megami

A KDE blackjack game.

Command: `megami`

Icon: `/usr/share/icons/hicolor/32x32/apps/megami.png`

KMahjongg

KDE's mahjongg game.

Command: `kmahjongg`

Icon: `/usr/share/icons/Bluecurve/48x48/apps/kmahjongg.png`

Atlantik

A Monopoly-esque game for network play.

Command: `atlantik`

Icon: `/usr/share/icons/crystalsvg/48x48/apps/atlantik.png`

Klickety

Kind of an inverse Tetris-like game in the Same Game genre.

Command: `klickety`

Icon: none

NOTE *As there is no specific icon for Klickety, you can make one of your own, download one, or use one from another application.*

KWin4

A KDE version of Four in a Row that can be played against the computer or on a network.

Command: `kwin4`

Icon: /usr/share/icons/Bluecurve/48x48/apps/kwin4.png

Utilities

IDLE

A graphical interface for the Python programming language. You don't have to use it to write programs in Python, but as some Python books make reference to it (or straight out tell you to use it), you might want to use it to follow along.

Command: `python /usr/lib/python2.2/site-packages/idle/idle.py`

Icon: `/usr/lib/python2.2/site-packages/idle/Icons/python.gif`

Kdeedu

If you chose to install the Kdeedu package mentioned in Chapter 17, then the following applications will also be installed in your system but hidden in the Main menu in GNOME.

FlashKard

A flash card program that lets you create cards and then use them to quiz yourself.

Command: flashkard

Icon: /usr/share/icons/crystalsvg/48x48/apps/flashkard.png

Kalzium

The periodic table goes graphic — relive your chemistry class days.

Command: kalzium

Icon: /usr/share/icons/crystalsvg/32x32/apps/kalzium.png

KEduca

A rather sophisticated flash card/interactive quiz application.

Command: keduca

Icon: /usr/share/icons/Bluecurve/48x48/apps/keduca.png

KGeo

Interactive geometry.

Command: kgeo

Icon: /usr/share/icons/Bluecurve/32x32/apps/kgeo.png

KHangMan

As the name implies, a KDE version of Hangman.

Command: khangman

Icon: /usr/share/icons/crystalsvg/32x32/apps/khangman.png

Kiten

Japanese-English, English-Japanese, Kanji dictionary and Kanji study tool.

Command: kiten

Icon: /usr/share/icons/crystalsvg/16x16/apps/kiten.png

KLettres

A very simple program for learning the sounds of the English, French, or Danish alphabets.

Command: klettres

Icon: /usr/share/icons/Bluecurve/32x32/apps/klettres.png

KMessedWords

Unscramble scrambled words with three levels of dictionary — kind of fun, actually.

Command: kmessedwords

Icon: /usr/share/icons/Bluecurve/32x32/apps/kmessedwords.png

KmPlot

A mathematical function plotter.

Command: kmplot

Icon: /usr/share/icons/crystalsvg/32x32/apps/kmplot.png

Modupedometa

Want to know how much distance your mouse actually travels? Yes, an odometer for your mouse, which shows both total and "trip" distances. Kind of dumb, but kind of fun.

Command: kodo

Icon: /usr/share/icons/Bluecurve/48x48/apps/kodo.png

KPercentage

Improve your skills in calculating percentages.

Command: kpercentage

Icon: /usr/share/icons/crystalsvg/32x32/apps/kpercentage.png

KStars

Very cool virtual star atlas, which lets you see the night sky from any point in the world — and even any time!

Command: kstars

Icon: /usr/share/icons/Bluecurve/48x48/apps/kstars.png

KTouch

Touch-typing tutor — also allows you to practice with different keyboard layouts.

Command: ktouch

Icon: /usr/share/icons/Bluecurve/32x32/apps/ktouch.png

KVerbos

Spanish verb trainer.

Command: kverbos

Icon: /usr/share/icons/crystalsvg/16x16/apps/kverbos.png

KVocTrain

Another flash card program, specifically for foreign language study.

Command: kvoctrain

Icon: /usr/share/icons/Bluecurve/48x48/apps/kvoctrain.png

KDE World Clock

World clock that shows areas of night and day and local times in cities of your choice.

Command: kworldclock

Icon: /usr/share/icons/Bluecurve/48x48/apps/kworldclock.png

B

RESOURCES

As Linux owes much of its growth and development to the Internet, it should come as no surprise that there is a wealth of information available to you online. In addition to the usual news sites, how-to site, and download sites, you will find a variety of tutorials, forums, mailing lists, and other useful information, all of which you can turn to as you use and learn more and more about your system.

Online Forums Appropriate for Beginners

All of these forums allow you to read messages and to post messages (once you register) about your system. Most also have a series of how-to lists or FAQs (frequently asked questions) that may answer any basic questions you have. Note that these forums are not Fedora specific, so make sure to mention the distro and version of Linux that you are running when you do post a message. And always seek clarification when you don't understand the advice you've been given.

JustLinux   www.justlinux.com

LinuxQuestions.org   www.linuxquestions.org

Linux Forum   www.linuxforum.com

Mailing Lists

Another way to get community feedback on your various questions and to learn the concerns of fellow Fedora users is via mailing lists. Postings are received and sent by email. You do not have to access a Web page in order to use this sort of service (except, in some cases, to sign up for the list). There are many such lists out there, so you might want to do an Internet search for "Fedora mailing lists." Yahoo Groups also has a number of Linux-, Fedora-, and Red Hat–specific lists available that you might want to check out. You can search through the various Yahoo Groups by going to http://groups.yahoo.com.

If you like, you can also give the "official" Fedora list a try by having a look through the list's archives, which can be accessed at www.redhat.com/mailman/listinfo/fedora-list. If the level of things seems to be in sync with your pace and understanding, you can sign up for the list at the same URL.

NOTE   *You may find that some people on mailing lists, especially those on the Fedora list, are rather fussy about "top posting." Top posting means replying to messages by adding your comments to the top of the previous poster's comments. The proper netiquette on this list is to "bottom post," which means that you reply to a previous poster's comments after the original comment. You should also remove any unnecessary text from your reply, such as signatures from the list, and so on. Take a look at the example in Figure B-1 to see what I mean.*

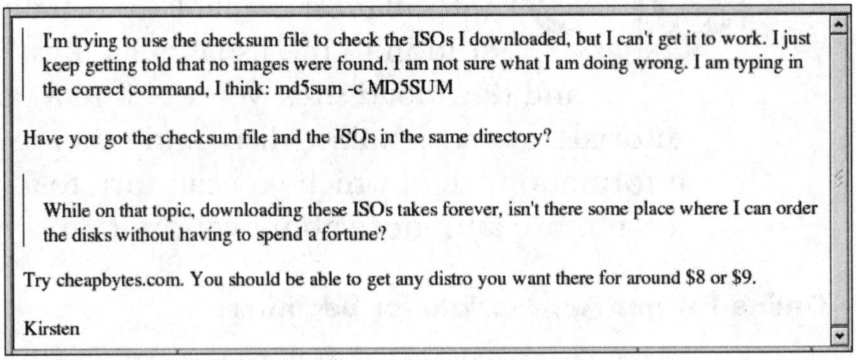

I'm trying to use the checksum file to check the ISOs I downloaded, but I can't get it to work. I just keep getting told that no images were found. I am not sure what I am doing wrong. I am typing in the correct command, I think: md5sum -c MD5SUM

Have you got the checksum file and the ISOs in the same directory?

While on that topic, downloading these ISOs takes forever, isn't there some place where I can order the disks without having to spend a fortune?

Try cheapbytes.com. You should be able to get any distro you want there for around $8 or $9.

Kirsten

Figure B-1: Example of bottom posting

Hardware Compatibility Issues

If you want to check to see whether or not your hardware is compatible with Linux, or you want to read up on other matters related to hardware support, take a look at the following sites:

Linux Compatible   www.linuxcompatible.org/compatibility.html
An alphabetical listing of all kinds of hardware, from motherboards to scanners. Listings are located near the bottom of the page.

LinuxPrinting.org   www.linuxprinting.org

Linmodems.org   www.linmodems.org

SANE Project (scanners)   www.sane-project.org

Linux on Laptops   www.linux-laptop.net

TuxMobil   http://tuxmobil.org

Wireless Related Sites

Wireless LAN Resources for Linux   www.hpl.hp.com/personal/Jean_Tourrilhes/Linux/Wireless.html

EZGoal HotSpots   www.ezgoal.com/hotspots/wireless
A listing of wireless hotspots throughout the United States and around the world — everything from hotels to city parks. Very cool.

Download Sites

If you find yourself looking for more applications to play around with, you should be able to find plenty of free software to download at one of these sites.

Applications and Other Packages

FreshRPMs   http://freshrpms.net/packages
A collection of add-on RPM packages that are specifically prepared for Red Hat Linux/Fedora and are grouped by version.

DAG   http://dag.wieers.com/packages
Another collection of add-on RPM packages prepared for Red Hat Linux/Fedora. Packages from DAG are designed to be compatible with those from FreshRPMs.

Fedora.us   http://download.fedora.us/fedora/fedora/1/i386/RPMS.stable
Another collection of add-on RPM packages, though not guaranteed to be compatible with those from FreshRPMs and DAG.

Planet CCRMA   http://ccrma-www.stanford.edu/planetccrma/software
Mostly specialty-music-related packages, many of which are not easily found on other sites. This is a good place to find things like music notation software and sequencers.

RPMFind   www.rpmfind.net/linux/RPM
An RPM file search tool you can use to find specific files you are looking for (perhaps to get you out of dependency hell?).

SourceForge.net   http://sourceforge.net
A source for RPM and tarball packages. Click the **software map** button for a category listing of what's available. Be aware that a few of the applications are only for the Windows environment.

FreshMeat.net   http://freshmeat.net
Similar to SourceForge.net. Click the **browse** link for a category listing of what's available.

GNOME.org   www.gnome.org/softwaremap
Applications specifically designed for the GNOME environment.

Customization

art.gnome.org   http://art.gnome.org
Customization files for the GNOME environment. (Wallpapers downloaded for use in GNOME can also be used in KDE.)

KDE-Look.org   www.kdelook.org
Customization files for the KDE environment. (Wallpapers downloaded for use in KDE can also be used in GNOME.)

X MultiMedia System   www.xmms.org/skins.php
Skins for the XMMS media player.

Winamp   http://classic.winamp.com/skins
Skins for the Windows Winamp2 media player that can also be used with XMMS.

Free Fonts

Font Freak   www.fontfreak.com

Font Paradise   www.fontparadise.com

Fontor.com   www.fontor.com

Divide by Zero Fonts   http://fonts.tom7.com

Linux Reference Sites

These are general sites, which are geared toward newbies, where you can learn a bit more about using Linux in general.

LinuxCommand.org   http://linuxcommand.org
If you've become interested in the Linux Command Terminal and the commands you use in it, this site has lots for you, including tutorials and explanations of other useful Linux commands.

NewToLinux.org www.newtolinux.org.uk
> Tutorials and other information for newbies, with a focus on helping migrants from the Windows world ease into Linux.

Linux Online www.linux.org
> All sorts of information about Linux, including information on Linux history, distributions, and links to various downloadable applications.

News and Information

These sites are mainly informational, keeping you abreast of what's going on in the Linux world. DistroWatch focuses on the various distributions available out there and what features they have, whereas Linux Today and LinuxPlanet are more of the online magazine/newspaper genre.

Linux Today http://linuxtoday.com

LinuxPlanet www.linuxplanet.com

DistroWatch www.distrowatch.com

Buying Linux CDs

In the future, if you want to get a newer version of Fedora (or any other distro), but you don't want or are not able to download it, you can order a full version on CDs for $5 to $10 from any of these sites.

CheapBytes www.cheapbytes.com

Linux CD www.linuxcd.org

LinuxInstall.org http://linuxinstall.org

INDEX

Media Access Control (MAC) address, 253

Megami game, 289

memory cards, 164

memory, computer, 14

mkdir command, 127

modems, 55–57

Modupedometa utility, 291

monitors
    compatibility, 13
    configuration of, 21
    old/unusual, *21*

motherboards, 13

mounting
    disks, 100
    USB storage devices, 168

mouse configuration, 21

Mozilla Flash plug-in, 140–41

Mozilla Mail, 65

Mozilla Web browser
    changing character encoding in, 239
    creating Web pages, 63–64
    Popup Manager, 63
    program launcher, 41
    tabbed browsing in, 61–63
    themes, 85–87

MP3 support for XMMS, 181–86

MPlayer program, 146–50

Mr. Project program, 216

mscorefonts folder, 233

multilingual login, 243

multilingual users and language learners, 237–50
    Chinese, Japanese, Korean, 243–46
    Kdeedu language-learning programs, 246–48
    nonstandard characters, 240–42
    read-only language support, 238–40
    StarDict dictionary, 248–50
    viewing system in another language, 242–43

music, 171–94
    Audacity program, 189–90
    audio formats, 171–72
    CDs
        burning, 104–5, 285
        duplicating, 106–8
        ejecting, 285
        playing, 103–4
        ripping, 175–77
    EasyTAG program, 188–89
    Grip program, 172–75
    MP3 support for XMMS, 181–86
    Rhythmbox audio player, 177–79

troubleshooting problems with, 285

XMMS audio player, 179–81

mv command, 127

myxfonts folder, 230

N

Nautilus program, 34–39
    bookmarks within, 37
    CD Creator window, 104
    changing file and folder permissions within, 37–39
    as Image Viewer, 34–36
    Side Pane of, 36–37
    using to view text and PDF files, 36

Navigator window, 209–10

netwave_cs driver, 256

network configuration, 22, 54, 259, 260

network connections, wireless. *See* wireless network connections

Network Device Control window, 261

network interface card, wireless, 261–62

new user account, 70–71

NewToLinux.org site, 297

NIC (wireless network interface card), 253, 255–57

nonstandard characters, 240–42

O

object code, 154

OEM (Original Equipment Manufacturer), 256

office suites
    KOffice, 214–15
    OpenOffice.org
        applications in, 211–14
        overview, 208–11

oily colors, problem solving, 286

online forums, 293–94

Open Link in New Tab option, 62

Open Link in New Window option, 61

Open Recent item, 40

OpenOffice.org office suite, 208–11
    applications in, 211–14
    making fonts available to, 229
    overview, 208–11

Original Equipment Manufacturer (OEM), 256

orinoco_cs driver, 256

outline font, 223

P

package installation, 23, 24–25

Package Management window, 115–19

GNU GENERAL PUBLIC LICENSE

Version 2, June 1991

Preamble

The licenses for most software are designed to take away your freedom to share and change it. By contrast, the GNU General Public License is intended to guarantee your freedom to share and change free software–to make sure the software is free for all its users. This General Public License applies to most of the Free Software Foundation's software and to any other program whose authors commit to using it. (Some other Free Software Foundation software is covered by the GNU Library General Public License instead.) You can apply it to your programs, too.

When we speak of free software, we are referring to freedom, not price. Our General Public Licenses are designed to make sure that you have the freedom to distribute copies of free software (and charge for this service if you wish), that you receive source code or can get it if you want it, that you can change the software or use pieces of it in new free programs; and that you know you can do these things.

To protect your rights, we need to make restrictions that forbid anyone to deny you these rights or to ask you to surrender the rights. These restrictions translate to certain responsibilities for you if you distribute copies of the software, or if you modify it.

For example, if you distribute copies of such a program, whether gratis or for a fee, you must give the recipients all the rights that you have. You must make sure that they, too, receive or can get the source code. And you must show them these terms so they know their rights.

We protect your rights with two steps: (1) copyright the software, and (2) offer you this license which gives you legal permission to copy, distribute and/or modify the software.

Also, for each author's protection and ours, we want to make certain that everyone understands that there is no warranty for this free software. If the software is modified by someone else and passed on, we want its recipients to know that what they have is not the original, so that any problems introduced by others will not reflect on the original authors' reputations.

Finally, any free program is threatened constantly by software patents. We wish to avoid the danger that redistributors of a free program will individually obtain patent licenses, in effect making the program proprietary. To prevent this, we have made it clear that any patent must be licensed for everyone's free use or not licensed at all.

The precise terms and conditions for copying, distribution and modification follow.

GNU GENERAL PUBLIC LICENSE
TERMS AND CONDITIONS FOR COPYING, DISTRIBUTION AND MODIFICATION

0. This License applies to any program or other work which contains a notice placed by the copyright holder saying it may be distributed under the terms of this General Public License. The "Program", below, refers to any such program or work, and a "work based on the Program" means either the Program or any derivative work under copyright law: that is to say, a work containing the Program or a portion of it, either verbatim or with modifications and/or translated into another language. (Hereinafter, translation is included without limitation in the term "modification".) Each licensee is addressed as "you".

    Activities other than copying, distribution and modification are not covered by this License; they are outside its scope. The act of running the Program is not restricted, and the output from the Program is covered only if its contents constitute a work based on the Program (independent of having been made by running the Program). Whether that is true depends on what the Program does.

1. You may copy and distribute verbatim copies of the Program's source code as you receive it, in any medium, provided that you conspicuously and appropriately publish on each copy an appropriate copyright notice and disclaimer of warranty; keep intact all the notices that refer to this License and to the absence of any warranty; and give any other recipients of the Program a copy of this License along with the Program.

    You may charge a fee for the physical act of transferring a copy, and you may at your option offer warranty protection in exchange for a fee.

2. You may modify your copy or copies of the Program or any portion of it, thus forming a work based on the Program, and copy and distribute such modifications or work under the terms of Section 1 above, provided that you also meet all of these conditions:

a) You must cause the modified files to carry prominent notices stating that you changed the files and the date of any change.

b) You must cause any work that you distribute or publish, that in whole or in part contains or is derived from the Program or any part thereof, to be licensed as a whole at no charge to all third parties under the terms of this License.

c) If the modified program normally reads commands interactively when run, you must cause it, when started running for such interactive use in the most ordinary way, to print or display an announcement including an appropriate copyright notice and a notice that there is no warranty (or else, saying that you provide a warranty) and that users may redistribute the program under these conditions, and telling the user how to view a copy of this License. (Exception: if the Program itself is interactive but does not normally print such an announcement, your work based on the Program is not required to print an announcement.)

These requirements apply to the modified work as a whole. If identifiable sections of that work are not derived from the Program, and can be reasonably considered independent and separate works in themselves, then this License, and its terms, do not apply to those sections when you distribute them as separate works. But when you distribute the same sections as part of a whole which is a work based on the Program, the distribution of the whole must be on the terms of this License, whose permissions for other licensees extend to the entire whole, and thus to each and every part regardless of who wrote it.

Thus, it is not the intent of this section to claim rights or contest your rights to work written entirely by you; rather, the intent is to exercise the right to control the distribution of derivative or collective works based on the Program.

In addition, mere aggregation of another work not based on the Program with the Program (or with a work based on the Program) on a volume of a storage or distribution medium does not bring the other work under the scope of this License.

3. You may copy and distribute the Program (or a work based on it, under Section 2) in object code or executable form under the terms of Sections 1 and 2 above provided that you also do one of the following:

a) Accompany it with the complete corresponding machine-readable source code, which must be distributed under the terms of Sections 1 and 2 above on a medium customarily used for software interchange; or,

b) Accompany it with a written offer, valid for at least three years, to give any third party, for a charge no more than your cost of physically performing source distribution, a complete machine-readable copy of the corresponding source code, to be distributed under the terms of Sections 1 and 2 above on a medium customarily used for software interchange; or,

c) Accompany it with the information you received as to the offer to distribute corresponding source code. (This alternative is allowed only for noncommercial distribution and only if you received the program in object code or executable form with such an offer, in accord with Subsection b above.)

The source code for a work means the preferred form of the work for making modifications to it. For an executable work, complete source code means all the source code for all modules it contains, plus any associated interface definition files, plus the scripts used to control compilation and installation of the executable. However, as a special exception, the source code distributed need not include anything that is normally distributed (in either source or binary form) with the major components (compiler, kernel, and so on) of the operating system on which the executable runs, unless that component itself accompanies the executable.

If distribution of executable or object code is made by offering access to copy from a designated place, then offering equivalent access to copy the source code from the same place counts as distribution of the source code, even though third parties are not compelled to copy the source along with the object code.

4. You may not copy, modify, sublicense, or distribute the Program except as expressly provided under this License. Any attempt otherwise to copy, modify, sublicense or distribute the Program is void, and will automatically terminate your rights under this License. However, parties who

have received copies, or rights, from you under this License will not have their licenses terminated so long as such parties remain in full compliance.

5. You are not required to accept this License, since you have not signed it. However, nothing else grants you permission to modify or distribute the Program or its derivative works. These actions are prohibited by law if you do not accept this License. Therefore, by modifying or distributing the Program (or any work based on the Program), you indicate your acceptance of this License to do so, and all its terms and conditions for copying, distributing or modifying the Program or works based on it.

6. Each time you redistribute the Program (or any work based on the Program), the recipient automatically receives a license from the original licensor to copy, distribute or modify the Program subject to these terms and conditions. You may not impose any further restrictions on the recipients' exercise of the rights granted herein. You are not responsible for enforcing compliance by third parties to this License.

7. If, as a consequence of a court judgment or allegation of patent infringement or for any other reason (not limited to patent issues), conditions are imposed on you (whether by court order, agreement or otherwise) that contradict the conditions of this License, they do not excuse you from the conditions of this License. If you cannot distribute so as to satisfy simultaneously your obligations under this License and any other pertinent obligations, then as a consequence you may not distribute the Program at all. For example, if a patent license would not permit royalty-free redistribution of the Program by all those who receive copies directly or indirectly through you, then the only way you could satisfy both it and this License would be to refrain entirely from distribution of the Program.

If any portion of this section is held invalid or unenforceable under any particular circumstance, the balance of the section is intended to apply and the section as a whole is intended to apply in other circumstances.

It is not the purpose of this section to induce you to infringe any patents or other property right claims or to contest validity of any such claims; this section has the sole purpose of protecting the integrity of the free software distribution system, which is implemented by public license practices. Many people have made generous contributions to the wide range of software distributed through that system in reliance on consistent application of that system; it is up to the author/donor to decide if he or she is willing to distribute software through any other system and a licensee cannot impose that choice.

This section is intended to make thoroughly clear what is believed to be a consequence of the rest of this License.

---

8. If the distribution and/or use of the Program is restricted in certain countries either by patents or by copyrighted interfaces, the original copyright holder who places the Program under this License may add an explicit geographical distribution limitation excluding those countries, so that distribution is permitted only in or among countries not thus excluded. In such case, this License incorporates the limitation as if written in the body of this License.

9. The Free Software Foundation may publish revised and/or new versions of the General Public License from time to time. Such new versions will be similar in spirit to the present version, but may differ in detail to address new problems or concerns.
Each version is given a distinguishing version number. If the Program specifies a version number of this License which applies to it and "any later version", you have the option of following the terms and conditions either of that version or of any later version published by the Free Software Foundation. If the Program does not specify a version number of this License, you may choose any version ever published by the Free Software Foundation.

10. If you wish to incorporate parts of the Program into other free programs whose distribution conditions are different, write to the author to ask for permission. For software which is copyrighted by the Free Software Foundation, write to the Free Software Foundation; we sometimes make exceptions for this. Our decision will be guided by the two goals of preserving the free status of all derivatives of our free software and of promoting the sharing and reuse of software generally.

NO WARRANTY

11. BECAUSE THE PROGRAM IS LICENSED FREE OF CHARGE, THERE IS NO WARRANTY FOR THE PROGRAM, TO THE EXTENT PERMITTED BY APPLICABLE LAW. EXCEPT WHEN OTHERWISE STATED IN WRITING THE COPYRIGHT HOLDERS AND/OR OTHER

PARTIES PROVIDE THE PROGRAM "AS IS" WITHOUT WARRANTY OF ANY KIND, EITHER EXPRESSED OR IMPLIED, INCLUDING, BUT NOT LIMITED TO, THE IMPLIED WARRANTIES OF MERCHANTABILITY AND FITNESS FOR A PARTICULAR PURPOSE. THE ENTIRE RISK AS TO THE QUALITY AND PERFORMANCE OF THE PROGRAM IS WITH YOU. SHOULD THE PROGRAM PROVE DEFECTIVE, YOU ASSUME THE COST OF ALL NECESSARY SERVICING, REPAIR OR CORRECTION.

12. IN NO EVENT UNLESS REQUIRED BY APPLICABLE LAW OR AGREED TO IN WRITING WILL ANY COPYRIGHT HOLDER, OR ANY OTHER PARTY WHO MAY MODIFY AND/OR REDISTRIBUTE THE PROGRAM AS PERMITTED ABOVE, BE LIABLE TO YOU FOR DAMAGES, INCLUDING ANY GENERAL, SPECIAL, INCIDENTAL OR CONSEQUENTIAL DAMAGES ARISING OUT OF THE USE OR INABILITY TO USE THE PROGRAM (INCLUDING BUT NOT LIMITED TO LOSS OF DATA OR DATA BEING RENDERED INACCURATE OR LOSSES SUSTAINED BY YOU OR THIRD PARTIES OR A FAILURE OF THE PROGRAM TO OPERATE WITH ANY OTHER PROGRAMS), EVEN IF SUCH HOLDER OR OTHER PARTY HAS BEEN ADVISED OF THE POSSIBILITY OF SUCH DAMAGES.

END OF TERMS AND CONDITIONS.

How to Apply These Terms to Your New Programs

If you develop a new program, and you want it to be of the greatest possible use to the public, the best way to achieve this is to make it free software which everyone can redistribute and change under these terms.

To do so, attach the following notices to the program. It is safest to attach them to the start of each source file to most effectively convey the exclusion of warranty; and each file should have at least the "copyright" line and a pointer to where the full notice is found.

<one line to give the program's name and a brief idea of what it does.>
Copyright (C) <year> <name of author>

This program is free software; you can redistribute it and/or modify it under the terms of the GNU General Public License as published by the Free Software Foundation; either version 2 of the License, or (at your option) any later version.

This program is distributed in the hope that it will be useful, but WITHOUT ANY WARRANTY; without even the implied warranty of MERCHANTABILITY or FITNESS FOR A PARTICULAR PURPOSE. See the GNU General Public License for more details.

You should have received a copy of the GNU General Public License along with this program; if not, write to the Free Software Foundation, Inc., 59 Temple Place, Suite 330, Boston, MA 02111-1307 USA

Also add information on how to contact you by electronic and paper mail.

If the program is interactive, make it output a short notice like this when it starts in an interactive mode:

Gnomovision version 69, Copyright (C) year name of author
Gnomovision comes with ABSOLUTELY NO WARRANTY; for details type `show w'.
This is free software, and you are welcome to redistribute it under certain conditions; type `show c' for details.

The hypothetical commands `show w' and `show c' should show the appropriate parts of the General Public License. Of course, the commands you use may be called something other than `show w' and `show c'; they could even be mouse-clicks or menu items–whatever suits your program.

You should also get your employer (if you work as a programmer) or your school, if any, to sign a "copyright disclaimer" for the program, if necessary. Here is a sample; alter the names:

Yoyodyne, Inc., hereby disclaims all copyright interest in the program `Gnomovision' (which makes passes at compilers) written by James Hacker.
<signature of Ty Coon>, 1 April 1989
Ty Coon, President of Vice

This General Public License does not permit incorporating your program into proprietary programs. If your program is a subroutine library, you may consider it more useful to permit linking proprietary applications with the library. If this is what you want to do, use the GNU Library General Public License instead of this License.

A NOTE ABOUT
FEDORA VERSIONS

Most operating systems, and Linux distributions for that matter, have a six-month to one-year life cycle before they are *versioned* up. The Fedora Project does things a little differently, however, by releasing a new version of Fedora Core every three to four months. This book, for example, which came out in March of 2004, is based on the then very recently released Fedora Core 1, and yet Fedora Core 2 is already out and Fedora Core 3 is soon on its way.

The idea behind this clearly rapid turnover cycle is that it provides the most cutting-edge distro available so that no one is kept waiting for the newest and coolest features available in the Linux world. Although this sounds great, it isn't a completely foolproof way of doing things, in that much less time is spent on beta testing and, more importantly, on fixing any bugs found during that period of testing. The result is that you get more new stuff, but you also get more bugs. Fedora Core 2 (FC2) is a good example of the mixed blessings that come from the trade off.

What's New in FC2?

Well, let's start off by focusing on what's new and, for the most part, cool in Fedora Core 2. Of course, the first thing you will learn even before you install anything on your computer is that Fedora Core 2 takes up four disks, compared to Fedora Core 1's three disks (the Publisher's Edition was only two). This seems to indicate that a lot of new stuff has been thrown into the mix, and this is pretty much the case; however, most of these extras are on Disk 4. To replicate everything you've done in this book, you'd still only need to use the first three FC2 install disks, so in terms of the average user, it is still pretty much a 3-CD distro. Still, there are quite a few changes once you do get everything installed, although only two or three of these are really of great interest to most users.

New Nautilus Window Browsing System

One of the first things you will notice after you install FC2 is that there is a new icon, called *Computer*, on your desktop. Basically, *Computer* is a GNOME version of the My Computer icon you find on Windows desktops. After double-clicking *Computer*, a window opens from which you can access your hard disk (labeled *File System*); floppy, CD-ROM, and/or DVD drives; removable storage devices (such as USB disks or thumb drives); and whatever local area network you happen to be on (Figure 1).

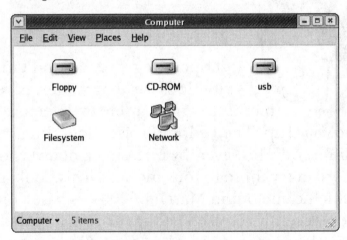

Figure 1: GNOME's new Computer window

Although the new *Computer* icon isn't really all that radical an addition, the new window browsing system that comes with FC2, specifically the new version of GNOME (2.6) it is bundled with, is quite different. Though the desktop *Computer* icon could arguably be called Windows-esque, the results of clicking folders within Nautilus's new windows reveal what some might call a rather Mac OS 8-ish feature: spatial-mode windows.

Of course, you might not be all that familiar with Mac OS 8, so let me explain. Basically, when you double-click a folder or desktop icon in this new spatial-mode world, a window appears, showing the content of the folder you've just clicked. So far, nothing new, right? Well, when you click the icon for a subfolder within that folder or any other folder window, you will spot the difference: the contents of that subfolder appear in yet another window, all its own. Thus, you can, as the GNOME folks put it, "think of the window as the folder."

Getting Things Back the Way They Were

Some people really love this new feature, while others prefer the more familiar browser-mode windows present in Fedora Core 1. Fortunately, the old browser-mode windows are still present in FC2. To open one up, just go to the Main menu, and select **Browse Filesystem**.

If you really hate the new spatial-mode windows and would like to do away with them altogether, you can do that too. To do this, just go to the Main menu and select **System Tools > Configuration Editor**. The editor window then appears along with a small message window telling you that using the editor isn't the best way to set your preferences. Well, in this case, you have no choice, so click **OK** in that window to get rid of it. Next, click the small arrow next to the **apps** folder in the left pane of the main editor window, and then do the same for the **nautilus** folder and the **preferences** folder within it. Finally, check the box next to **always_use_browser** in the right pane of the window. Once you've done all that clicking, the editor window should look like the one in Figure 2. If it does, go ahead and quit the editor, at which point the spatial-mode windows become but a memory.

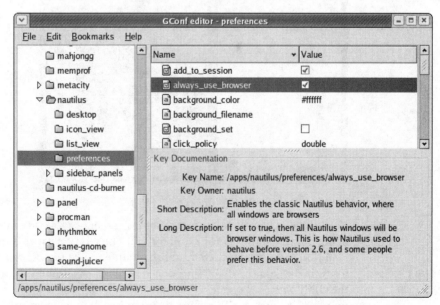

Figure 2: Saying goodbye to spatial-mode windows via the Configuration Editor

The GIMP Grows Up

One of the best things about FC2 is that it includes The GIMP 2.0 (the FC1 version is only 1.2). Now although many application upgrades don't make much of a difference to the majority of average users, GIMP 2.0 is definitely not one of them. The new version of the GIMP has a new, easier-to-use, and arguably, more attractive interface, as you can see in Figure 3. This new interface consists of only two windows, in contrast to the four or more windows that appear when you open earlier versions. Needless to say, this results in a good deal less desktop clutter.

Figure 3: The clean new look of the GIMP 2.0

Now if all this talk of clutter-free desktops and handsome new interfaces doesn't impress you, I am sure my next point will. The GIMP 2.0 now utilizes the *font-config* font subsystem, which means that, quite unlike before, you can now install fonts via the "easy method" introduced in Chapter 16, and you can use them in the GIMP without any geekin' around. That being the case, you have practically no reason to bother with the older and more cumbersome Core X font subsystem anymore. This is a pretty cool thing if you're in touch with your artistic "kitten" side.

Lightening Up with XFCE

One other interesting change in FC2 is the addition of XFCE, which is a lightweight alternative desktop environment to GNOME and KDE. Unlike those two environments, however, you can't install XFCE directly during the installation process or via the Package Manager at some time after that. Instead, you must install it directly from the RPM files located on Disk 4. If you want to give it a try while still using FC1, you can do that too, because XFCE is available for FC1 (as you can see in Figure 4) via Synaptic from the DAG repository.

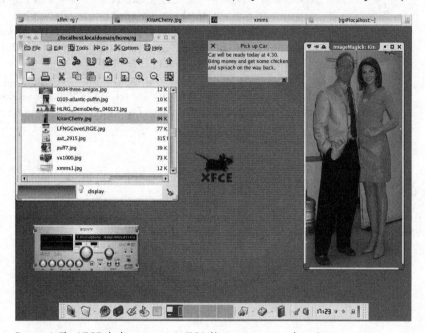

Figure 4: The XFCE desktop in action (FC1/Synaptic version shown)

So What's Not Cool about FC2?

The folks at the Fedora Project may consider FC2 cutting edge, but I can't help but wonder if you can really call something cutting edge if it doesn't work right. Sure FC2 works, and at first glance, it seems to be even smoother and slicker than FC1 . . . but then the bugs start crawling out.

Some of the bigger crawlers are associated with CD handling (particularly writing), package installation via the Package Manager window, changing keyboard layouts, and changing themes, to name but a few. Of course, some people fail to notice these bugs because they fall outside the realm of what they normally do in the course of their computing chores. Still others don't mind spending time geekin' around to find a fix for this bug or that — the fun of finding the bug fix, oh yeah! Whether or not you'll find the bugs to be a problem (or think finding fixes for them is fun) really depends on what it is you do with your system. For my part, I passed on using FC2, because its bugs seemed to be designed specifically to keep me from doing what I normally do. Lucky I'm not paranoid, one might say.

Thus my final verdict is that FC2 has the feel of a beta project rather than a finished distro — it's a real "no wine before it's time" sort of package. The only really wish-I-had feature is the GIMP 2.0, so unless you desperately need that right now, I'd suggest that you just hold off and wait for a more stable version of Fedora in the near future.

How Do I Get My Own FC2?

Okay, so you want to ignore me and install FC2 anyway. Fair enough, but I'd really recommend that you work through this book with FC1 before you do so. At least that way you'll have some Linux experience under your belt and will thus be able to logically tackle the few differences that pop up here and there in FC2. You'll practically be an expert by then, after all.

Assuming you do heed my advice, you can then get your FC2 disks in one of three ways: download the ISOs from www.fedora.redhat.com/download/ and then burn your own disks, order a set of disks from one of the services listed in Appendix B, or take advantage of the special offer included on the last page of this book.